HUMAN RIGHTS AND HUMAN
DIVERSITY

HUMAN RIGHTS AND HUMAN DIVERSITY

An Essay in the Philosophy of Human Rights

A. J. M. Milne

State University of New York Press

First published
in USA by
STATE UNIVERSITY OF NEW YORK PRESS
Albany

For information, address State University of New York
Press, State University Plaza, Albany, NY 12246

Printed in Hong Kong

Library of Congress Cataloging-in-Publication Data
Milne, A. J. M. (Alan John Mitchell), 1922–
Human rights and human diversity.
Bibliography: p.
Includes index.
1. Civil rights (International law) – Philosophy.
2. Law – Philosophy.   I. Title.
K3240.4.M56   1986   342'.085'01   86–5804
ISBN 0–88706–366–7 (hc)   342.28501
ISBN 0–88706–367–5 (pbk)

10   9   8   7   6   5   4   3   2   1

To my Anita in loving memory

Contents

Contents

Preface

I first conceived the idea of this book in the autumn of 1978. I had been invited by Professor Frank Dowrick of the Law Department in the University of Durham to give a public lecture on the idea of 'human rights'. This was part of the series of lectures and seminars held in the university to commemorate the 30th anniversary of the United Nations Declaration of Human Rights. Although I had previously written about both rights in general, and human rights in particular, while working on my lecture I became dissatisfied with my earlier work. I should like to thank Professor Dowrick and all who contributed to the lectures and seminars, for the stimulus which they have given me. Over the next seven years I had the opportunity on a number of occasions to try out the arguments and ideas in this book in the form of seminar and conference papers and lectures. I should like in particular to acknowledge my intellectual debts to the following: the members of the Politics Department in the University of York, Professor David Evans and members of the Philosophy Department in the Queen's University, Belfast, Dr Moorhead Wright of the Department of International Politics, University College of Wales, Aberystwyth, together with the members of the conference at Gregynog, Wales, in July 1984 which he organised, and Professor Neil MacCormick, together with the members of his Jurisprudence Conference at the University of Edinburgh. To all of these I owe much in the way of critical comment and suggestion. I should also like to thank my colleagues in the Politics Department here at Durham and also in the Philosophy Department, for comments and criticisms on some of the arguments in this book which I have presented to them.

I am glad to have the opportunity to express my thanks for the practical help I have received in preparing the typescript for publication. I am especially indebted to Dr Wolfgang von Leyden, Mr Neville Rigby, Mr Kimmett Edgar and Mrs Susan Elkan for assisting me in preparing the final draft. I am greatly indebted to Mrs Hilda Winn, Mrs Dorothy Anson and Mrs Jean Richardson for producing the final typescript on the departmental word-processor — it was, in fact, the first book to be done on our new machine. I am especially grateful to Dr R. W. Dyson for correcting the proofs. Finally, I should like to mention my late wife, in whose memory this book is dedicated. She did not live to see its completion but I would like to record here my profound gratitude for her support, loyalty and help not only in writing this book but in all my work over the past 37 years.

University of Durham   A.J.M.M.

Introduction

0.1 OBJECTIONS TO THE IDEA OF HUMAN RIGHTS

0.1.1   The idea of human rights is one of the most prominent in Western political rhetoric today. A regime which protects human rights is good. One which violates them, or, worse still, does not acknowledge them at all, is bad. There is a basis for the rhetoric. Talk of human rights can today be supported by such documents as the United Nations Universal Declaration of Human Rights of 1948 together with later covenants which supplement it, and by the European Convention on Human Rights of 1953. Earlier it was often supported by eighteenth-century documents, notably the Virginia Declaration of Rights of 1776, and the French Declaration of the Rights of Man, 1790. All these documents make use of the idea of human rights, but in none of them is it analysed and critically examined. This is not surprising, since their aims were practical and political, not academic and philosophical. Their authors assumed that the idea was straightforward. The problem was to give effect to it. But this assumption was mistaken. There are objections to the idea of human rights which I shall briefly indicate. They are not, however, insuperable. In this book I shall argue that there is a rationally defensible idea of human rights. It is at once less straightforward and more modest than anything in the documents but not on that account without significance. Just what its significance is, however, is something else which I shall consider in this book, which is an essay in the philosophy of human rights. It is concerned with the answers to two related questions: 'What can be meant by human rights?' and 'How should we think of them?'

0.1.2   If the adjective 'human' is taken seriously, the idea of human rights must be the idea that there are certain rights which, whether or not they are recognised, belong to all human beings at all times and in all places. These are the rights which they have solely in virtue of being human, irrespective of nationality, religion, sex, social status, occupation, wealth, property, or any other differentiating ethnic, cultural or social characteristic. Article 2 of the UN Declaration appears to support this suggestion:

Everyone is entitled to all the rights and freedoms set forth in this Declaration without distinction of any kind such as race, colour, sex,

1

language, religion, political or other opinion, national or social origin, property, birth or other status.

But a passage in the preamble shows that the authors had something else in mind.

Now therefore the General Assembly proclaims this Universal Declaration of Human Rights as a common standard of achievement for all peoples and all nations to the end that every individual and every organ of society keeping this declaration constantly in mind, shall strive by teaching and education to secure respect for these rights and freedoms, and by progressive measures national and international, to secure their effective recognition and observance . . . .

This shows that the idea of human rights which the authors had in mind was that of an ideal standard which every human community should try to reach. Article 2 simply affirms the universality of the standard. What it requires is respect for all the rights set forth in the Declaration. As a cursory reading is enough to show, these embody the values and institutions of modern liberal-democratic industrial society. As we shall see, this gives rise to a problem.

Thus Article 8 affirms equality before the law: 'Everyone has the right to an effective remedy by the competent national tribunals for acts violating the fundamental rights granted to him by the constitution or the law.' Article 10 provides for freedom of expression and inquiry: 'Everyone has the right to freedom of opinion and expression. This right includes freedom to hold opinions without interference and to seek, receive and impart information and ideas through any media and regardless of frontiers.' Article 21 provides for democratic political procedures: 'Everyone has the right to take part in the government of his country directly or through freely chosen representatives . . . .' Articles 22–30 set forth economic and social rights. They embody the values and institutions characteristic of what has come to be known as the 'Welfare State'. This Article 23 states, 'Everyone has the right to work, to free choice of employment, and to protection against unemployment . . . .' According to Article 24, 'Everyone has the right to rest and leisure, including reasonable limitation of working hours, and to periodic holidays with pay.' Finally, Article 25 lays down that 'Everyone has the right to a standard of living adequate for the health of himself and his family, including food, clothing, housing and medical care . . . .'

Because the ideal standard consists of rights which embody the values and institutions of liberal-democratic industrial society, it implicitly includes those values and institutions. The preamble is by implication calling upon all nations to become liberal-democratic industrial societies. The 'progressive measures, national and international' which they are urged to take must be directed towards this end. But the majority of humanity do not live in such societies and have never done so. Nor are they likely to be able to do so in the foreseeable future. That possibility is precluded by present economic and cultural conditions. Unfortunately this has been ignored by the authors. The result is that, in the case of many nations, and notably those which make up the so-called 'Third World', the ideal standard is inevitably utopian. To them many of the rights set forth in the Declaration, despite its claim to universality, are simply irrelevant. So much the worse, then, for the Declaration. An account of human rights which makes many of them irrelevant to much of humanity is not a rationally defensible account.

The European Convention makes no claim to universality. Its preamble states that the signatories, certain Western European governments, acknowledge 'allegiance to a common heritage of political traditions, ideals, freedoms, and the rule of law'. The rights set forth in the Convention are therefore restricted to citizens of the states which share the common heritage. They do not extend to the people of Third World nations. Much less are they the rights of all human beings at all times and in all places. This is borne out by the rights themselves. They consist of the main constitutional and political rights characteristic of liberal-democratic states, and include most, although not all, of the rights set forth in the first twenty-one articles of the UN Declaration. They contain a number of explicit references to 'democratic society': notably in Articles 9, 10 and 11. What is the justification for calling them 'human rights' as distinct from 'liberal-democratic rights'? Presumably it is that, in the opinion of the signatories, the common heritage which the rights embody represents a standard of excellence which other nations would do well to try to emulate. They are saying in effect, 'We who have approximated to this standard, think that all nations would do well to try to reach it, but, however that may be, we intend to maintain it.' The idea of human rights upon which the Convention is based is thus at least implicitly that of an ideal standard. Since it is a standard which for the foreseeable future is out of reach of much of humanity, the account of human rights in the Convention is open to the same objection as that in the Declaration.

0.1.3   There is another objection to equating human rights with liberal-democratic and modern social-welfare rights. The particular values and institutions which these embody have their roots in the Western tradition of culture and civilisation. But the Western is only one of a number of such traditions. Others are the Islamic, the Hindu and the Buddhist, to name only three, each of which is based upon a great religion.[1] Western civilisation may be pre-eminent in science and technology, and in industry and commerce. But that does not justify erecting certain of its values and institutions, with their associated rights, into a universal standard. West may be best for Westerners; but to assume that it must be so for humanity at large is unwarranted. This objection casts doubt upon any idea of human right which presents it as a universal ideal standard. Such an ideal, with its constitutive values and institutions, must, if it is to be coherent, be drawn from a particular tradition of culture and civilisation. Those who belong to a different tradition have no reason to accept it.

These considerations point to an objection to the idea of human rights which I sketched at the outset: that of certain rights which belong to all human beings at all times and in all places. This idea ignores the social basis of an individual's identity as a human being. A man becomes the person and the human being that he is by growing up in a particular community, learning to speak its language, and to participate in its life. There must be some community for him to grow up in if he is to become a person and, in more than a purely zoological sense, a human being at all. But what community it is makes an important difference. If his native community had been different, in important respects he would have been a different person from the one he has in fact become. His native language would have been different. So would many of the ideas, beliefs and values in terms of which he has been brought up to think and act. Hence no human being can be socially and culturally neutral. He is always the product of some social and cultural milieu. Different traditions of culture and civilisation are different ways of being human. It follows that rights which belonged to all human beings at all times and in all places would be rights which they had as 'desocialised' and 'deculturised' beings. Since they are not and cannot be such beings, there cannot be such rights.

A different but complementary argument is developed by Alasdair MacIntyre in *After Virtue*, when discussing the idea of human rights. According to him, not only are there no human rights: the notion of a right itself is not found in every society. After pointing out that claims to the possession of rights presuppose the existence of a set of socially established rules, he goes on, 'Such sets of rules only come into existence at particular historical periods and in particular social circumstances. They are in no way universal features of the human condition.'[2] He supports this by pointing out that

> There is no expression in any ancient or medieval language correctly translatable by our expression 'a right' until near the close of the Middle Ages. The concept lacks any means of expression in Hebrew, Greek, Latin, Arabic classical or medieval, before about 1400, let alone in Old English or in Japanese as late as the mid-nineteenth century.

As he understands 'human rights', 'They are supposed to attach equally to all human individuals whatever their sex, race, religion, talents or deserts.' In view of the linguistic facts to which he has referred, he considers that 'It would of course be a little odd that there should be such rights attaching to human beings simply *qua* human beings ....' Referring to the same linguistic facts, he then comments, 'From this of course it does not follow that there are no natural or human rights, it only follows that no one could have known that there were ....' He concludes that 'There are no such rights', adding that 'Every attempt to give good reasons for believing that there are such rights has failed.' His verdict is that 'Natural or human rights are fictions', and that 'belief in them is at one with belief in witches and unicorns'.

0.2   HUMAN RIGHTS AS A MINIMUM STANDARD

0.2.1   A rationally defensible idea of human rights must be able to meet all these objections. They may be briefly summarised as follows.

(a)   The idea of human rights as that of an ideal standard consisting of liberal-democratic and modern social-welfare rights makes many of such rights irrelevant to much of humanity, including the peoples of the Third Word.

(b)   The idea of human rights as any kind of ideal standard ignores cultural diversity. If the ideal is to be coherent, it must be drawn from a particular tradition of culture and civilisation and those who belong to other traditions have no reason to accept it.

(c)   The idea of human rights as those which belong to all human beings at all times and in all places, ignores not only cultural diversity but also the social basis of personal identity. It presupposes homogeneous desocialised and deculturised human beings and there are no such beings.

(d)   MacIntyre's objections, of which there are three. The first is that the notion of a right is not found in every society and is not necessary for social life as such. This is supported by the fact that in no ancient language and in no medieval language until near the close of the Middle Ages is there any expression correctly translatable by our expression 'a right'. The Greeks did not have a word for it! The second objection is that, if there are human rights, no one could have known that there are before the modern era. The third is that there are none, because all attempts to give good reasons for the belief in human rights have failed. Belief in them is like belief in witches or unicorns.

The idea of human rights which I shall argue is rationally defensible is not that of an ideal but that of a minimum standard. More accurately, it is the idea that there are certain rights respect for which is required by a universal minimum moral standard. They are not, however, liberal-democratic and modern social-welfare rights. Hence, so far as (a) is concerned, there is no case to answer. What about (b)? Must not a minimum, no less than an ideal, standard be drawn from a particular tradition of culture and civilisation? No, if the minimum standard has its roots in certain moral requirements of social life as such, irrespective of the particular form it takes. I shall argue that this is the case, that the minimum standard is applicable to all cultures and civilisations, irrespective of the differences between them. If my argument is sound, objection (c) is answered. A minimum moral standard which is applicable to all cultures and societies does not deny that every human being is largely made what he is by his particular cultural and social experience. It does not presuppose homogeneous desocialised and deculturised human beings. Rather it presupposes social and cultural diversity and sets minimum moral requirements to be met by all societies and cultures. Such requirements set moral limits to the scope of diversity but in no way deny its existence. The universal applicability of the minimum moral standard entails that the rights for which it requires respect should be universally recognised. In an intelligible sense, they are the moral rights of all human beings at all times and in all places: that is, universal moral rights. But this appears to run straight into MacIntyre's objections.

0.2.2   According to him, Greek, along with other ancient languages, had no word for our expression 'a right'. But in the *Phaedo* Socrates's last words are 'Crito, I owe a cock to Asclepius: will you remember to pay the debt?' Now, to say that something is owed is to say that payment of it is due to whomever it is owed to. This is equivalent to saying that the latter is entitled – that is, has a right – to have it paid. While the Greeks did not have a single expression literally translatable by our expression 'a right', they clearly had a working understanding of the concept. This is shown by the fact that they had an expression literally translatable by our 'is due'. Moreover, our expression 'a right' is not univocal. According to Wesley N. Hohfeld, it expresses four distinct conceptions. These are claims, privileges or liberties, powers, and immunities (see 6.2.1–4 for a discussion of Hohfeld). Each is a right when respect for it is due to its possessor, this being prescribed by law, morality or custom. But what must be done to show respect, and by whom, are different in each case. Too much should not be read into the fact that an expression in one language has no single equivalent in another. There may be other expressions in the second language the use of which shows that its speakers have a working understanding of the concept for which in the first language there is a single expression. The linguistic fact cited by MacIntyre as evidence for his contention that the notion of a right is not found in every society is not decisive.

In fact his contention is mistaken. This can be seen by considering the implications of the institution of property and the practice of promising. Some form of the institution of property is necessary for social life as such. Without it, the members of a community would have no way of coming to possess, of distributing, using and maintaining the material things necessary for their corporate and individual survival. The practice of promising is equally necessary. Without it, the members could not make agreements and give undertakings. They would be unable to engage in systematic co-operation and such co-operation is one of the constituents of social life. Now, both the institution and the practice are constituted by rules and these necessarily confer rights, whether or not there is a single linguistic expression for them. Property rules must entitle people to acquire, and to transfer, material goods and services. The rules of promising must entitle promisees to have promises kept.

In denying that sets of rules which confer entitlements are found in every society, MacIntyre must have forgotten about property and promising. Apart from this, the notion of a right is part of the concept of social membership. Part of what it is to be a member of any social group, whether it be a community, an association or a family, is that certain things are due to you from fellow members and due to them from you. If nothing at all is due to you, if you can be treated arbitrarily, you cannot have the status of member of the group. In English today, this is expressed by saying that, as a member, you have rights and obligations *vis à vis* your fellow members. In other languages it may be expressed in terms not literally translatable into English as 'rights and obligations'. But the root idea is the same: that of there being certain acts and forbearances which are due to and from fellow members in virtue of their membership. In this elementary but fundamental sense, the notion of a right is necessary for social life as such.

There remain MacIntyre's other objections. His equating of belief in human rights with belief in witches or unicorns is mistaken. Whether or not there are witches or unicorns is an empirical question. An affirmative answer must be supported by evidence in the form of independent reports that creatures having the characteristics of witches or unicorns have been observed on certain occasions in particular places: reports which are sufficiently detailed and precise to be publicly checked by further independent observations. Whether there are human rights, respect for which is required by a universal minimum moral standard, is not an empirical question. Rather it is a question about the implications of social life as such and whether these include such a standard. The answer turns on the outcome of an inquiry into the nature of morality and its role in social life. This must include an inquiry into moral and social concepts, into what we are saying and doing in using them, and into what they commit us to. MacIntyre's comment, that, if there are human rights, before the modern era no one could have known that there are is beside the point. People are invariably unaware of many of the implications of even the most familiar ideas in terms of which they regularly think and act. They acquire such ideas unself-consciously in the course of growing up and have a working understanding of them and the concepts they contain, sufficient for the practical business of living, but that is all. If and when some of these implications are made explicit so that many people become aware of them, that marks an increase in self-knowledge and understanding and makes possible more informed thought and action. MacIntyre's comment shows only that, if there are human rights, the modern era differs from earlier ages in making possible thought and action informed by knowledge of them.

0.2.3   MacIntyre's demand for good reasons to show that there are human rights is of course justified. In this book I shall do my best to meet it. His claim, which I do not dispute, that all attempts so far have failed, while not showing that the task is impossible, suggests that it is formidable. However, the idea of human rights as part of a universal minimum moral standard reduces its difficulty, or so I hope to show. In that connection, a problem so far glossed over is worth briefly mentioning here. It is not enough to show that the minimum standard has its roots in certain moral requirements of social life as such. That shows only that it is applicable within every human community, not that it is universally applicable: that is, to relations between different communities and between their respective members. It must be shown that the minimum standard is applicable to human relations as such: not only to all transactions between fellow countrymen or between co-religionists, but also to all those between inhabitants of different countries or between 'true believers' and infidels and heretics. I shall attempt to demonstrate that there is such a universal standard.

Is the attempt worth making? Does it matter whether good reasons can be given to show that there is a universal minimum moral standard? In the past, when the various traditions of culture and civilisation were relatively self-contained and contact between them was limited and sporadic, it mattered less than today, which is not to say that it did not matter at all. If there are good reasons for such a standard and in the past they had been widely appreciated, then it is at least possible that the cruelty and suffering inflicted on human beings by human beings would have been less than it actually was. Be that as it may, it certainly matters today. This is because our era is one of global interdependence brought about by modern science and technology. No longer are the various traditions relatively self-contained. There is continuous contact between them, which generates both co-operation and conflict. A universal minimum moral standard, because it only sets minimum requirements, would still be compatible with considerable cultural diversity. To show that there are good reasons for such a standard is to make at least an intellectual contribution to fostering human co-operation and to lessening human conflict. In the age of nuclear weapons and increasing danger to the natural environment, such a contribution, although modest, is not negligible. The attempt then is worth making not only for the sake of its intrinsic philosophical interest but also because it can help us to understand matters which today are of vital human concern.

0.2.4   In order to show that respect for certain rights is required by a universal minimum moral standard, it is necessary to show that there is such a standard. As we have seen, that means inquiring into the nature of morality and its role in social life. It must be shown that the standard has its roots in the moral requirements of social life as such, and is applicable not only within every community but to all human relations. In this book, the aim of Part I, 'Morality', embracing Chapters 1–5, is to do this. It must also be shown what the rights are, respect for which is required by the standard. That means inquiring into the nature of rights and how people come to have them. These matters are dealt with in Part II, 'Rights', embracing Chapters 6–9. The prominence of the idea of human rights in Western political rhetoric today was noted at the outset. In Chapter 9 I shall say something about the significance for politics of the idea of human rights as a minimum standard. While less than might be supposed from contemporary rhetoric, it is not wholly negligible. To justify the claims to have a right, reference must be made either to a set of rules or to a principle which is its source. Rules and principles are important not only in morality and in law but in all rational conduct. An initial discussion of them is necessary as a preliminary to what is to follow. This is undertaken in Chapter 1.

There is one matter about which a preliminary word is necessary. It concerns something already pointed out: that rights respect for which is required by a universal minimum moral standard are in an intelligible sense universal moral rights. Because the universal standard is a minimum one, it is compatible with much cultural and moral diversity. Universal moral rights – that is, human rights – must therefore be contextually interpreted. This is necessary to take account of the diversity. This means that what is a violation according to one moral code is not necessarily so according to another. But there must be some acts which always and everywhere violate the right, because failing to meet the minimum moral requirements of the universal standard. If a particular moral code permits such acts, then in that respect it is morally defective. As an example, consider the right to life. If anything is a human right, it is. But, as a right of all human beings at all times and in all places, it can only be the right not to be wantonly killed and not to be exposed to unnecessary danger. But what counts as 'wanton' killing is not the same in every culture or according to every moral code. Consider the blood-feud, duelling and abortion. The taking of life which they involve is justified according to some moral codes, unjustified or 'wanton' according to others. But killing for purely private gain or for sadistic pleasure is always 'wanton'. Any moral code which does not condemn it is in that respect defective. Similar considerations arise in the case of necessary and unnecessary dangers. But here circumstances as well as moral and cultural values are important.

This is, however, only a preliminary comment. Clearly much more needs to be said about contextual interpretation and the application of the minimum standard, and that will be done in the course of this book, especially in Chapter 8. I mention it here to show that my position differs from the famous and venerable doctrine of Natural Law. According to that doctrine, Natural Law is a universal moral standard but not a minimum one. The 'natural' rights of which it is the source are universal moral rights but are not subject to contextual interpretation in the light of particular moral codes and cultural values. I shall have more to say in Chapter 8 about how my position differs from Natural Law in its failure to take cultural and moral diversity seriously. My position is not open to that criticism. Does taking cultural and moral diversity seriously entail cultural and moral relativism, and, if so, does it matter? These questions will also be taken up in Chapter 8. It is clear from all this that, in order to show that there is a rationally defensible idea of human rights and to assess its significance, it is necessary to inquire into a number of issues in moral, social and political philosophy. Some consideration must also be given to certain topics in the philosophy of law. About all these matters, however, I shall say no more than is necessary for my own purposes. What I have to say about each is therefore limited and partial. I claim only that it is correct so far as it goes and would find a place, albeit in a modified form, in a fuller account. The partial treatment of related issues is inevitable in any philosophical inquiry. One merit of human rights as the topic of such an inquiry is that many of the related issues are themselves intrinsically interesting and even a partial treatment of them may be illuminating. I at least have found this to be so and hope that the reader will too.

Part I
Morality

1 Rules, Principles and Conduct

1.1 RULES

1.1.1 Both morality and law are guides to conduct but there is an obvious difference between them. If I am caught breaking the law, I shall be brought before a court, sentenced and punished. But, if I am discovered acting immorally but not illegally – for instance, lying or betraying a confidence – there is no court which can sentence me. I shall incur blame, disapproval and perhaps hostility, but that is all. Law is backed by official sanctions imposed and carried out by judicial and penal authorities. Morality is backed only by the informal sanction of public opinion. But, although distinct, the two overlap. Actions which are prohibited by the criminal law are for the most part morally wrong whether or not they are illegal. Obvious examples are killing for private gain, rape, theft and unprovoked violence. The relation between law and morality is worth exploring further. But first something must be said about rules and principles and about rule-governed and principle-governed action. It is through the rules and principles which they contain that morality and law are guides to conduct. In this section I shall be concerned with rules, in the next with principles, before returning in the final section of the chapter to morality and law.

A rule is stated in the imperative mood. So is a command. A command tells a person or a number of persons to do something on a particular occasion. 'Shut the door!' 'Stand up!' 'Stop talking!' The simplest kind of rule is a generalised command. It tells people to do something or not to do something, not merely on a particular occasion but on all occasions of a specified kind, or sometimes on all occasions without qualification. 'Always shut the door when you leave the room!' 'Always stand up when a lady enters!' 'Never talk in the library!' 'Always tell the truth!' 'Never commit adultery!' A rule in the form of a generalised command is applied to a situation of the kind which it covers by giving the appropriate command: that is, by telling people to do an action of the kind it prescribes or not to do one of the kind it forbids.

1.1.2 Rules in the form of generalised commands are first-order or primary rules. They are directly concerned with what is to be done and must be distinguished from rules of another kind. These are second-order or secondary rules. They are directly concerned not with what is to be done but with who decides. They confer authority to make rules and give commands, and specify who is subject to this authority. Thus, while they contain generalised commands, they also contain something more. They tell people subject to authority always to comply with its prescriptions. But they also confer the authority to make the prescriptions.[1] Constitutional law, which is concerned with legislative, executive and judicial authority, largely consists of secondary rules. Criminal law, which is directly concerned with what should be done and, more especially, what should not be done, largely consists of primary rules. In morality it is primary rules which are most conspicuous and familiar: for instance, rules about keeping agreements, telling the truth and refraining from bullying. But there are also secondary moral rules: for instance, those conferring parental authority. It is because they contain generalised commands that secondary rules can be applied to particular situations. This is done by telling people on a particular occasion to do what the authority to which they are subject has ordained: to carry out the order of a court, to obey police directives, to comply with parents' decisions.

There is another distinction which, while it may appear similar to, must not be confused with, that between primary and secondary rules. This is the distinction between regulative and constitutive rules.[2] Regulative rules, as their name implies, regulate action. Their defining characteristic is that the actions which they cover, are logically independent of them. An example is the rule limiting the speed of vehicles in built-up areas to 30 miles per hour. This presupposes that vehicles can be driven in built-up areas irrespective of any rule regulating their speed. The rule then regulates it by setting a limit to it. In the case of constitutive rules, the opposite is true. The actions they cover are logically dependent upon them. The rules of games are examples. The game of chess is constituted by rules specifying what the pieces are, how they can be moved and what the purpose of the game is. Without the rules, there could be no such game and no chess moves. Not only games but all institutions exist in virtue of constitutive rules. Take the most ubiquitous of all institutions, that of language. Without lexical, grammatical and syntactical rules, there could be no speech because no possibility of formulating sentences. Individual speech acts such as statements, questions, requests, appeals and commands must observe more or less correctly the constitutive rules of the language in which they are uttered.

A simple example of constitutive rules in the field of law is provided by the legal institution of property. Legal rules about acquisition, use and transference are necessary to constitute it. Theft is a breach of these rules and without them there could be no such offence. Bentham understood this: 'Legislation must first determine what things are to be regarded as each man's property before the general rule of ethics on this head can have any particular application.'[3] But Proudhon did not. His aphorism 'Property is theft' betrays a failure to understand that the prohibition of theft is a constitutive rule of the institution of property. Unless there is property there cannot be theft, because there is nothing to steal. Hence property as such cannot be theft. An individual case of theft is logically dependent upon the institution of property, including the constitutive rule prohibiting theft. A simple example from the field of morality is provided by the institution or practice of promising. The rule that promises must be kept, is a constitutive rule of this institution. It is part of what makes promising possible, and every promise is logically dependent upon it. It cannot be a regulative rule because it is already contained in what *per impossibile* it is supposed to regulate.

The actions covered by regulative rules must be logically independent of them. But regulative rules can regulate actions and activities which are made possible by constitutive rules and which are therefore logically dependent upon them. Examples of regulative rules which do this are the tactical rules of games, rules of literary style and rules imposing customs and excise duties. All regulative rules are primary rules because they are directly concerned with what is to be done. All secondary rules are constitutive because without them there could be no authority to enact rules and give commands. The having of such authority is logically dependent upon the secondary rules which confer it. But not all primary rules are regulative rules. Many are constitutive. An example is one which we have just discussed: the rule that promises must be kept. It is a constitutive rule of the practice of promising. But it is also a primary rule because it is directly concerned with what is to be done. The same is true of the rule prohibiting theft. It is both a primary rule and a constitutive rule of the institution of property. Another example is the constitutive rules of a language. They are primary rules because they say what must be done in order to speak the language: that is, how words are to be used and sentences formulated.

The following is a summary of what has been said so far.

(a) Every rule is either a primary or a secondary rule. It is either about what is to be done or who decides. If the former, it is a primary rule; if the latter, a secondary rule.

(b) Every rule is either regulative or constitutive. It is regulative if what it covers is logically independent of it, but constitutive if what it covers is logically dependent on it.

(c) All regulative rules are primary rules and all secondary rules are constitutive rules. But a primary rule may be either regulative or constitutive, and a constitutive rule may be either primary or secondary.

(d) Primary rules, whether regulative or constitutive, have the form of generalised commands. But secondary rules, because they confer authority, are more than simply generalised commands. It may be thought that many constitutive primary rules have the form of definitions rather than generalised commands: for instance, rules of vocabulary, scoring-rules in games, and eligibility rules for membership of voluntary associations. But generalised commands are implicit in the definitions. Rules of vocabulary say how words should be used; scoring-rules tell referees and players how and when points should be awarded; and eligibility rules say who can and who cannot be considered for membership. Every rule must contain a generalised command implicitly if not explicitly. If it did not, it would have no imperative force and could not be a guide to conduct.

1.1.3 What has been said about secondary rules shows one way in which rules can come into being. They may be enacted by a person, an agency, or a rule-making body, with authority to enact them. Examples are statutes enacted by legislatures, the rules of a game enacted by its governing body, and the rules of a club enacted by its members at its annual general meeting. Secondary rules as well as primary rules can be enacted: for instance, a statute enacted by a legislature conferring authority upon a local council to make byelaws; or a rule passed by the annual general meeting of a club conferring authority upon its management committee to make rules about the use of its facilities. But there are many rules which have never been enacted. An example is the rules of a language. They are part of the language and came into being as the language came to be spoken. Grammarians may have codified them but this codification is not enactment. It is the systematic recording and presentation of what those who speak the language are already doing. Linguistic rules, that is to say, are discovered not enacted. Other examples are the rules of custom, of traditional practices and of morality. Their origin lies in the origins of custom, tradition and morality, and, as these change, so they change. For convenience I shall call such rules 'conventional' to distinguish them from enacted rules. The term 'convention' is used in the sense in which Dicey used it when writing of the conventions of the British Constitution.[4] This was to distinguish constitutional conventions from positive laws.

Conventional rules are prior to enacted rules in the sense that without conventional rules there could be no enacted rules, but there could be conventional rules without there being any enacted rules. This priority is logical. An enacted rule must be formally stated. It therefore presupposes language and linguistic rules. Apart from the special case of technical language, linguistic rules can only be conventional. They cannot be created by enactment because there must already be language and linguistic rules in which to state them. But enacted rules also presuppose conventional rules in the form of customary, traditional and moral rules. A rule can be enacted only if a secondary rule confers the authority to enact it. It is possible for this secondary rule itself to be an enacted rule, but only if one of two conditions is satisfied.

One is that there is another secondary rule which is conventional and which confers the authority to enact the first secondary rule. An example is the convention of the British Constitution which confers authority upon 'The Crown in Parliament' to enact statutes, including ones which delegate legislative authority to subordinate bodies such as local councils. The other is that the enacted secondary rule is part of a written constitution: for instance, of a nation state or a voluntary association. To come into operation, a written constitution must either be officially approved through a referendum, or else officially adopted at an inaugural meeting summoned for the purpose. A referendum presupposes a moral commitment to abide by the result and therefore that moral rules already exist. The official adopting of a constitution at an inaugural meeting presupposes the moral rule that agreements should be kept. This is because those who adopt it are agreeing to its provisions and to be bound by them. The holding of a meeting also presupposes rules of procedure. Such rules can be codified and some can be created by enactment. But they cannot all be. A meeting summoned to draw up new procedural rules would have to operate according to existing ones while drawing them up. Some procedural rules at least must be conventional. This is a particular case of the logical priority of conventional to enacted rules.

1.1.4   Something must be said about what Rawls calls 'summary rules'.[5] These are rules based upon summaries of, or generalisations from, experience. Examples are rules of health and hygiene, and of technique and skill. They are regulative not constitutive rules because the kinds of action they cover must be logically independent of them. If this were not so, there would be no experience from which to generalise or to summarise. Such rules may be incorporated into traditional practices but they cannot be merely conventional. This is because conscious thought must have gone into their formulation. The experience upon which they are based must have been systematically considered. On the other hand, although they may be codified in textbooks, such rules cannot have been created by formal enactment. This is because they are arrived at through empirical inquiry and trial and error. No secondary rule is needed to confer authority to make them. What is necessary is the requisite experience and thought. Summary rules are best described as being informally enacted. Informal enactment is a third way, over and above formal enactment and convention, through which rules can come into being. Nor is it only summary rules which originate in informal enactment. The same is true of all informal rules, such as those which a man makes for himself, or those which an informal group spontaneously associating for the sake of a common purpose may make for carrying it out.

    Informally enacted rules must be formulated in words. Like formally enacted rules, they presuppose language. This is also true of customary, traditional and moral rules. Although conventional in origin, it must be possible to say what they are. Otherwise they could not be taught and learned. Nor would it be possible to say when they have been obeyed or broken. Without language, there could be no rules at all. But, as we have seen, language is itself rule-governed. In order to speak, one must more or less correctly observe linguistic rules. It follows that linguistic rules are logically prior to all other rules. All other rules are formulated by means of linguistic rules, and linguistic rules themselves must be observed in their own codification by grammarians. But this priority is not only logical. It is also temporal in the sense that one must learn to speak before one can learn other rules and understand what it is to obey or to break them. Finally, before turning to the subject of principles, it must be stressed that what has been said here about rules is far from being a complete account. I have drawn attention only to those features of rules which have a bearing upon what is to come later.

1.2 PRINCIPLES

1.2.1 The notion of principles is familiar in both theoretical and practical contexts. The student of an academic subject encounters it at the outset: for instance, principles of mathematics, principles of economics, principles of literary criticism. They are the fundamental ideas of a subject which enable it to be understood in detail. In practical contexts, principles provide the basis for action informed by understanding. They do this by laying down certain requirements which such action must meet. Consider the following examples: the moral principle of beneficence, the political principle of constitutional opposition, the strategic principle of 'the offensive'.

The first requires that, between good and evil, good should always be chosen; that, between goods, the greatest good; and, between evils, the least evil. Meeting these requirements is essential in morality. Not to understand that they must be met is not to understand an elementary but fundamental part of morality. The second is a principle of representative government. According to it, while there is an obligation to obey the government of the day, there is no obligation to agree with it. There must be freedom to express in public both support for and opposition to the government, freedom to form and to join political parties, and freedom to contest elections. To show respect for these freedoms is a requirement which all who engage in politics must meet. Not to understand that this is a requirement is not to understand representative government. The third is a principle for the conduct of war. It says that an important aim must be to gain and hold the initiative, making the enemy fight under conditions not of his choosing, and allowing him no respite. These who plan and conduct military operations are required to pursue this aim. Not to understand that this is a requirement is not to understand how war should be conducted. Action which is intended to meet the requirements of beneficence is action informed by an understanding of morality. The same is true of the other examples. Action intended to meet the requirements of constitutional opposition is informed by an understanding of representative government. Action intended to meet the requirements of 'the offensive' is informed by an understanding of how to conduct war.

1.2.2 Rules also lay down requirements for action, but there is a significant difference between following a rule and acting on a principle. Someone following a rule has no discretion about what to do. The rule tells him. He must keep his promise, must not exceed the speed limit, must comply with the local fire regulations. Someone acting on a principle has discretion. The principle lays down a requirement but does not tell him how to meet it. He must decide that for himself. A moral agent must identify the evils confronting him and decide which is the least. A political party out of office must decide whether to support or to oppose the government on a particular issue and the government must decide how to answer its critics. Generals must decide what to do to gain the initiative and how best to exploit it. It is because discretion must be exercised in deciding how to meet its requirements that a principle provides the basis for action informed by understanding. Because a rule allows no discretion, it cannot provide such a basis. In order to follow a rule, all that is necessary is to know what it is, and to be able to recognise the occasion on which it applies. Rule-governed action is simply right or wrong. A rule is either kept or it is broken.

There is a sense in which principle-governed action is also either right or wrong. It is right when an attempt is made to act on an appropriate principle, wrong when the principle is ignored: for instance, when no thought is given to which alternative is the greater good, or when what is acknowledged to be the greater evil is deliberately chosen; when a government refuses to answer its critics, when it persecutes them, or when a political party turns to subversion; or when a general remains on the defensive without making any plan to counter-attack. But while it is right to attempt to act on a principle, what is attempted may be well or ill conceived and executed. A man may misjudge the character of the evils confronting him. A political party may play into the government's hands by ill-considered or intemperate opposition. A general may surrender the initiative by attacking in the wrong place or at the wrong time. Principle-governed action may be better or worse, as well as being right or wrong. Some understanding of what a principle is a principle of, and of why it requires what it does, is necessary if there is to be any attempt to act upon it at all. But the

quality of the understanding which actually informs an action intended to meet
a principle's requirements can vary from excellent to poor.

   The perspective of rule-governed action is confined to what situations have
in common. What matters about any situation is what the rules are for situations
of that kind. Actions of the kind prescribed for situations of that kind must be
done, those forbidden not done. No account need be taken of it as an individual
situation. Its details, its particular features and circumstances, can be ignored.
The perspective of principle-governed action is not confined to what situations
have in common. Attention must be given to the individual situation. Its details,
its particular features and circumstances, are clearly important in deciding how
best to meet the requirements of principles applying to situations of that kind.
What evils do the possible alternatives involve and which is the least? What is
the best line to take about a particular issue, bearing in mind the policy the
government is pursuing and public reactions to it? Where is the enemy most
vulnerable and what resources are available to take advantage of it? Such
questions can be answered only by paying attention to the details of the
situation. The requirements of rules are specific and can be formulated in
definite prescriptions and prohibitions. Those of principles are at a higher level
of generality and need contextual interpretation. That is why discretion must be
exercised and why, as we have already seen, principles provide the basis for
action informed by understanding. But, if the requirements of principles are to
be met, understanding must be addressed to the individual situation, which is
what contextual interpretation means.

1.2.3   Every situation is an individual situation however much it resembles
others. This suggests that rule-governed action, because its perspective is
confined to what situations have in common without taking account of them as
individual situations, is an inadequate, or at least an incomplete, form of action.
There is a core of truth in the suggestion. Rule-governed action is uniform
action: always doing the same thing on all occasions of the same kind. There is
no room for choice, let alone spontaneity, initiative, and innovation. A man who
tried to live by rules alone would be condemning himself to a life of
monotonous routine. It may be objected that he is a man of straw. No one
seriously advocates trying to live by rules alone. Granted; but that only
emphasises an important point contained in the suggestion. That is not that
rule-governed action is an inadequate form of action, if that means that we can
do without it. If there were no constitutive rules, there could be no language
and no institutions. If there were no regulative rules, conduct would be
unpredictable and past experience could not be summarised and made available
for present use. Rather, the point is that not all action can be rule-governed.
That this is the case is implicit in rule-governed action itself.

Constitutive rules point beyond themselves in the sense that actions which conform to them are also something more. They are necessary elements in the activities which the rules make possible. While there is no choice about what to do so far as the rules are concerned, there is in the activities of which they are the rules. People talking to one another are necessarily obeying linguistic rules, but that is not all they are doing. They are conversing, discussing, arguing, quarrelling, negotiating, asking and answering questions, or in some other way communicating with one another. While they cannot talk without obeying linguistic rules, the rules cannot tell them what to talk about. That is up to them. A game cannot be played unless, for the most part, the players keep to the rules. But in playing they are not simply keeping to the rules: they are making moves, attacking and defending, feinting and manoeuvring, in ways permitted by the rules. A description of the course of a game is a description of these moves, including the skill and judgement, the flair and finesse, which the players display. The rule that promises must be kept does not tell people what to promise or to whom. They must decide that for themselves in the course of their dealings with one another. The description of an act as 'keeping a promise' is incomplete. One needs to know the context and why that particular promise was made. Accounts of property transactions are not accounts of the laws of property. They are accounts of buying and selling, borrowing and lending, in which the laws are observed but which are entered into for commercial or financial reasons.

In the case of regulative rules, matters are similar but not identical. The activities which they regulate must be logically independent of them. Otherwise there would be nothing to regulate. Actions conforming to them are not necessary elements in these activities, because the latter can be carried on in the absence of any regulative rules. When they are performed, they are parts of these activities. There is no choice about what to do so far as the rules are concerned. But there is in the activities which the rules regulate. A law prescribing that one third of earned income must be paid in tax does not tell people how to earn their living. Traffic laws do not tell people where to drive to, when to drive, or whether to drive at all. It follows that rule-governed action, whether the rules are constitutive or regulative, is always incomplete. It points beyond itself to activities which involve choice and decision. These activities, because they involve choice and decision, cannot be merely rule-governed, although they are either made possible or are regulated by rules, or both. Nor is the enacting of a rule itself a rule-governed act. There must be a secondary rule conferring authority to enact it and prescribing obedience to what is enacted. But there cannot be a rule prescribing what rule to enact. That is for the rule-maker to decide within the limits of his jurisdiction. It follows that to think of all action as essentially rule-governed must be mistaken.[6] Such a view ignores the difference between rules and principles. It also ignores actions which neither follow rules nor implement principles: for instance, impulsive actions and actions promoted by strong emotions, such as jealousy or revenge.

1.2.4   The place of principles is in the activities which constitutive rules make possible and which regulative rules regulate. But not in all of them. There is no need for principles in essentially spontaneous activities or in those which do not call for reflective understanding: for instance, casual conversation or going for a walk. Where they are needed is in activities which cannot be engaged in without systematic understanding. They are arrived at by reflecting upon the nature and significance of an activity, analysing what those who engage in it are committed to trying to do, and formulating the results in requirements which they must try to meet in their actions. What is formulated when a principle is formulated is something implicit in the activity itself. In being formulated, it is made explicit and thus becomes the basis for action informed by understanding. It follows that the relation between principles and the activities of which they are the principles is a logical one. To engage in these activities is to act on their principles. But the relation between constitutive rules and the activities which they constitute is also a logical one. The activities are logically dependent upon the rules. How does this differ from the logical relation between principles and the activities of which they are the principles? An answer can be given in terms of 'necessary' and 'sufficient' conditions.

A necessary condition for being able to engage in an activity constituted by rules is to be able to obey the rules. No one can play a game unless he knows and can obey its rules. No one can speak a language unless he can comply with its grammar. But being able to obey the rules is not enough. In the case of a game, one must know how to attack and manoeuvre; in the case of a language, how to communicate with other speakers. But being able to engage in an activity is a sufficient condition for being able to obey its constitutive rules. If you can play a game, you must be able to obey its rules. If you can communicate in a foreign language with native speakers, you must be able to comply with its grammar. This relation is reversed in the case of regulative rules. A sufficient condition for being able to engage in activity regulated by rules is that you can obey these rules. If you can drive at a speed not exceeding 30 miles per hour in a built-up area, you must be able to drive. But being able to engage in activity is only a necessary, not a sufficient, condition for being able to obey any rules which may happen to regulate it. There may not be any rules. If there are, you can still engage in the activity without obeying them. When you exceed the speed limit, you are necessarily driving. It is not difficult to see why the relation in the one case must be the reverse of what it is in the other. It is because constitutive rules are logically prior to the activities which they constitute, while, in the case of regulative rules, the activities which they regulate are logically prior.

Being able to act upon the principles of an activity is both a necessary and a sufficient condition for being able to engage in it. This is because it is by acting on its principles that the activity is engaged in. This relation is symmetrical. Being able to engage in an activity is both a necessary and a sufficient condition for being able to act on its principles. But more needs to be said. A man who adopts a particular course because he judges it to be the least evil is acting morally. But acting morally is not confined to acting on the principle of beneficence. There are other moral principles: for instance, 'respect for human life' and justice. The same is true of our other examples. Constitutional opposition is not the only principle of representative government. Others are the principles of 'the rule of law' and of the accountability of the government to the governed. 'The offensive' is not the only principle of strategy. Others are 'the maintenance of the objective' and 'the maintenance of the strategic reserve'. For the sake of simplicity, each example has so far been confined to a single principle. But, in any activity which cannot be engaged in without understanding, there are likely to be a number of principles. This must not be omitted from an account of principle-governed action.

A man acting on principles must be able to decide on any given occasion which is the appropriate principle for that occasion. Unless he can do this, he cannot know what the requirements are which he must try to meet. Much less can he decide how best to meet them in the individual situation confronting him. It remains true that being able to engage in an activity of which there are principles, is both a necessary and a sufficient condition for being able to act on those principles. But being able to act on these principles includes being able to decide on any given occasion which is the appropriate principle for that occasion. Being able to act morally is therefore both a necessary and sufficient condition for being able on a particular occasion to know which moral principle is appropriate for that occasion, as well as being able to make and carry out a decision about how best to meet its requirements. What has been said about 'necessary' and 'sufficient' conditions can now be summarised. Being able to obey constitutive rules is a necessary but not a sufficient condition for being able to engage in the activities which they constitute. Being able to obey regulative rules is a sufficient but not a necessary condition for being able to engage in activities which they regulate. Being able to act on principles is both a necessary and a sufficient condition for being able to engage in the activities of which they are the principles. To this must be added that to be able to use language and therefore to obey linguistic rules is a necessary condition not only for all other rule-governed action but for any principle-governed action at all. The reason is that without language there can only be rudimentary thought:

certainly not the developed thought needed for acting on principles. This is a corollary of the logical and temporal priority noted in section 1.1.

1.2.5   It follows that to know the principles of an activity is not only to know what each of them is, but to know how each of them is related to the others. This is necessary in order to be able to decide on any given occasion which is the appropriate principle for that occasion. To know its principles is to understand an activity. But such understanding can never be complete. There is always the possibility of coming to understand it better. Further analysis may lead to the formulation of new principles or to the improved formulation of old ones. An activity may change in character owing to developments in related fields so that it becomes necessary to rethink its principle. A contemporary instance is the implications for military strategy of the development of nuclear weapons. Moreover, there may be different and to some extent conflicting views about the nature and significance of an activity. There will then be no unanimity about its principles and how they are related. As we shall see in later chapters, this is true of morality. All this does not mean that there are no immutable universal principles. On any view of morality, beneficence is a moral principle. Expediency and economy are general principles of instrumental action at all times and in all places. But it does mean that many principles are mutable in the sense of being open to improved or revised formulation as understanding increases or circumstances change. Many are of only restricted universality since they presuppose shared ideas and values. These matters need to be kept in mind in considering the role of principles in practical contexts.

One role which they have is to justify the breaking of rules. A man following a rule has no discretion about what to do. The rule tells him. We have seen that the perspective of rules is confined to what situations have in common. No account is taken of the details of the individual situation. But special circumstances may mean that obeying a rule is self-defeating because frustrating the activity of which it is a rule. This is obvious in the case of regulative rules. Owing to special circumstances, obeying a technical rule may yield poor results. Breaking it and doing something more efficacious is then justified by the principle of expediency. But there are also occasions when breaking a constitutive rule is justified: for instance, breaking a promise in order to remain at the scene of an accident and render assistance to the injured. This is justified by the principle of beneficence. Promising is a moral practice, but on this occasion its requirements are incompatible with more important moral demands. All this, however, depends upon whether the principle cited in justification for breaking a rule is widely accepted. This may not be the case, and, if it is not, breaking the rule will be controversial. But more about that later.

Before concluding this section, a reservation similar to that made at the end of the last is necessary. What has been said here about principles and principle-governed action is far from being a complete account. Attention has been confined to those features which have a bearing upon what is to come later. There is, however, one further matter about which a word is needed. We all know the expression 'It is a matter of principle!' When this is said, what is meant is not merely 'It is a matter in which there is a basis for action informed by understanding.' While this is not excluded, it is not what is primarily intended. That is something like 'It is a moral matter, as distinct from one of prudence or expediency.' This is an elliptical way of saying that a moral principle is involved and we cannot simply suit ourselves. In other words, it is a way of calling attention to the proper context in which a matter should be considered. When thus interpreted, the expression is not incompatible with anything said here. But, because it is elliptical, it needs to be interpreted.

1.3　LAW AND MORALITY

1.3.1　This chapter began with a reminder of an obvious difference between law and morality. Law is backed by official sanctions, imposed and carried out by judicial and penal authorities. Morality is backed only by the informal sanction of public opinion. This characteristic of law suggests that it must consist of enforceable rules: that is, rules breaches of which can be publicly ascertained and publicly dealt with. Examples of such rules already referred to are the primary rules of criminal law and the secondary rules of constitutional law. But the content of law need not be confined to enforceable rules. It is possible for a principle to be legally enforced. This can be done by specifying a minimum standard which people are required to meet when acting on it. An example is provided by the legal fault of negligence. The law requires people to exercise 'reasonable care' and the courts are authorised to adjudicate disputes about whether or not it has been exercised. The exercise of 'reasonable care' is a special requirement of the general principle of social responsibility. It is up to people to decide for themselves how best to meet this requirement in the light of individual circumstances. The fault which a court declares a man convicted of negligence to have committed is either to have disregarded the requirement or not to have met it in a way which satisfies the minimum standard.

　　There are also principles concerned with legal procedures and the administration of justice. They must be acted upon by those responsible for these matters: that is, law officers, judges and the police. An example is the principle of 'equality before the law'. According to it, all who are subject to a given system of law stand on an equal footing. No one is above the law in the sense of being exempt from the obligation to obey the law. Nor is anyone below the law in the sense of being denied its protection, or any facilities that it may afford. Another is the principle that no one should profit from wrong-doing. This applies in assessing legal liability and in sentencing. It may be thought that such principles cannot be legally enforced because they are presupposed in the enforcement of the law. But this does not preclude their being enforced in particular cases. If one of them is disregarded on a particular occasion, this can be publicly ascertained and dealt with by the courts. Such incidents, however, must be isolated cases if the whole legal system is not to break down. Law, then, consists of both rules and principles. As we have seen, morality also contains both rules and principles: the constitutive rule of promise-keeping, the principles of beneficence, 'respect for human life' and justice. But so far nothing has been said about virtues. They are usually thought of as belonging to, or having to do with, morality.

1.3.2   The concept of virtue is best understood as a special case of the wider concept of merit. 'Merit' is a term of favourable appraisal. To ask about the merits of something – for instance, a car, a book, a performance, a proposal – is to ask 'What are its good points? What, if anything, is there about it to commend?' It is also by implication to ask about its defects: that is, 'What, if anything, is wrong with it?' An appraisal can only be made with reference to a relevant standard or set of standards. To say of a car that it has certain merits and certain defects is to say that, with reference to the appropriate standards for cars, this one meets some of them and fails others. To say 'Your proposal has certain merits' is to say something like 'Your proposal is in certain respects suitable for the matter in hand.' What is essential in making an appraisal is to be able to give reasons for it: that is, to be able to show in what respects the appropriate standards are met or not met. If you say that X has certain merits and certain defects, you must be able to show what the merits are and why they are merits, and what the defects are and why they are defects.

Two kinds of appraisal which can be made of people need to be distinguished. One is of their abilities: that is, their various talents and skills, or their lack of them. A man is said to have certain merits and certain defects in a particular capacity – as an administrator, a teacher, a manager, a shop-steward, a doctor, a salesman, a musician, a mountaineer or a cricketer. Judged by the standards appropriate to a particular field, or to a particular role, post or job, he is good at certain things, not so good at others. The second is of people's characters. A man is of good character to the extent that he can be depended upon to act morally, of bad character to the extent that he cannot. Hence moral standards are the appropriate ones in such appraisals. It is in such appraisals that the concept of virtue is typically used. Virtues are character merits, vices character defects. A particular virtue is a particular character trait or disposition normally involved in, or necessary for, some aspect of moral conduct. A particular vice is a particular character trait or disposition normally either incompatible with, or an obstacle to, such conduct. An appraisal of a man's character must therefore be an appraisal of the character traits and dispositions he displays in his conduct. Those among them which are morally relevant are his personal virtues and vices.

To possess a virtue is to be able and willing, whatever the temptations to the contrary, to act on the principles and follow the rules of the aspect of morality with which it is connected. As examples, consider the familiar virtues of integrity, courage and loyalty. Integrity is the virtue of truthfulness, not only in word but also in deed. It means not lying, deceiving, cheating or stealing: on the positive side, keeping your word, admitting errors and failures, and being open and straightforward in your dealings. Courage consists of mastering fear and facing what you are afraid of. It is a virtue because needed whenever acting morally involves danger, real or imagined. But courage is not confined to people of good character. A scoundrel can exhibit it in the course of his nefarious activities. Hence it is a character trait necessary for, rather than involved in, moral conduct. Nor is it the same as, although it is intimately connected with, fortitude, which consists in being able to withstand suffering. Loyalty is the readiness to stand by and stand up for persons with whom you are associated, organisations to which you belong and causes which you support, if necessary at the expense of your safety and security. It is a virtue because necessary for meeting moral commitments in such relationships. But it is like courage in not being confined to moral commitments or, more accurately, to commitments which are morally justified. There can be loyalty between thieves and between conspirators.

While various virtues are connected with various aspects of morality, they are also connected among themselves. Morality cannot be cut up into water-tight compartments, each with its own special virtue. Loyalty clearly presupposes both integrity and courage. We have just seen that courage and fortitude are intimately associated. Moreover, one virtue, the most elementary of all, is necessary for morality as such. This is self-control. But these matters cannot be pursued further here. There is, however, one point which is important. As merits of character, virtues are logically distinct from talents and skills. Not that they are unrelated. Certain virtues are necessary for the developments of any talents and the acquisition of any skills: for instance, self-discipline, perseverance and, in many cases, courage.[7] Even a highly gifted man is unlikely to make much of his gifts without them. But morality and ability are not the same. A man of good character need not be especially talented or skilled. He can have many virtues and few vices without being particularly good at anything. But he will be good, for instance, as a husband, a colleague, a neighbour, a friend and a citizen.[8] He will be good, that is to say, in roles and relationships which make moral demands because he has the qualities of character necessary to meet them. What is perhaps misleadingly called 'moral education' is the attempt to instil and foster in children the various character traits and dispositions which make up the virtues. To cultivate and practice them is a basic moral obligation. Whether they are all compatible, or whether the development of some must be at the expense of the development of others, is a question which cannot, however, be pursued here.

1.3.3 'Obligation' is a key concept in both morality and law. Its central idea is that of having to do something because it is the right thing to do. To say of someone that he is under an obligation to do something is to say that he must do it whether he wants to or not, because it is morally or legally right. It may not be in his interest to do it, but that makes no difference if he is under an obligation to do it. Obligations and interests sometimes conflict, sometimes coincide, but are always logically distinct. If a man is under a moral obligation to do something, he has morally no choice about whether or not to do it, although he may have about how, when and where to do it. If he is under a legal obligation, the law may permit him some choice about the time, place and manner of complying, but none about whether or not to comply. The moral and legal exclusion of choice does not, however, exclude it physically and psychologically. A man may decide to break a promise because keeping it is inconvenient, or to exceed the speed-limit because he is in a hurry. In the first case his decision is morally wrong; in the second, legally wrong. But he can always choose to do wrong, although of course he ought not to. Particular moral obligations arise out of the detailed requirements of morality, particular legal obligations out of the detailed requirements of law. In the one case they are obligations to act upon moral principles, to obey moral rules and to cultivate and practice moral virtues; in the other, obligations to obey legal rules and act upon legal principles.

Morality is logically prior to law. There can be morality without law but not law without morality. This is because, while law can create particular obligations, it cannot create the general obligation to obey law. A law prescribing obedience to law would be pointless. It presupposes the very thing it is intended to create: the general obligation to obey law. That obligation must necessarily be moral. Without it, obedience to law could be a matter only of prudence, not of having to do the right thing. A system of positive law can come into being only where morality is already a going concern: that is, in a community most of whose members acknowledge that they have moral obligations and for the most part are able and willing to meet them. Without the moral obligation to obey law, there could be no legal obligations properly so-called. There could only be legal requirements backed by force. Furthermore, the maintenance of a system of positive law depends upon the integrity of those responsible for its administration and enforcement: that is, judges, the police and the legal profession. To the extent that these become corrupt, the operation of law is weakened. People cannot count upon receiving equal protection from it and upon being able to avail themselves of the facilities it affords.

The logical priority of morality to law can be presented in another way. This is as a special case of the logical priority of conventional to enacted rules (see 1.1.3 above). Every legal system must contain secondary as well as primary rules. This is because in every legal system there must be a judiciary to declare the law in disputed cases and to decide when it has been broken. Secondary rules are necessary to constitute and confer judicial authority. If much of the law in a given system takes the form of statutes – that is, consists of enacted rules – there must also be secondary rules constituting and conferring legislative authority. This is not a necessary feature of a legal system as such. Like the English Common Law, it can consist only of conventional rules. But without a judiciary there cannot be a legal system properly so-called at all. Hence the necessity for secondary rules to constitute and confer judicial authority. These secondary rules can be either conventional or enacted. If they are enacted, they presuppose conventional rules and, in particular, moral rules. If they are conventional, they must themselves be moral rules.

As enacted rules, they may be part of a written constitution. But we have seen (in 1.1.3) that a written constitution presupposes conventional rules and, in particular, the moral rule that agreements must be kept. Otherwise the constitution could not be adopted and come into operation. But they can be enacted without being part of a written constitution – for instance, rules enacted by a hereditary monarch. This, however, presupposes a moral secondary rule prescribing obedience to what the monarch ordains. Otherwise there could be no obligation to obey him. Again, they may be enacted by a representative meeting of the leaders of a community. That presupposes not only the moral primary rule that agreements must be kept but also moral secondary rules defining the relations between the people and their leaders. To put the matter generally, enacted secondary rules presuppose conventional rules which must include either moral secondary rules or the moral primary rule about keeping agreements. What is true of the general case is true of the particular case of enacted secondary rules conferring judicial authority. On the other hand, these secondary rules can themselves be conventional. But, if so, the judiciary must be a traditional institution of which they are the constitutive rules. In such a case they must be moral rules, since otherwise there would be no obligation to obey the judiciary.

The logical priority or morality to law is also a necessary part of the concept of crime. To commit a crime is to do wrong both legally and morally: legally, because it is to commit a legally punishable offence; morally, because of the moral obligation to obey the law and therefore not to commit legal offences, whether punishable or not. But this is not all. Apart from special circumstances, an act which is a crime would still be morally wrong even if it were not a crime – that is, not a punishable legal offence. Murder, rape and theft are breaches of moral rules whether or not there are laws prohibiting them. The justification for bringing a class of acts within the scope of the criminal law is that such acts are morally wrong. Not that all morally wrong acts should *ipso facto* be made punishable legal offences. Other considerations, especially enforceability, are important. But, unless there are moral rules and principles, there cannot be morally wrong acts and hence no justification for creating punishable legal offences. Moral rules and principles are not as such enforceable: that is, they need not be enforceable in order to be moral. What then is it which makes them moral? While this chapter has given a number of examples of moral principles and rules, the idea of morality and 'the moral' has not yet been investigated. It has been treated as a familiar idea, which of course it is. But its familiarity in everyday thought and action does not make it immune from critical scrutiny. Its importance for the idea of human rights makes such scrutiny necessary.

2 Morality and Society

2.1 WHAT MORALITY IS

2.1.1 Morality consists of virtues which there is an obligation to cultivate and practice, of principles upon which there is an obligation to act, and of rules which there is an obligation to follow. 'Obligation' is the primary moral concept. To say that something is a moral matter is to say that there is an obligation concerning it. It is a matter which must be attended to, irrespective of convenience, expediency or prudence. Not to attend to it would be wrong. An objection to this emphasis upon 'obligation' is that it takes no account of the moral achievements of saints and heroes.[1] Not so: saintliness and heroism are displayed in acts which 'go beyond the call of duty'. But there must be duty before there can be acts which go beyond its call. The concepts of 'saintliness' and of 'heroism' presuppose the concept of 'obligation'. Saints and heroes do more than is morally required of them. But, in order to identify and appreciate the 'more' which they do and their achievements in doing it, we must know what is morally required of them: that is, what their obligations are.[2]

To say that 'obligation' is the primary moral concept is not to deny that there are others. It is to say that 'obligation' is logically prior to these others, that they presuppose it and are intelligible only with reference to it. This is borne out by what was said about the concept of 'virtue' in the last chapter. Moral virtues are character traits and dispositions which are either involved in or necessary for moral conduct: that is, acting on moral principles and following moral rules. Moral principles and rules are therefore logically prior to moral virtues. It is with reference to them that those character traits and dispositions which there is an obligation to cultivate and practice can be identified. It is because there is an obligation to act upon the principles and follow the rules that there is an obligation to cultivate and practice such traits and dispositions. Hence the concept of 'obligation' is logically prior to the concepts of 'moral principles', 'moral rules' and 'moral virtues'.

2.1.2 Not all principles, rules and virtues, are moral. There are non-moral as well as moral imperatives. According to Kant, the distinction between the moral and the non-moral corresponds to a distinction between two kinds of imperatives: 'categorical' and 'hypothetical'.[3] Categorical imperatives are moral: that is, obligations. Hypothetical imperatives are non-moral. Hypothetical imperatives are well illustrated by the case of instrumental action: that is, 'means to ends' action. If I have adopted a certain end and a particular action is the best means of attaining it, I must do the action. But this imperative is conditional upon my having adopted the end. If I have not, there is no imperative upon me to do the action. Furthermore, I can release myself from the imperative by abandoning the end. This gives the key to the character of hypothetical imperatives. They are imperatives which are conditional upon the agent's decisions. He is subject to them by his own choice and, if he chooses, can release himself from them by abandoning what he hopes to gain by complying with them. It is up to him to decide in the light of what he wants and what he judges to be in his interest.

It is tempting to conclude that categorical imperatives are those which are not conditional upon the agent's decisions. Truthfulness is such an imperative. People must be truthful, irrespective of their interests and inclinations. But this will not do, because there are moral imperatives which in part are dependent upon the agent's decisions. An example is promise-keeping. If I have promised to do something, there is a moral imperative upon me to do it; not so, if I have not promised but only stated an intention to do it. The moral imperative is conditional upon my promise: that is, upon my prior decision. But, while I can abandon my intention, I cannot cancel my promise. Once I have promised, I am under an obligation: that is, subject to an imperative from which I cannot release myself. This is the respect in which obligations are categorical imperatives. They are imperatives which, once they have been incurred and irrespective of how they have been incurred, are not conditional upon what the agent wants to do or what it is in his interest to do. They are imperatives from which he cannot release himself, or, more accurately, from which he can only release himself by complying with them.[4] Kant's distinction between categorical and hypothetical imperatives is the distinction between imperatives from which the agent cannot release himself except by complying, and imperatives from which he can release himself without complying. As an account of the distinction between moral and non-moral imperatives, this is correct. Kant's development of the idea of categorical imperatives based on the principle of universalisability is another matter. But more about that in Chapter 5. Let us now look more closely at instrumental action and its imperatives, since these are *prima facie* cases of non-moral imperatives and according to Kant are hypothetical imperatives.

2.1.3   There are two general imperatives of instrumental action: expediency and economy. Of these, expediency is the more elementary, economy the more advanced. Expediency is addressed to an agent with a single end in view. It requires him to choose as a means that course of action which is most likely to attain the end successfully. Where techniques are available, this will be to follow the appropriate technical rules. Where they are not, the agent must find out for himself what course of action is most expedient. Economy is concerned with the allocation of finite resources with alternative uses among competing ends. It is addressed to an agent with a number of ends in view and with limited material resources for attaining them: for instance, time, energy and money. It requires him to do two things: first, to make up his mind about the relative importance of his various ends; second, to allocate his available resources among them in such a way that each is attained, not with perfect completeness, but as fully as its relative importance warrants. Economy may often require some sacrifice of expediency. The technically best way of attaining a given end may be too extravagant, leaving too few resources available for attaining other ends of at least equal importance. Instead of flying to New York by Concorde, I may have to make do with a 'stand-by' flight. But the requirements of expediency are always relevant. In any given case, they must first be known before any decision can be made about the extent to which they may have to be compromised for the sake of economy.[5]

Economy and expediency are rational imperatives of instrumental action. To undertake such action is to be rationally committed to them. But they are not as such moral imperatives. It is foolish to waste one's time, money and energy. It is foolish not to take advantage of available techniques. But foolishness and immorality are not identical. Certain character traits and dispositions are necessary for being good at instrumental action. The name given to them is 'efficiency'. It is the special virtue of instrumental action. But it is not as such a moral virtue. An efficient man is not necessarily a moral man. He may be dishonest or cruel. The same is true of 'prudence'. It is both a principle and a virtue. As a principle, it requires that risks should be minimised. As a virtue, it is the disposition to 'look before you leap'. It is foolish to take unnecessary risks and foolish not to look out for possible dangers. But, once more, foolishness is not identical with immorality. A prudent man is not as such a moral man. His prudence may lead him to evade meeting a particular obligation if meeting it would expose him to danger.

It is, however, incorrect to describe the imperatives of instrumental action as hypothetical. Such a description implies that people can always release themselves from them if they choose to do so, but that is not the case. Sometimes they can, but often they cannot. This is because meeting an obligation often involves instrumental action. If I have promised my companions on a walking-expedition to provide the food, I must undertake the instrumental action necessary to provide it. In undertaking this action, I am committed to the imperatives of economy and expediency. I cannot release myself from them, because in virtue of my promise I am under an obligation to undertake instrumental action and they are the imperatives of such action. Matters are different if I am going walking alone. I need to provide myself with food and must undertake the necessary instrumental action. But, if, for some reason, such as a change in the weather, I want to abandon my intention to go walking, I am free to do so. Because no obligation is involved, I can release myself from the imperatives of instrumental action by simply not undertaking the instrumental action which would have been necessary if I had not changed my mind. But, while people may be able to release themselves from the imperatives of instrumental action on particular occasions, much of life is inevitably taken up with such action. Quite apart from moral considerations, we are continually having to do things not for their own sake but for the sake of what they bring about. This is necessary not only to enable us to do what we enjoy or find worthwhile, but simply to stay alive. These are additional reasons why it is incorrect to describe the imperatives of instrumental action as hypothetical. Such action, together with its imperatives, is inescapable in the conduct of life.

Because meeting obligations often involves instrumental action, efficiency is a necessary although not a sufficient condition for morality. A completely inefficient man would be incapable of morality because incapable of the instrumental action involved in acting morally. Efficiency is not a sufficient condition because, as we have seen, an efficient man is not as such a moral man. Moreover, efficiency is a matter of degree. What morality requires is a reasonable degree of efficiency rather than the highest possible level. The imperative of efficiency is therefore not hypothetical. There is an obligation to cultivate it in order to be capable of meeting moral demands, but it must not be elevated to more than it is: an instrumental not a moral virtue. Similar considerations apply to prudence. A prudent man is not as such a moral man. But a completely imprudent man would be completely irresponsible and thereby unfitted for any position of trust. There is an obligation to cultivate the virtue of prudence because it is required not only for the sake of self-interest but also for the sake of morality. It follows from all this that the distinction between categorical and hypothetical imperatives is inadequate as the key to the distinction between the moral and the non-moral. It fails to capture the complexity of the relation between them.

2.2   THE SOCIAL BASIS OF MORALITY

2.2.1   Instrumental action is necessary for human life. Enjoyment and activities and experiences which are worthwhile for their own sake, while not strictly necessary, are desirable. Life totally devoid of them would not be worth living. What about morality? What is its contribution to human life? Why does there have to be morality at all? The short answer is that without it there could be no social life. A moment's reflection on the institution of property and the practice of promising is enough to show why. Both are essential in every human community, whatever its social structure and organisation. Without some form of the institution of property, material things could not be owned, used or maintained, and the members could not produce and distribute what they need for their corporate survival. Without the practice of promising there could be no agreements and therefore no joint undertakings and systematic co-operation. But both property and promising are constituted by moral rules. Without morality and its constitutive rules, there could be no such institution and no such practice (see 1.1.2 above). Hence, because both are essential in every community, without morality there could be no communities and therefore no human life, since human life is necessarily carried on in communities.

But, while this is true, it does not capture the full significance of morality for the life of human communities. To appreciate what that is, consider the concept of trust. It is a concept which presupposes morality. To trust a man is to be willing to act towards him in the belief that he will always do his best to meet his obligations: for instance, to be willing to take his word, to make agreements with him and, more generally, to co-operate with him. Not to trust him is to be reluctant to act towards him in such ways because of doubts about his moral character. He may be a liar and a cheat who has no scruples about using other people for his own ends. To say that a man is untrustworthy is to say in effect that he has no conception of the 'right thing to do', or that, if he has, it plays very little part in his conduct. You never know when he may 'do you down'. An untrustworthy man is one with whom it is prudent to have nothing to do, or, failing that, as little to do as possible. If there were no morality, there would be no obligations, no idea of the 'right thing to do' and therefore no basis for trust. In the absence of trust, human relations would be dominated by suspicion. Everyone would regard everyone else as a potential enemy who, given the opportunity, might 'do him down'. Such a state of affairs was imagined by Hobbes and stated in a memorable passage:

> In such a condition there would be no place for industry because the fruit thereof is uncertain and consequently no cultivation of the earth, no navigation nor use of the commodities that may be imported by sea, no commodious buildings, no instruments for moving and removing such things as require much force, no knowledge of the face of the earth, no account of time, no arts, no letters, no society and which is worst of all, continual fear of danger and violent death, and the life of man, solitary, poor, nasty, brutish and short.[6]

2.2.2   Hobbes thought that this condition, which he called the 'state of nature', was one in which human beings would be in the absence of government:

without, in his words, 'a common power to keep them all in awe'.[7] This, however, is mistaken. Morality is logically prior to government as well as to law (see 1.3.3 above). While there cannot be social life without morality, there can be without government. The significance of the Hobbesian 'state of nature' lies in its picture of what things would be like in the absence of trust. In such a situation everyone would be condemned to a solitary and poor existence because there would be no co-operation. No one would want to have anything to do with anyone else. Hence there would be no society, no possibility of industry, of commodious buildings, of arts and letters.

It may be thought that in the Hobbesian 'state of nature' human life would not only be short; it would rapidly come to an end. There would be no families, no domestic environment in which the next generation could be brought up. This is no doubt true. But it only reinforces the main point, which is that without trust people cannot live together. They need to be able, for the most part, to rely upon one another to tell the truth, to keep agreements, to refrain from violence, theft and deception, and, more generally, not to take unfair advantage of one another. This mutual reliance is, however, possible only between people each of whom acknowledges that it is right to act in such ways and believes that the others acknowledge it too. They must, that is to say, be moral agents who share and are aware that they share common ideas about right and wrong conduct. This shows what the fundamental role of morality in a human community is. It provides the necessary basis for trust between the members, without which they would be unable to carry on the various forms of co-operation which make up the corporate life of their community. This does not, however, mean that morality is essentially instrumental in character. It is not a means to the end of social living. Rather it is part of what is involved in living socially. To be a member of a community is *inter alia* to be a moral agent. People become moral agents as they grow up in and become members of their community. Early in life they learn that they cannot simply do as they like. Certain ways of acting are right, others wrong, and they are required to do what is right and to refrain from doing what is wrong.

2.2.3 It may be thought that trust is not an essential prerequisite for co-operation. Common interest is sufficient. If a number of people all want something and can get it only by working together, it is in their common interest to do so. In deciding to co-operate, they become partners in a joint enterprise and must treat one another accordingly. That means not only refraining from harming one another but also giving each other help and support. This holds whether the purpose for which they co-operate is good or evil. Hence the need for 'honour among thieves', something of which Plato was well aware. In *The Republic* Socrates asks Thrasymachus, 'Do you think that any group of men, be it a state, an army, a set of gangsters or thieves, can undertake any sort of wrong-doing if they wrong each other?' Then, answering his own question, he says, 'Their prospect of success is greater if they don't wrong each other.'[8]

Common interest alone, however, is a precarious basis for co-operation. Unless all are trustworthy, there is a danger that one of them may 'double-cross' the others in order to get more for himself. That all have an interest in common does not entail that all are trustworthy. Whether something is in a man's interest, and whether he is honest, are separate questions. The answer to the first is distinct from, and has no bearing upon, the answer to the second. Admittedly, to say that trust is an essential prerequisite for co-operation is too strong. It is an essential prerequisite for social life in the sense that, if there were no such thing as trust, there could be no human society at all. But circumstances can make co-operation necessary with people about whose trustworthiness one has doubts: for instance, in an emergency. In such circumstances, which in the nature of the case will be exceptional, one can only be 'on one's guard'. But, granted that without trust there could be no social life, the importance of common interest is undeniable. It generates many forms of co-operation – business enterprises, trade unions and pressure groups being familiar contemporary examples. Moreover, it may be thought that the interest of a community must be reducible to the common interest of its members. What else could it be? This is, however, worth exploring further.

2.3 ON A COMMUNITY'S INTEREST AND ITS MORAL IMPLICATIONS

2.3.1 Human life is always and everywhere carried on in communities – necessarily so, because otherwise there could be no next generation and human life would cease. Communities can take, and historically have taken, different forms. Tribes, kingdoms, city states, the principalities and duchies of medieval Europe, the nation states of the modern world. There are, however, certain characteristics which any human group must possess if it is to be any form of community at all. It must be a group of people living together on certain terms which are known to them all. These define the status of membership and enable each member to know what is due from him to the other members and from them to him. What this is in detail is specified by the principles and rules of the institutions and practices which give the group a definite structure and corporate existence. One thing, however, is due from every member of any community, whatever its form and irrespective of its particular institutions and practices. This is a practical concern for the well-being of all fellow members.

Each must regard it as important that, subject to the terms upon which they are living together, every member should be able to live as well as possible. If some are suffering, their fellow members have an obligation to take practical steps to relieve their distress. This practical concern is required by the principle of fellowship, a principle to which every member is committed by virtue of his membership. There can be no community where people are indifferent to one another's lot. They can constitute a community and live together as its members only to the extent that they are committed to the principle of fellowship and acknowledge an obligation to do their best to meet its requirements.

Certain other characteristics are also necessary. A community must have a viable economy to enable it to provide for the material needs of its members: that is, enough food, clothing and shelter to keep them alive. The division of labour is a necessary concomitant of a viable economy.[9] It makes possible both specialisation and co-operation, and is the foundation of all exchange. But the pattern and scale of division of labour varies greatly. In a small tribal community with a subsistence economy, it is rudimentary. In a modern national community with an advanced industrial economy, it is far-reaching. We have already seen that some form of the institution of property is necessary (see 2.2.1 above). It can take many different forms: communal, familial, personal, corporate, private and public, as well as many variants and combinations of these. The institution of the family is also necessary to provide for the care and upbringing of the next generation. But this too can take, and historically has taken, a variety of forms.

It is in the interest of a community that conditions, both internal and external, should be established and maintained which will enable every member to live as well as possible upon the terms which define his status as a member. This is entailed by the principle of fellowship. But the qualification 'upon the terms which define his status as a member' is important. It means that, for instance, peasants should live as well as possible in the manner appropriate to peasants, artisans in the manner appropriate to artisans, landowners in the manner appropriate to landowners and merchants in the manner appropriate to merchants. Fellowship does not require that peasants should live like landowners, or artisans like merchants. Admittedly this rests on the assumption that the terms on which the members are living together are of such a kind that every status position which they define offers to those who occupy it some prospect of living well: that the manner of life appropriate to peasants or artisans is intrinsically worth living. But, if the assumption is unjustified, it will be a requirement of fellowship that the terms of membership be revised so that it becomes justified, so that every status position offers to those who occupy it reasonable prospects of living well.

There is a straightforward sense in which the interest of a community is reducible to the common interest of its members. A community consists of and is nothing apart from its members. Hence its interest must be identical with the interest which, as members, they have in common. The expression 'the interest of a community' is simply an abbreviation for 'the common interest of the members of a community'. This is perfectly compatible with what has been said in previous paragraphs. Each member of a community, in virtue of his membership, is committed to the principle of fellowship. Because of his commitment, it is in his interest that there should be conditions which will enable every member to live as well as possible. What is true of each member is true of them all. The interest which all members have *qua* members and which is therefore common to them all – that is, their common interest as members – is an interest in establishing and maintaining these conditions. Two qualifications, however, must now be made. The first is that not every human being who resides in a community is for that reason a member. There can be many who live in a community without being members of it. Slaves are an obvious example. As they are not members, there is no necessary connection between the community's interest and their interest. The second is necessary to forestall any misunderstanding. To say that the interest of a community is identical with the common interest of its members is not to say that it is identical with their common self-interest as individual persons. These are not identical because a man's interest as a member of a community is not identical with his self-interst as an individual person. Not only are these two not identical: they can come into conflict.[10]

2.3.2   The perspective of a man's self-interest is confined to what is best for him. The conditions which are in his self-interest are those which will enable him personally to live as well as possible. This is not necessarily a narrowly selfish standpoint. He may well be concerned about the well-being of his family, his friends and, more generally, all those with whom he is in intimate or regular contact. They contribute directly to the quality of his personal life, and his well-being is to a greater or lesser extent bound up with theirs. The conditions which are in his self-interest will then include those which will enable them to live well. But, in the case of all the other members of his community with whom he is not in intimate or regular contact, matters are different. In a modern nation state, these may number many millions. From the perspective of his self-interest they are an anonymous multitude with whose joys and sorrows, hopes and fears, he has nothing to do. They do not contribute directly to the quality of his personal life and his well-being is not bound up with theirs. He cannot afford to be completely indifferent to their lot. He is linked to them through the impersonal system of the division of labour and it is in his self-interest that they should do their work efficiently within that system. Over and beyond this, however, what is in his self-interest is not that they should live as well as possible but that they should not make trouble by threatening the conditions which enable him and his personal associates to live well. The perspective of self-interest ignores the moral character of community membership. The principle of fellowship is not totally excluded. But its scope is confined to those who are in intimate or regular contact.

It may be thought that the distinction between self-interest and interest *qua* member is not a necessary characteristic of communities as such. It arises when a community is too big for all its members to be in intimate or regular contact. For each member, there must be others who do not contribute directly to the quality of his personal life and whose well-being is not bound up with his. Where there are no such others – for instance, in a small nomadic community all of whose members know and are dependent upon one another – it does not arise. Personal self-interest and interest *qua* member are then identical. But it is not merely a question of size. The members of a small nomadic community may not consciously draw the distinction but it can still be drawn. Occasions can arise when personal self-interest and interest *qua* member are not identical. An extreme case is when the survival of the community depends upon certain of its members being willing to sacrifice their lives. Suppose that it is being attacked by a superior force intent upon subjugating it and enslaving its members. But it may be able to escape and survive as a community if a small detachment covers its retreat, holding back the enemy by fighting to the last man and the last round. It is in a man's interest *qua* member that the detachment should succeed in holding up the enemy and he may think it an honour to be included in it. But it cannot be in his self-interest to be included. What is in his self-interest is that others and not he should be selected, so that he can have the chance of escaping with the rest of the community.

An objection to this is that it equates self-interest with personal physical survival – or, more accurately, that self-interest is identified as necessarily being an interest in the conditions favourable to such survival. This identification, however, is not always warranted. Suppose that, in our example, belief in personal immortality is part of the community's religion. Suppose further that, according to this religion, those who sacrifice their lives in defence of the community are assured of the most honoured status in the hereafter. It will then be in a man's self-interest to be included in the detachment in order to achieve that status. But this does not affect the distinction between personal self-interest and interest *qua* member. It only changes the relevant considerations. Not everyone can be included in the detachment. It is in the interest of the community that most able-bodied men should stay with it and escape so that it can continue to exist as a community. For able-bodied men, therefore, self-interest and interest *qua* member are not identical. They will coincide for a man who is selected for the detachment but not for those who are not and have to stay with the community. The latter are doing what the interest of the community requires but not what is in their personal self-interest according to their religious belief. Most communities, however, are too big for all the members to be in intimate or regular contact. In them, the distinction between self-interest and interest *qua* member is not one which arises only occasionally: it is present all the time.

The distinction between self-interest and interest *qua* member does not mean that the two never coincide. That his community should continue to exist is not only in a man's interest *qua* member but also in his self-interest. He is economically dependent upon its system of division of labour. He shares in its culture and can turn to it for help and support. Certain conditions which are necessary for a community's continued existence are clearly not only in every member's interest *qua* member but in the self-interest of each *qua* individual person. In a modern nation state, they include not only security of person and property but also such things as efficient sanitation and hygiene provisions, efficient means of transport and communications. With respect to these and similar conditions, the interest of a community coincides with the common self-interest of its members as individual persons. But this does not affect the truth of what was said earlier. It is indeed in a man's self-interest that his community should continue to exist, but not that it should do so in a form which will enable *all* its members to live as well as possible. What is in his personal self-interest is that it should continue to exist in a form which will enable him and his personal associates to live as well as possible. So far as his self-interest is concerned, the lot of his fellow members who are not personally associated with him is a matter of indifference, so long as they do not make trouble. There is no pre-established social harmony which guarantees that what is best for each is necessarily best for all. The economic fact of limited resources excludes such a harmony. If all are to have enough, not everyone can have a lot. If some are to have more, others must have less.[11] All this applies to the economic interests of different groups and classes within a community – the interest of farmers in agricultural prosperity, of trade unionists in higher pay and better working-conditions, of businessmen in profitable commercial enterprise. The interest of the community is of no concern to any of these groups except to the extent that it has a bearing upon their respective sectional interests.

All this brings out another aspect of the role of morality in the life of a human community. We have already seen that it is not instrumental, not a means to the end of social living but part of what is involved in living socially. A person becomes a moral agent in the course of growing up in and becoming a member of a community (see 2.2.2 above). In becoming a moral agent, he learns that he has obligations. We have seen (in 1.3.3) that the central idea in the concept of 'obligation' is that of having to do something irrespective of inclination or self-interest. One obligation which every member of a community has is to give precedence to its interest over his self-interest whenever the two conflict. To do this is a requirement of another principle to which every member of a community is committed in virtue of his membership. It is distinct from, although implied by, the principle of fellowship. This is the principle of social responsibility. As a member a person is responsible to his fellow members, not only for giving precedence to the community's interest over his personal self-interest, but also to do whatever he can to assist in promoting the community's interest. Without an obligation to act on the principle of social responsibility, a community's interest would largely go by default and its continued existence as a community would be in jeopardy. Social responsibility does not require people to abandon the pursuit of personal self-interest. But they must pursue it in ways compatible with the community's interest. The same applies to the sectional interests of groups and classes within the community. They must be adapted to, and not pursued at the expense of, the community's interest.

2.3.3   Suppose a man says that he does not see why he should give precedence to the interest of his community over his personal self-interest. He only lives once and it is rational for him to make the most of his life.[12] He agrees that the continued existence of his community is in his self-interest and he is in favour of other people meeting their obligations and giving precedence to the community's interest. But he does not see why he should be concerned about, much less put himself out for, the many members of his community with whom he is not personally associated. More generally, he does not acknowledge that he has any obligations. He will act on moral principles and follow moral rules when it is in his self-interest to do so. But, when it is not and he can get away with it, he will disregard them. He is unmoved by the objection that, if everyone acted like him, trust would break down and the continued existence of his community would be undermined. He is not saying that everyone should be like him. On the contrary, it is not in his self-interest that they should. His position is that of an amoral egoist, although it is not in his self-interest to admit it. He will profess to uphold morality and the precedence of the community's interest over self-interest. But he will only practise what he professes when it is necessary to avoid being found out. It is not in his self-interest that anyone else should be an amoral egoist. But, provided that the great majority of people are not, it is in his self-interest to be one.

Now, like himself, every other member of his community, and for that matter every other human being, only lives once. If, in view of this, it is rational for him to be an amoral egoist, then it is rational for everyone else to be one. But is it rational for anyone to be an amoral egoist? The principle of practical reason requires that like cases should be treated alike and that there should be differential treatment only where there are relevant differences. Suppose that, if no one else is an amoral egoist, it is in a man's self-interest to be one. It still would not be rational for him to be one, because that would be in breach of the practical-reason principle. It would be in effect to say that what he can do no one else should do, when there are no relevant differences between him and them. It is then not rational for anyone to be an amoral egoist. This is not to deny that, given that he only lives once, it is rational for a man to try to make the most of his life. What is not rational is to interpret 'making the most of his life' as 'being an amoral egoist'. The rational interpretation is to live as well as possible as a member of a community and a moral agent, this being the interpretation which meets the requirements of the practical-reason principle.

The reply to the man who says that he does not see why he should not be an amoral egoist is that to be one is to claim an arbitrary privilege: arbitrary because there are no rational grounds for it. To be an amoral egoist is to be a 'free rider': that is, someone who takes the benefits of social life without meeting his share of its burdens. It is only as a member of a community that a man can become an individual person and be in a position to pursue his personal self-interest at all. He is being a free rider if he does not give precedence to the community's interest over his personal self-interest. It may be objected that an amoral egoist will be unmoved by the charge of being a free rider. That is, however, beside the point, which is that amoral egoism is rationally indefensible. This can be highlighted by showing that it entails being a free rider. Whether something is rationally defensible and whether it influences people's conduct are separate questions. The first turns on logical and conceptual issues, the second on empirical facts about human behaviour. It is with the first that I have been concerned here. But the empirical character of the second is a reminder of the relevance of empirical facts to the practical question of whether to trust someone. Although trust is an essential prerequisite for social life, it does not follow that an individual man is trustworthy. Whether he will always do his best to meet his obligations is an empirical question, to answer which one needs evidence about his character and behaviour. Hence the importance of character references.

2.3.4   To conclude this chapter, a word is necessary about fact and value, or, more precisely, about 'is' and 'ought'. Since Hume, it has been a philosophical commonplace that facts cannot entail values, that from 'what is the case' there can be no valid inference to 'what ought to be done'. It may be thought that such an invalid inference is lurking in my contention that every member of a community is committed to the principles of fellowship and of social responsibility. That this is not so can be seen by briefly considering a distinction between two orders of fact: 'brute' facts and 'institutional' facts.[13] Brute facts are physical descriptions: for instance, that a man is bald, or six feet tall. In their case, Hume's dictum holds. There can be no valid inference from a brute fact to a value, from a physical description to a prescription. Institutional facts are facts about statuses, roles, offices, posts, occupations and the like. They are not only descriptive but also necessarily prescriptive. This is because part of what they describe is the obligations people are under in virtue of occupying a certain status, office, role or other social position. You cannot say what someone is, as a husband, a priest or a member of Parliament, without saying something about what he ought to do. Hume's dictum therefore does not apply in the case of institutional facts. To say that every member of a community is committed to the principles of fellowship and of social responsibility is to state a general institutional fact about community life. As we shall see, the notion of institutional facts is important, not least in connection with rights.

3 Moral Universality and Moral Diversity (i)

3.1 WHY MORAL DIVERSITY CANNOT BE TOTAL

3.1.1 According to the argument of the last chapter, there must be morality wherever there is social life. This is in fact the case. Morality is universal in the sense that in every community there are virtues which the members have an obligation to cultivate and practise, principles upon which they have an obligation to act, and rules which they have an obligation to follow.[1] But, while everywhere there is morality, there is not everywhere the same morality. The virtues, principles and rules are not always and everywhere the same. There exists and always has existed a 'diversity of morals'.[2] This can be illustrated by the institution of the family and the moral virtues, principles and rules connected with it. It exists in every community but not in the same form. It takes one form in urban North America, another in rural India. In many respects it is markedly different in modern Europe from what it used to be in medieval Europe. At different times and in different places, relations between husbands and wives, between parents and children and between near and distant kinsfolk have been based upon different principles. There are and have been different rules about eligibility for marriage, about whether, and if so for what reasons, it can be terminated, about the scope and limits of parental authority, as well as about many other details of family life.

There is nothing surprising about this. We know that human life is necessarily carried on in communities and that these can take and historically have taken different forms. The terms upon which people live together are not, and need not be, always and everywhere the same. The same therefore holds for moral virtues, principles and rules. They differ from age to age and from place to place, depending upon what form social life takes and upon the ideas and values, the knowledge and understanding, upon which it is based. Historically religion has been an important factor in moral diversity and it is by no means negligible today. Different religions generate different ways of life: for instance, Christianity, Judaism, Islam, Hinduism and Buddhism, to mention only the most familiar cases. Religion is not, however, the only factor in moral diversity.[3] But more about that in the next chapter. First, it is important to appreciate that moral diversity cannot be total. Certain moral principles are necessary if there is to be any social life at all, irrespective of its particular form. We have already encountered two of them; the principles of fellowship and of social responsibility (see 2.3.1–2 above). Again, this is not surprising. We have already seen (in 2.3.1) that every community must possess certain characteristics if it is to be a community properly so-called at all. Moreover, as we shall see, with some qualifications the same moral principles are necessary in any form of human association.

3.1.2   There are nine moral principles which are essential for social life as such, and it is convenient to divide them into two groups. The first contains three, the second six. The three are beneficence, respect for human life, and justice; the six, fellowship, social responsibility, freedom from arbitrary interference, honourable conduct, civility, and child welfare. There are also virtues associated with these principles, but more about that later (see 3.4.3). Of the first group, beneficence and respect for human life are straightforward. But justice needs to be discussed at some length. There can be no doubt about the necessity for beneficence. Without it, an essential prerequisite for trust would be missing. No one can be trusted who does not acknowledge an obligation always to choose good and not evil, and, when faced with a choice of evils, always to choose the lesser. To the extent that the commitment of beneficence is not met, a community is exposed to avoidable and perhaps irreparable harm. Respect for human life, in the limited form of respect for the lives of fellow members, is also clearly necessary. Without it, another essential prerequisite for trust would be missing. The principle does not mean that the life of a member can never be taken. It prohibits wanton killing and requires that no member's life should ever be unnecessarily endangered. It requires that the taking of a member's life must always be justified: for instance, as an officially prescribed punishment, in self-defence, or to vindicate personal honour.

3.1.3   Justice in the elementary form of 'to each his due' is an essential moral principle in any community. It requires that each member should render what, in virtue of his status as a member, is due from him to his fellow members, and should receive what is due to him from them. Without this principle there could be no such status as that of 'member' and hence no community. What in detail is due to and from each member depends upon the character of the community: upon its terms of membership, its values and institutions, and the various roles connected with them. Thus, while the abstract principle of justice is a moral principle of social life as such, its content varies from one community to another. This difference in content, which gives rise to different conceptions of justice, is a reflection of moral diversity. But there is one thing which is always due to and from every member, irrespective of the particular culture and values of a community. This is fair treatment. The idea of fairness is integral to the concept of justice in all its forms. John Rawls saw this and summed it up in his elaborate theory of justice under the head of 'justice as fairness'.[4] But, surprisingly, he did not conduct any systematic examination of the idea of fairness. Whether, if he had done so, his theory of justice would still have taken the form it did is an interesting question, although not one which can be pursued here.

Fairness is right and unfairness wrong. It is right, because fair, that all should be given an equal slice of the cake; wrong, because unfair, that some should have bigger slices than others. But fairness and unfairness are not the only kinds of right and wrong. Truthfulness is right and lying is wrong. However, this is because they are cases not of fairness and unfairness but of honesty and dishonesty. Fairness and unfairness are a particular kind of right and wrong. To see what kind, we must go back to the practical-reason principle (see 2.3.3 above). That principle requires that cases which are alike in all relevant respects must be treated alike and that cases which are relevantly different must be treated differently, their differential treatment corresponding to their relevant differences. Fairness and unfairness are concerned with the application of the principle in the treatment of people. They are treated fairly when it is properly applied, unfairly when it is not. But, in the treatment of people, comparative differences or differences of degree are very important. To take account of this, the principle must be reformulated with greater precision and in a way suitable for contexts in which people are involved. That can be done by following Aristotle and formulating it as the 'proportionate-equality' principle.[5]

3.2   ANALYSIS OF 'JUSTICE' AS 'FAIR TREATMENT'

3.2.1   The proportionate-equality principle requires

(a)   that all cases which are equal in the special respect relevant to the kind of treatment which is appropriate in a particular context must be treated equally;
(b)   that all cases which are unequal in this respect must be treated unequally;
(c)   that the comparative inequality of the treatment must be proportional to the comparative inequality of the cases.

Proportionate equality is thus a principle for deciding when treatment is to be equal, when unequal, and, where unequal, in what degree. For it to be applicable, there must be a context involving people in which the appropriate kind of treatment is variable: that is, in which treatment can be either equal or unequal. For analytical purposes, it is helpful to consider such contexts under four heads: distribution, adjudication, criticism, and competition. Each heading both picks out a kind of context and indicates the kind of treatment which is appropriate in it, these being necessarily connected. But, as we shall see, the headings are not mutually exclusive and some qualifications will be necessary. Before considering them, it is worth pointing out that they are the kinds of contexts in which questions of fairness typically arise. In connection with distribution, we speak of 'fair shares'; in connection with adjudication, of 'a fair trial' and, more fundamentally, of 'the fair apportioning of blame'. In connection with criticism, we speak of 'a fair assessment'; in connection with competition, of 'fair play', as well as of competition itself being 'fair'.

3.2.2   People are involved in a distributive context when something has to be allocated among them. The appropriate treatment is distributive in the sense of being concerning with allocating to each his share. Certain conditions are necessary to create a distributive context. There must be something to be allocated. This may consist of benefits or burdens. But, whether desirable or undesirable, it must be finite and divisible. There must also be constitutive rules of eligibility. These define those who are eligible for inclusion in the allocation and prescribe that all those and only those who are eligible are to be allocated a share. There must also be a principle for carrying out the allocation which is appropriate to what has to be allocated: for instance, according to need in the case of benefits, according to capacity in the case of burdens. These conditions are necessary to make allocation possible but they do not ensure that it will be fair. For that, proportionate equality is necessary. It requires that, in carrying out the allocation, equals must be treated equally and unequals unequally in proportion to their degree of inequality. Thus it is fair that those in greater need should receive more and that the stronger should carry heavier loads. It follows that reallocation is justified when the existing allocation is unfair: when those in greater need are receiving less, or when the weaker are carrying the heavier loads. Matters are not, however, always so straightforward as this. But more about this later (see 7.3.4). Natural assets and defects are necessarily excluded from distributive contexts because they lie outside the scope of human allocation and reallocation. It is not unfair that some are more handsome or more intelligent than others but simply that some have been luckier than others in the genetic lottery.

An adjudicative context is one in which either credit or blame has to be apportioned. In such apportioning, there must be adjudication. Hence the appropriate treatment is adjudicative. For there to be an adjudicative context, there must either be something for which people deserve credit or else something for which they deserve blame: in the one case something good which was their achievement, in the other something bad which was their fault. The concepts of 'credit' and of 'blame' contain constitutive rules which must be followed in the apportioning: all those and only those who have made a positive contribution are to be given credit; all those and only those who are at fault are to be blamed. But, if the apportioning is to be fair, proportionate equality is also necessary. This requires that credit and blame be apportioned according to comparative desert: credit among those who contributed in proportion to the comparative value of their respective contributions; blame among those at fault in proportion to the degree to which each was at fault. Tribunals and law courts are institutions for ascertaining legal fault and apportioning legal blame. The requirements of what are called the principles of 'natural justice' ensure that, so far as possible, the apportioning will be fair. These requirements are that all interested parties must be heard, that the judge must not be an interested party, that his decision must not be according to the existing law. A 'fair trial' is one which is conducted according to 'natural justice', and, in the case of a tribunal, the same is true of a 'fair hearing'.

A critical context is one in which some human characteristic is being assessed. It may be an individual's merits and defects: his character, his professional competence, his performance of a particular task or in a particular role. It may be the merits and defects of an organisation: its efficiency, the quality of its service or its products, the extent to which it has been successful in accomplishing what it was set up to do. An assessment must be made with reference to a relevant standard, and the appropriate treatment is what this entails. It is 'critical' because necessarily involving judgements of 'good and bad', 'better and worse'. The concept of assessment contains a constitutive rule: all those and only those considerations which are relevant to what is being assessed must be taken into account. Unless this rule is followed, no assessment can be correct. But if it is to be fair, proportionate equality is also necessary. It requires

(a)   that each relevant consideration must be rated positively or negatively according to whether it is favourable or unfavourable;
(b)   that those of equal worth must be rated equally, those of unequal worth unequally in proportion to their unequal worth;
(c)   that those which are unfavourable must be rated negatively in proportion to the degree to which they are unfavourable.

In a competitive context people contend for something according to constitutive rules which prescribe the conditions of the contest and define success and failure. Races, games, tournaments, 'competitive' examinations, quizzes and raffles are familiar examples. Commerce and industry may also be carried on under competitive conditions. A contest in which there are no rules, in which 'anything goes', is not a competition but a fight. If 'All's fair in love and war', then neither love nor war is a competition properly so-called.

Appropriate treatment in a competitive context is that which must be accorded by the officials to the competitors and by the competitors to one another. The former must apply the rules impartially and the latter must compete according to them. There is, however, another condition which must be met if a contest is to be a competition properly so-called. This is that the constitutive rules must give every competitor an equal chance of winning so far as the conditions of the contest are concerned. The concept of competition, that is to say, contains the proportionate-equality principle and therefore the idea of fairness.

An unfair competition – that is, one whose constitutive rules do not give every competitor an equal chance, because the conditions they lay down favour some at the expense of others – is, in the language of economics, an 'imperfect competition'. Proportionate equality allows for handicapping as in golf and racing, in order to give competitors of unequal ability an equal chance. But the handicapping must be fair: in other words, proportional to the unequal ability of the competitors. An analogue in the case of industry is government assistance to companies in 'depressed' areas through tax exemptions, grants and the like. 'Fair play' means competing according to fair rules. To cheat is to try to gain an 'unfair' advantage; that is, an advantage not allowed by the rules.

3.2.3   To show that there has been unfairness, it must be shown that a requirement of 'proportionate equality' had not been met. In the four contexts, there are two ways in which this can happen. The first is when all the conditions for the application of the principle in a particular context have been met but the principle is wrongly applied: for instance, in a distributive context, when the comparative needs of those receiving benefits have been wrongly estimated, so that some get more and others less than they should; in an adjudicative context, when all those at fault have been blamed but not according to their comparative deserts; in a critical context, when all considerations relevant to an assessment have been taken into account, but when the significance of some of them has not been fully appreciated; or, in a competition, when some competitors cheat without being caught, or when officials fail to apply the rules impartially. The second is when a rule constitutive of a context has been broken: for instance, when an eligible man is excluded from an allocation; when the innocent man has been blamed; when a consideration relevant to an assessment has been ignored; or when the rules of a competition give some competitors an advantage over others.

That all those and only those eligible should be included in an allocation is a requirement of proportionate equality. It is not, of course, the only requirement. The allocation must be according to comparative need or capacity. But, unless the eligibility rule is followed, proportionate equality cannot be applied. Thus, when an eligible man is excluded, the allocation is necessarily unfair. Those included receive greater benefits or have to carry heavier burdens because of his exclusion. He himself is treated unfairly in being excluded, because he is being treated unequally when in the relevant respect, eligibility, he is equal. When an innocent man is blamed, the apportioning of blame is necessarily unfair. Those at fault either escape it altogether, or receive less than they deserve. The innocent man is being treated unfairly in being blamed because he is being treated unequally when in the relevant respect, innocence, he is the equal of all who are not at fault. An assessment is necessarily unfair when a relevant consideration has been ignored. The significance of those taken into account is wrongly estimated, and, because one has been ignored, equals are not being treated equally. A competition the rules of which give some competitors an advantage is necessarily unfair. Equals in the relevant respect, that of being competitors, are not being treated equally.

Both distributive and adjudicative contexts involve criticism. In competitive contexts, there is adjudication and may also be criticism. Competition can be involved in a critical context. This is why the four headings are not mutually exclusive. If allocation is to be according to need, the need of each person eligible for inclusion must be assessed. Before credit can be apportioned according to comparative desert, the value of each person's contribution must be assessed. In competitions, there is adjudication when referees or umpires have to apportion blame for breaches of the rules. There is criticism when, for handicapping purposes, officials have to assess each competitor's ability. Criticism may also involve competition. The knowledge and potential of scholarship candidates may be assessed on their performance in a competitive examination. All this shows that the source of unfairness is not always in the immediate context. An unfair allocation may be owing to an unfair assessment of individual need; an unfair apportioning of credit, to an unfair assessment of an individual contribution; an unfair assessment of knowledge and potential, to the examination itself being unfair.

My account of the kinds of contexts in which the proportionate-equality principle is applicable has been illustrative, not exhaustive. More could be said about each of them, but, for my present purpose, the elucidation of 'fairness' as 'proportionate equality', what has been said is sufficient. To show this in the case of adjudication, consider the question of 'fair compensation'. As a matter of justice, compensation is due from one party to another when, without an adequate excuse, the former has harmed the latter: for instance by negligence or not keeping an agreement. But justice also requires that the compensation be fair. This means that proportionate equality must be applied in deciding the kind and amount of compensation. It must be in proportion to the harm for which the offending party is to blame.[6] While this is clearly a matter for adjudication, it is not merely a matter of apportioning blame. That, however, is necessarily involved. The extent to which the offending party is to blame must be ascertained. Is it solely his fault, or are there mitigating circumstances? Criticism is also involved. The seriousness of the harm for which the offending party is to blame must be assessed. If compensation is to be fair, proportionate equality must be properly applied in deciding the kind and amount. But it cannot properly be applied in making this decision if it is misapplied either in ascertaining the extent to which the offending party is to blame, or in assessing the seriousness of the harm: for instance, if the blame is exaggerated or the seriousness of the harm underestimated.

3.2.4   Consider the familiar slogan, 'A fair day's pay for a fair day's work.' Restated in terms of proportionate equality, it is the following contention: 'All whose work in a given job is up to standard, should be paid the going rate for that job. But any whose work is sub-standard should be paid less in proportion to the degree to which it is sub-standard.' Proportionate equality cannot, however, say what the going rate should be. Nor can it say what the appropriate standard is. Another familiar slogan, 'Equal pay for equal work', is of no help. It requires that all whose work is of the same kind and equal in amount and quality should be paid the same. This is a direct application of proportionate equality. All who are equal in the relevant respect, doing work of the same kind and equal in amount and quality, should be treated equally – that is, paid the same. But, again, this says nothing about what the rate of pay should be. These considerations suggest that fairness is a second-order value. It presupposes first-order values: in other words, substantive values which do not themselves presuppose other values. This suggestion is supported by the compensation example. That there should be compensation for culpable harm is a first-order requirement of justice. The question of what kind and amount is fair can arise only if it is right that there should be compensation.

    That the suggestion is correct, that fairness is a second-order value, is clear when we turn from particular examples to the four contexts. In each, proportionate equality is applied to the treatment appropriate in that context. But what this is is not a question of proportionate equality. In distributive contexts, it must be right that, for example, allocation should be according to need in the case of benefits; according to capacity in the case of burdens; and, in the case of pay, according to 'supply and demand', perhaps modified by collective bargaining. Only then can proportionate equality be applied in making the allocation. The same holds of the other contexts. In adjudication, it must be right that credit is given for achievement, blame for harm. In criticism, there must be appropriate standards with reference to which merits and defects can be assessed. In competition, the contest itself must be worthwhile. That fairness is a second-order value in no way diminishes its importance. It vitally affects people's experience of first-order values. But its limitations must also be appreciated. If there is disagreement about what treatment is appropriate – for instance, whether medical care should be allocated according to need or according to ability to pay, or whether something counts as an achievement for which credit should be given – there will be irreconcilable conflicts about what is fair. Fairness presupposes agreement about relevant first-order values and cannot settle conflicts over them. Nevertheless it is essential for social life as such. A group of people who did not have a practical understanding of the proportionate-equality principle could not constitute a community at all. They would have no understanding of competition, would be incapable of criticism and of rational distribution, and could not apportion either credit or blame.

3.3   EXPOSITION OF THE MORAL PRINCIPLES OF COMMUNITY

3.3.1   Justice in its general form of 'to each his due' includes the principle of respect for life in the sense that such respect is due from every member of a community to every other member. But the two principles need to be distinguished. Unjust treatment need not be and usually is not at the expense of life. A man can be unfairly blamed without his life being in any way endangered. Beneficence is distinct from both principles. It may sometimes be the lesser evil to acquiesce in unfair treatment: for instance, to accept not being given all the credit you deserve rather than making a fuss and causing embarrassment. It may even be the lesser evil for the lives of some members of the community to be sacrificed so that the rest can survive: for example, under siege conditions when there is not enough food and water to go round. Justice in its general form also includes the six principles in the second group because acting on each of them is due from every member of a community in all his dealings with fellow members, and is therefore also due to them. But they need to be distinguished both from justice and from each other: from justice, because they are not the same as fair treatment; from each other, because it is for a different reason that each is essential for social life as such. It will be recalled that they are: fellowship, social responsibility, freedom from arbitrary interference, honourable conduct, civility, and child welfare (see 3.1.2 above).

3.3.2   We already know about fellowship (see 2.3.1). If the members of a group are totally indifferent to one another's well-being, they cannot constitute a community at all. We also know about social responsibility (see 2.3.1). Each member has an obligation to give precedence to the community's interest over his personal self-interest. Each also has an obligation to do what he personally can to promote the community's interest. Each member is responsible to his fellow members for meeting these obligations. A community may be able to tolerate considerable social irresponsibility, especially when this is owing to carelessness or laziness. But no community can survive if all its members completely repudiate the requirements of social responsibility. If that happened, its interests would go by default and the conditions necessary for it to survive as a community would be undermined. The obligations of fellowship can overlap with those of social responsibility. Social-welfare services are a case in point. It is in the interest of a modern industrial community to organise them, thereby making the relief of distress owing to unemployment, sickness, poverty and old age a responsibility to be borne by all adult members of the community not themselves in distress. Questions of fairness in allocating the costs of these services and about who is eligible and for how much will also arise. The respective principles, however, remain distinct.

'Freedom from arbitrary interference' requires that any interference with the freedom of action of a member of a community must be justified, whether the interference is by fellow members or by the community through agents acting on its behalf. 'Arbitrary' interference is unjustified interference. The justification must always be moral, although, in a community with a system of positive law, it may also be legal. To interfere with a man, by force if necessary, to prevent him from committing a crime is both legally and morally justified: legally, because he is about to break the law; morally, because crime is morally as well as legally wrong. Laws which restrict freedom of action for the sake of the interest of a community – for instance, public health laws, factory laws, 'anti-trust' laws and conservation laws – are for that reason morally justified. Without the principle of freedom from arbitrary interference, the personal security essential for social life would be missing. The weaker would be at the mercy of the stronger. All would be in constant danger of molestation and would be unable to go about their business in safety. 'Freedom from arbitrary interference', however, although necessary for, is not identical with, 'freedom' as a primary moral and political value. It is not, that is to say, identical with 'freedom' as that has come to be understood in modern Western society. If it were, every community would by definition be a free society and this is clearly not entailed by the meaning of the term in the West today.

'Honourable conduct' requires truthfulness in deed as well as in word. It forbids stealing, lying, cheating and duplicity of any kind. Positively, it requires keeping one's word, and integrity in all transactions and undertakings. Without it there would be no basis for trust and, instead of social life, only a Hobbesian 'state of nature'. A community may be able to survive considerable dishonourable conduct on the part of some of its members. But it could not survive if the principle of honourable conduct were expressly repudiated and none of its members acknowledged any obligation to act on it. 'Civility' requires people to treat one another with respect in all their dealings. They must refrain from unprovoked violence, from shocking, insulting and humiliating one another. Positively, they must treat one another with courtesy, which means not only observing conventions of good manners but also showing consideration and sensitivity. Again, a community may be able to tolerate considerable incivility among some of its members, but, if there were no conventions of good manners, no obligation to show consideration and sensitivity, no obligation to refrain from insulting, abusive and humiliating behaviour, co-operation would give way to conflict, and social life to the Hobbesian 'state of nature'.

All these principles, the three in the first group and the five so far discussed in the second, are essential not only in every form of community, but also in every kind of limited association − for instance, in business enterprises, professional associations, clubs, trade unions, churches and universities. This is obvious in the case of 'beneficence' and 'respect for life'. 'Justice' is also essential, especially in the form of 'fair treatment'. The benefits and burdens of an association must be allocated fairly among its members. 'Fellowship' is also essential, because an association cannot be carried on if its members are totally indifferent to one another's fortunes in participating in it. Social responsibility, in the limited form of responsibility for promoting the corporate interest of the association and subordinating personal self-interest to it is likewise essential, as is 'freedom from arbitrary interference': an association cannot carry on if its members are continually interfering with one another without justification. Finally, both 'honourable conduct' and 'civility' are essential. If an association is not to break down, not only must the members be able to trust one another, but they must treat one another with courtesy and consideration. The sixth principle of the second group − 'child welfare' − however, applies to communities rather than to associations.[7] Bringing up children is invariably a family responsibility in every community, whatever its form of family life. But, if a community is to survive, it cannot afford to neglect the well-being of the next generation. It is in its interest that this well-being should be adequately provided for: for instance, by organising and maintaining education, by arranging for the care of orphans and protecting children from abuse by adults. These and kindred matters entail obligations not only upon families but upon all adult members of the community.

3.3.3   Certain rules as distinct from principles are also necessary for social life as such. Promise-keeping, truth-telling and refraining from theft are examples. What makes them necessary is that they are constitutive rules of practices and institutions which are themselves necessary for social life as such. Promise-keeping is a constitutive rule of the practice of promising which is itself necessary for any systematic co-operation. Truth-telling is a constitutive rule of communication; the prohibition against theft, of the institution of property. Without communication and co-operation, there could be no social life. The same is true of the institution of property. But property can take different forms: communal, corporate, personal, public and private, as well as many variants of these. Hence there is no single principle of property which is necessary for social life as such. There is only the necessity for property in some form. The same is true of the institution of the family. As we have seen, it can take and historically has taken different forms (see 3.1.1 above). Hence there is no single principle of family life which is necessary for social life as such. But the institution of the family in some form is necessary so that children can be looked after and brought up. Associated with the institution of the family are rules of sexual conduct. What these are depends upon the particular form the institution takes. But there is one which is universal because constitutive of sexual conduct as such. This is the prohibition of rape.[8]

Rape is an extreme form of personal assault and its prohibition is required by the principle of 'civility'. Other rules of sexual conduct, whatever they may be, also fall under the principle of civility. Obedience to the other rules of socially necessary institutions and practices is a requirement of one or more of the nine moral principles of community which we have been discussing in this chapter. Refraining from lying and theft are requirements of 'honourable conduct'. Promise-keeping is another such. Respect for the institution of property in whatever form it takes in a particular community, and therefore obedience to its rules both constitutive and regulative, are requirements of 'civility'. Respect for the institution of the family, whatever form it takes, and hence obedience to its particular rules are requirements of both 'civility' and 'child welfare'. But a family is also a 'micro-community', consisting, as it does, of people living together. Hence all the moral principles of community are applicable to it in the sense that, in appropriate contexts, the members of a family must meet their respective requirements. Within the wider framework of social life, there can be occasions when the requirements of one moral principle of community may conflict with those of another. 'Honourable conduct' requires me to keep my promise to my colleagues to attend a meeting to speak on their behalf. 'Fellowship' and perhaps also 'respect for life' require me to stay at the scene of an accident and do what I can to help, which would mean missing the meeting. In such cases, the principle of beneficence must be the basis for deciding which requirements are to take precedence. It is the master moral principle in the sense of being the one which provides the basis for deciding what to do when faced by a conflict of moral principles.

3.4 COMMON MORALITY AND PARTICULAR MORALITY

3.4.1 For the sake of brevity, I shall henceforth call the moral principles of community – that is, the nine moral principles which are essential for social life as such and which we have been discussing in this chapter – 'common morality'. The adjective 'common' is appropriate because the principles are common to all communities, irrespective of the differences between them. Christians, Jews, Muslims, Hindus and Buddhists alike have a general obligation to act upon them in their respective communities. So do communists and socialists, conservatives and liberals. They have this general obligation not because of their particular religious and political allegiances, but because they are members of communities. Morality, however, is never confined to common morality, although it always includes it. This is because every community is an individual community with its own distinctive way of life, its own terms of membership, institutions and values. These generate further principles and also rules and virtues, together with further obligations relating to them. Such principles, rules and virtues, with their attendant obligations, I shall henceforth call 'particular morality'. The actual morality of any community always consists of a union of common morality with particular morality. The former consists of the moral principles which it has in common with every other community in virtue of being a community; the latter, of the principles, rules and virtues related to its particular way of life. It is differences between the particular moralities of individual communities which give rise to moral diversity. That diversity is the moral dimension of differences in their respective ways of life.

3.4.2 Communities are not like air-tight compartments hermetically sealed from one another. Much of the history of any community is concerned with its relations, both peaceful and hostile, to other communities. Nor are communities eternal entities. They interact with, interpenetrate, transform, absorb and grow out of one another. The nation states of modern Europe grew out of the kingdoms, principalities and duchies of medieval Europe. The latter emerged from the break-up of the Roman Empire. The Roman Empire itself came into being through the conquest and absorption of previously independent although in many cases interrelated communities: the city states of Greece and North Africa, the tribes of the Iberian peninsula and of Gaul. All this was accompanied by the spread of ideas, beliefs and values, of knowledge and of art, of institutions and practices, and of crafts and techniques. But the spread was neither uniform nor one-way. New ideas, beliefs and values were more readily absorbed in some places than in others. Conquerors not only taught but also learned from the conquered.

This 'cultural diffusion' means that the ways of life of different communities have features in common as well as their own peculiarities. Many of these common features have their source in the dissemination of a particular religion: Christianity in Europe, Islam in North Africa and the Middle East, Buddhism in Asia. But the same religion may be differently interpreted not only from one community to another, but also within the same community. A particular religion, therefore, may well be the source of differences as well as of common characteristics in the ways of life of individual communities. Sectarian differences in Christianity have given rise to differences between ways of life all of which profess to be Christian, and the same is true for other 'world' religions. All this is reflected in the particular moralities of individual communities. There are common features as well as differences among them. There are also likely to be differences within each of them. The particular morality of an individual community is rarely homogenous. It is likely to contain discrepant, perhaps antagonistic, characteristics within a framework of shared principles, rules and virtues. The origins of these discrepant characteristics lie in the community's history, and their effect upon its existing way of life is a matter requiring detailed empirical investigation. But, if the community is to hold together and not become polarised into conflicting sectarian groups, those principles, rules and virtues of its particular morality which all its members share must be more important to them than, and receive precedence over, the sectarian values which divide them.

3.4.3   Returning to common morality, we have already seen that the detailed requirements of 'justice' in its general form of 'to each his due' depend upon the way of life of an individual community with its particular terms of membership, institutions, roles and values (see 2.1.3 above). This is true of all the principles of common morality. Because they are applicable to every community, in the case of each individual community their requirements must be contextually interpreted. In the case of 'beneficence', what counts as the greater good or the lesser evil depends upon an individual community's values, upon its particular morality and upon the detailed requirements of the other principles of common morality within its way of life. Similar considerations apply to 'respect for life': notably, upon what grounds an individual community's particular morality justifies the taking of life. The detailed requirements of 'fellowship' depend upon the extent to which, within a community, there is organised provision for the relief of distress, as well as upon the varying life prospects which its terms of membership afford to the different classes of its members. What 'social responsibility' in detail requires depends upon the particular internal conditions which it is in a community's interest to establish and maintain. These vary from one community to another, depending upon a community's economy, its geography and climate, as well as upon its institutions and values.

We have seen that the justification for interfering with the freedom of action of any member of a community must always be moral and can also be legal. Moral diversity means that interference which is morally and legally justified in one community is not in another. In the USA during the 1920s, the manufacture and sale of alcoholic liquor was prohibited by law. Interference by the police to stop it was then morally justified. Not so in other countries, in which there was no such prohibition. In most Roman Catholic countries, the sale of contraceptives is prohibited by law and the police are morally and legally justified in interfering to stop it. Not so in most non-Catholic countries. In communist states, public criticism of the government is forbidden and agents of the state are morally justified in suppressing it. Not so in Western democratic states, where the people are free both to support and to oppose the government publicly. It may be thought that the requirements of honourable conduct are the same everywhere, but here too the context makes a difference. Business competitors are not required to be as candid with one another as are personal friends. Nor are diplomats in their dealings with foreign governments.

That the detailed requirements of 'civility' vary from one community to another is well known to every foreign traveller. 'They do things differently abroad.' Conventions of polite behaviour differ from one community to another. They may also differ between social classes in the same community. What is normal courtesy according to one code of manners may be an insult according to another: for instance, declining the food offered to you in a stranger's house. The detailed requirements of 'child welfare' also vary from one community to another. They depend in part upon the particular form of family life, in part upon what provision is made for education and other social services. Of particular importance is how, according to a community's values, children are thought of and what is considered appropriate for them: that they 'should be seen and not heard' or that youth should unreservedly be 'given its head'. We have also seen that sexual morality depends upon the particular form of family life. The latter varies from one community to another and so do the detailed requirements of the former. There may also be differences in the form of family life and in sexual morality between different social groups and classes within the same community.

3.4.4   The distinction between 'common' and 'particular' morality enables the implications of the concept of community to be reconciled with the fact of moral diversity. It is philosophical, not practical. People do not need to understand it in order to meet their obligations as members of communities. On the contrary, being able to meet those obligations is a necessary, although not a sufficient, condition for being able to understand the distinction. In fact most people are unlikely to be aware of the distinction, let alone understand it. This is because they encounter common morality not as the moral principles of social life as such, but as contextually interpreted in terms of the values and institutions of their particular community. To them, its obligations are just some, albeit among the more important, of their many obligations as members of that community. In other words, while morality in any community is always a union of a particular morality with common morality, the members do not see it as such a union. To them, morality is the body of principles, rules and virtues which, as members of that community, they are required to act upon, to follow and to practice. They have been brought up to meet these requirements and accordingly acknowledge them as obligations of membership. They will indeed be aware of any discrepancies in their community's particular morality. But these they will recognise to be manifestations of sectarian differences among themselves, or, if not sectarian, then class differences, which they must tolerate, such toleration being itself an obligation of membership. They will also be aware of moral diversity in the sense of knowing that in other communities the members have obligations which, in various respects, are different from theirs. Their attitude towards this will be coloured by how, according to the ideas, beliefs and values of their community, foreigners and foreign ways are regarded.

Certain virtues are associated with the principles of common morality: impartiality with fair treatment; compassion with fellowship; integrity and loyalty with honourable conduct; firmness, consistency and kindness with child welfare. 'Social responsibility' and 'civility' are the names of virtues as well as of principles. We have already seen (in 1.3.2) that self-control is necessary for all moral conduct, and courage whenever acting morally involves facing pain or danger. However, all these character traits and dispositions must be fostered and cultivated within the framework of an individual community's way of life. They must therefore be harmonised with the special virtues called for by its particular morality: for instance, with piety and humility; with self-reliance and self-respect; with asceticism and spirituality; with humaneness and tolerance. The cultivation of specific character traits and dispositions is of central importance in personal emotional development. Becoming a moral agent involves not only acquiring the capacity to follow rules and act upon principles but also the disposition to feel and respond in appropriate ways. What these are depends upon the character of the community's way of life and especially upon its particular morality. This emotional dimension is vital. Without it, there would be nothing to energise moral conduct. A moral agent must care about doing 'the right thing'. An account of morality which ignored it would be inadequate.

4 Moral Diversity (ii): Religion and Ideology

4.1 RELIGION

4.1.1 In the last chapter I said that religion was an important factor in moral diversity (see 3.1.1). To see how, something must be said about religion and religious morality.[1] There are certain conditions, each of which separately is necessary and all of which together are sufficient to constitute what is known as a religion. They are the following:

(a) belief in the reality of the supernatural;
(b) belief in the dependence of the natural upon the supernatural;
(c) belief in the supernatural origin of certain instructions for living, in virtue of which there is an obligation to comply with them;
(d) belief in the truth of a definitive statement, either in writing or in an oral tradition, of not only the instructions in (c) but also at least enough about the attributes of the supernatural, and of the dependence of the natural upon it, to make the supernatural origin of these instructions intelligible;
(e) a group of people who hold a belief of the kind in (d);
(f) an association based upon (d) and maintained by the group in (e), for the sake of enabling its members to give practical expression to their commitments in (c) and (d).

When all these conditions are satisfied, there is a religion and a religious morality. The latter is the particular morality of the group in (e) and consists of the general obligation in (c), together with other obligations entailed by membership of the association in (f). These will either include expressly, or at least will be compatible with, the obligations of common morality. Why should the supernatural origin of certain instructions for living give rise to an obligation to comply with them? The short answer is, because of the dependence of the natural upon the supernatural. The following first-person statement is an elaboration of that answer: 'I have received certain instructions for living which have a supernatural origin. As a natural being, I am dependent upon the supernatural. Not to comply with instructions from what I am dependent upon would be to deny my dependent status and *a fortiori* a fundamental part of what I am. To do that would be wrong, so the right thing to do is to comply. What applies to me applies to all who have received the same instructions. They too have an obligation to comply.'

A first-person statement is appropriate because religious belief is necessarily personal belief. Thus the Nicene Creed opens with the words, 'I believe in God, maker of heaven and earth. . . .' But only those who have received the same instructions have an obligation to comply. What about those who have received different instructions, or no instructions at all? Different religions answer this question in different ways. Some, but not all, teach that there is an obligation to spread the word. The instructions are universal and must be conveyed to all. Hence the activities of missionaries. Different answers to the question are a manifestation of religious diversity. The source of that diversity lies in different definitive statements of the kind in (c) and (d) – and therefore in different accounts of the attributes of the supernatural, of how the natural is dependent upon it, and of the supernatural origins of instructions for living – as well as in differences in these instructions themselves. The latter give rise to differences in the form and organisation of the associations in (f). Hence the differences between churches, temples, mosques and other centres of religious practice.

It is because of religious diversity that religious morality is a source of moral diversity. The content of instructions for living, as well as their scope and precision, varies from one religion to another. But, in order to be instructions for living at all, they must consist of principles, rules and virtues. Their scope depends upon their comprehensiveness – that is, upon how much of life they cover and how much they leave to people to decide for themselves; their precision, upon how much of what they cover is subject to the detailed specification of rules and how much to the guidance of principles. But, while it makes differences in religious morality intelligible, religious diversity itself poses a problem. This arises in connection with (d) and (e). The adherents of each religion believe in the truth of its particular definitive statement. How can a number of different definitive statements all be true? Two mutually exclusive answers suggest themselves. The first is that only one is really true, while all the others are false. The second is that each is a different figurative expression of an underlying fundamental truth.

4.1.2   The trouble with the first answer is that there is no rational method for critically assessing the claims to truth of different definitive statements. Neither empirical nor logical considerations are adequate. Empirical tests are inapplicable. Unlike a scientific or historical hypothesis, a definitive statement of religious belief is not held provisionally, subject in principle to falsification by experimental results or the discovery of new evidence. It is an absolute commitment, held unconditionally. That is why it is said to be a 'belief in . . .', not a 'belief that . . .'. Nor are purely logical considerations sufficient. Definitive statements of religious belief must be self-consistent if they are to be intelligible. But self-consistency, although necessary, is not sufficient for truth. It is of no help in finding out which, if any, of a number of different self-consistent definitive statements is true. The first answer, then, will not do, which leaves us with the second. This is that, while no definitive statement is literally true, each is a different figurative expression of an underlying fundamental truth. There can be no doubt about the figurative character of religious language. It abounds in analogies and metaphors. Theistic religions characteristically use personal and political analogies: 'God the Father', 'the Lord of Hosts', 'the King of Kings', 'the will of Allah'. In Buddhism, a non-theistic religion, a mechanistic metaphor, 'the Wheel of Existence', is of central importance.

There is no problem about the descriptive use of metaphors and analogies in ordinary language: that is, the socio-temporal language of events and things, of persons and society. They can always be 'cashed'. A metaphor can be translated into literal terms and the partial resemblance in an analogy made explicit. The point of using them is to convey briefly and vividly what, if stated literally, would be long-winded and tedious. Matters are different in the case of religious language. Its reference is to the supernatural, and the supernatural by definition is neither spatial nor temporal. Literal descriptions of the supernatural in ordinary language are therefore impossible. Nor can they be given in the technical language of natural science, because that too is spatio-temporal. Nor, again, is a formal symbolism of any help. It does not describe anything but is solely concerned with logical relations. It follows that religious language can describe the supernatural only through the use of metaphors and analogies. But these cannot be 'cashed'. There are not and cannot be any literal supernatural terms into which to translate them and make them explicit.

This makes religious diversity intelligible. Apart from the logical requirement of self-consistency, the only limits to the number and variety of different definitive statements are those of creative imagination. What then is the underlying fundamental truth of which they are supposed to be different figurative expressions? Is it what is believed in (a) and (b): the reality of the supernatural and the dependence of the natural upon it? Now, it is a fundamental truth that the existence of the universe cannot be explained in terms of the natural order of the universe, because all naturalistic explanations presuppose that the universe already exists. The natural sciences, through their detailed inquiries into the composition and structure of the universe, can increase our understanding of how the natural order works, but they cannot tell us why the universe should exist, or, indeed, why there should be anything at all. The universe is simply there and we do not and cannot know why. This fundamental truth is epitomised in the title of a book by Sir James Jeans, *The*

Mysterious Universe.[2] But (a) and (b) do not simply endorse the mysterious universe. They affirm a belief in something behind the mystery, the expression of this belief being necessarily figurative. The second answer must then be amended. Different definitive statements are not different figurative expressions of an underlying fundamental truth. They indeed presuppose a fundamental truth: the mysterious universe. But what they are different figurative expressions of is a belief in something behind the mystery, and the significance of that something for human life.

4.1.3 The conclusion entailed by this amended second answer is that religious belief is non-rational or, perhaps better, 'extra-rational'. That is why it is properly called 'faith'. Rational inquiry can take us as far as the mysterious universe but no further. To be religious is to go beyond reason and make 'the leap of faith'. Whether to leap at all, let alone in which direction to leap, is a question which cannot be answered by rational inquiry. The logical outcome of rational inquiry is agnosticism: that is, the acceptance of, and acquiescence in, the fundamental truth of the mysterious universe. This is not to deny that reasons can be given for a particular religious commitment. To the question, 'Why are you a Christian?', an answer along the following lines may be given: 'Most of my fellow countrymen are Christians and I was brought up as one. Being a Christian is part of what I am, my personal and social identity.' These are, however, personal and social reasons, not religious ones. There cannot be religious reasons for being religious. To answer, 'I am a Christian because I believe in the definitive statement of Christianity', is not to give a religious reason. It is to affirm a religious commitment which, once made, opens the way for religious reasons. It may be objected that reasons cannot be given for being rational. To be disposed to consider reasons is already to be rational. Rationality itself, no less than religion, is an extra-rational commitment. This is true but there is a difference. The commitment to rationality in the form of self-consistency and respect for evidence is a prerequisite for thought and action as such. Not so in the case of religion. People can think, speak and act without being committed to the definitive statement of any religion.

Because religious belief is extra-rational, there cannot be an obligation either to believe or not to believe. There cannot be an obligation to make the leap of faith at all, let alone to make it in one direction rather than another. There is an obligation not to deny what there are rational grounds for believing to be true, and not to affirm what there are rational grounds for believing to be false. But, in the case of religious belief, there can be no such grounds one way or the other. In religious language, 'true' and 'false' are metaphors, and metaphors which cannot be 'cashed'. Subject to a qualification, religious belief is logically prior to religious morality. A Christian has an obligation to comply with

Christian instructions for living because he is a Christian, a Muslim with Islamic instructions because he is a Muslim, a Jew with Judaic instructions because he is a Jew. As we have seen, the obligation is part of the commitment entailed by religious belief. It is in virtue of the fact that he believes, together with what he believes, that a religious believer has an obligation to comply with his particular religion's instructions for living.

The qualification concerns the social aspect of religion. In a community whose way of life is centred round a particular religion, that religion's instructions for living will be incorporated in the community's particular morality. This means that members who do not believe in the religion at all, or who are merely nominal believers, have an obligation to comply with its instructions for living because these are part of the community's particular morality. They have this obligation *qua* community members, not *qua* religious believers. Although not committed Christians, as members of a professing Christian community they have an obligation to comply with its particular version of Christian instructions for living. This has implications for the exercise of compulsion. People cannot be compelled to believe something, although they may say that they are through fear of being penalised for being suspected of not believing. But they can be compelled to comply with instructions for living and this compulsion can be justified on social grounds: namely, that for the sake of social stability a minimum standard of compliance must be observed. The members ought to comply without compulsion as a requirement of social responsibility. In the case of those who ignore this requirement, compulsion is justified to secure the minimum standard of compliance.[3]

These conclusions prompt three questions: two about religion in the past, one about it today. The first concerns the historical ubiquity of religion: the fact that it has figured prominently in the life of every known community. If religious belief is extra-rational, if there is no obligation to believe, why should this have been the case? The second concerns the fact that religion has been a major source of conflict, both between and within communities. Again, why should this have been the case if religious belief is extra-rational, if there is no obligation to believe? The third concerns the fact that in most parts of the world religion is no longer a major source of conflict – which is not, however, to say that it plays no part in conflict at all. But there can be no doubt that, generally speaking, religion is no longer the potent source of conflict which it once was. This is of course to be welcomed, but what is the explanation for it?

4.1.4   A simple answer to the question about the historical ubiquity of religion is that it enabled people to feel at home in the world. It did this by supplying answers to certain questions which the human capacity for self-conscious, reflective thought leads people to ask: questions about the ultimate nature of things and the place and destiny of humanity within it. The fact that these answers were extra-rational was either not understood at all, or only imperfectly understood, so that its implications were not appreciated. In any case, most people, not being intellectually sophisticated, were not interested in the scope of rational inquiry. What they wanted concerning ultimate questions were answers which would give significance to human life, and these religion supplied, including what was of great practical importance: instructions for living. But, in order to supply them, it had to be already there. How did it orginate in the first place? The historian H. A. L. Fisher, writing about the rise of Christianity, remarked that 'Religions are founded by laymen and organised by priests.'[4] This draws attention to the creative role of individuals in religious innovation. But it glosses over the fact that the great historical religious innovators, such as Moses, Buddha, Jesus and Mahomet, did not start from scratch but started from an already existing religion. An inquiry into the origins of religion would involve an inquiry into the origins of the capacity for self-conscious, reflective thought, and, more generally, the origins of human culture. That cannot be undertaken here. Our simple answer must stand. Whatever the origins of religion, the reason for its historical ubiquity is that it enabled people to feel at home in the world.

The great religious innovators must have accepted the first of the two answers to the question about religious diversity. Each must have been convinced that the particular definitive statement which he advocated was true and that all others were false. Otherwise he could not have inspired people to follow him. His followers must have accepted the first answer on his authority. Similar considerations must have applied to ordinary, intellectually unsophisticated people in the absence of religious innovation. They readily accepted the religion traditionally practised in their community, or in that section of it to which they belonged. They were initiated into it in childhood and, in the course of growing up, learned to think of the world and themselves in terms of its particular definitive statement. That this statement was true and all others were false was something which they would have taken for granted. If this is roughly true, it enables us to see why, historically, religion has been a major source of conflict. The attitude of most people to other religions would have depended upon the spirit and content of the definitive statement of their own religion. But, because they accepted the first answer, there would have been a strong inclination to regard those of different faiths as at best misguided, at worst as enemies. Hence the potential for religious conflict. The misguided had to be shown the error of their ways and made to see the truth. Enemies had to be neutralised or, failing that, destroyed. This applied with special force to those who subscribed to different definitive statements of the same religion. They were heretics and were a threat to the orthodox. The distinction between orthodoxy and heresy presupposes the first answer with respect to a particular version of the definitive statement of a given religion. That version alone is true, others being 'perversions' which must be stamped out to protect the truth.

Why is religion no longer a major source of conflict in most countries? What has just been said suggests an explanation. Most people today, at least in the West, accept not the first but the second answer to the question about religious diversity. They need not understand all the implications of the figurative character of religious language. If they accept the unamended second answer and understand, albeit intuitively, that no definitive statement can be literally true, that is enough to remove the incentive to quarrel about religion. They do not regard as misguided either those who are of different faiths, or those who subscribe to different versions of their own. Nor do they feel threatened by them. They are content if there is mutual respect between those of different religious traditions. This, however, only makes intelligible what has happened, not why it has happened. Why do most people today accept the second answer, rather than, as did their forebears, the first? How have they come to acquire the intuitive understanding not possessed by their forebears, that no definitive statement can be literally true? A general answer must suffice, which, however, is probably on the right lines. People today are aware, to a much greater extent than their forebears, not only of religious but also of cultural diversity. This increased awareness is owing to greatly improved communications, to increased contact between people of different cultures, and, in the Western world at least, to near-universal literacy. These developments in turn have been made possible by the growth of scientific knowledge since the eighteenth century, and by the development of new industrial techniques and the consequent expansion of trade on a world-wide scale during the eighteenth and nineteenth centuries.

There is, however, a simpler and cruder explanation of the fact that religion is no longer a major source of conflict. This is that religion no longer has the importance today which it used to have. Because it matters less to them, people are unwilling to fight about it. But this is not incompatible with the explanation given in the last paragraph. People who accept the second answer may well not attach so much importance to religion as people who accept the first. Realising that no definitive statement can be literally true and that their own religion is only one among a number of alternatives, it is understandable if they do not feel particularly strongly about it. In fact this is how many people, especially in the Western world, feel today. Outside the communist world, where religion, although not forbidden, is officially discouraged, most people today still profess some form of religious commitment. Only a handful admit to having no religion at all. But, in the West at least, only a minority take their religious commitments seriously. The majority regard them as merely nominal. They lead secular, not religious lives, only infrequently attending public worship and rarely, if ever, engaging in prayer.[5] While they may comply with some of their religion's instructions for living – for instance, those concerned with marriage and the family – they do so because these are part of their community's particular morality, not because they are religious instructions. They are *de facto* although not *de jure* agnostics: that is, agnostics who are unwilling to admit it and to sever their formal connection with organised religion.

4.1.5   Why do they remain *de facto* agnostics instead of going the whole way and becoming *de jure*? Why do they bother to retain a purely nominal religious commitment? Probably, in many cases, for personal and social reasons. But it may also be that they are unwilling to face the implications of *de jure* agnosticism. Unlike religion, agnosticism cannot enable people to feel at home in the world. It provides no instructions for living. Its answer to ultimate questions is simple and stark. Human beings are on their own in the mysterious universe, without supernatural protection and guidance. Their destiny can only be death. But there is also a positive side, to which the name of 'humanism' is appropriate. It is up to human beings to make the most of human life within the limits permitted by the natural order. Whatever significance human life has can only be given to it by human beings themselves. *De facto* agnostics are trying to have it both ways. They accept the humanism of agnosticism but avoid its simple and stark answer by retaining a nominal religious commitment. While such a position is intellectually indefensible, it is emotionally understandable that those who accept the unamended second answer about religious diversity should want to adopt it. They want to have the best of both worlds, which is a natural and amiable human characteristic.

It is important not to misunderstand what is being said here. Agnosticism is the logical outcome of rational inquiry into religious diversity. But it is not entailed by the amended second answer. What that entails is that religious belief is extra-rational and that to be religious is to make the 'leap of faith'. To make the leap is therefore an alternative to agnosticism. No doubt some, perhaps many, of those who today take their religious commitments seriously accept the amended second answer and make the leap with an understanding of what they are doing. Others, especially evangelicals, are indifferent to the problem of religious diversity and, like their forebears, accept the first answer. Again, many of those who take their religious commitments seriously do not find this incompatible with accepting in practice much of the humanism of agnosticism. Accepting that it is up to them to make the most of human life, they do their best to respond to the challenge. How far they are at liberty to do this, and how they interpret it, depends upon the content, scope and precision of the particular instructions for living of their own religion. In any case, the seriousness with which religious commitments are taken is a matter of degree. All sorts of positions are possible between complete dedication and nominal adherence. These are reflected in the extent to which, and the ways in which, people take it upon themselves to give significance to human life. These considerations amplify the explanations already given but they do not change them. Most people today, and especially in the West, accept the second answer in either its unamended or its amended form. Religion no longer has the importance in human life which it used to have. Hence it is no longer a major source of conflict.

4.2 IDEOLOGY

4.2.1   While religious diversity makes moral diversity in the past intelligible, what about today, when religion is no longer so important? A suggestion worth considering is that religion has been replaced by ideology. Ideological diversity is now the key factor in moral diversity. A brief elucidation of the notion of 'ideology' must therefore be attempted. The word 'ideology' was originally a technical term in Marxism and then later in what Karl Mannheim called the 'sociology of knowledge'.[6] This is how it is still used by some contemporary Marxists and sociologists. But today it is no longer confined to jargon, as is shown by the fact that Marxism itself is commonly referred to as an ideology. Thus Patrick Corbett, who cites Marxism as one of a number of examples, characterises an ideology simply as 'A set of beliefs about the conduct of life and the organisation of society.'[7]

According to this, any comprehensive social and political doctrine is an ideology. In particular, attention is drawn to the programmatic character of such doctrines. Something else, however, needs to be emphasised. What are called ideologies always contain a justification for what they advocate. Alasdair MacIntyre draws attention to this, picking out as a central feature of an ideology 'An account of the relationship of what is the case, and how we ought to live, between the nature of the world, and morals, politics and other guides to conduct.'[8] A similar point is made by Kenneth R. Minogue, who, contrasting academic and ideological thinking, writes, 'An ideology then is a description of the world designed to determine action, couched in apparently academic technicalities which nevertheless contain signals which are necessarily unsubtle, of the attitude we should adopt.'[9] It follows that, while ideologies must contain descriptions, these cannot be 'value-free'. If there is a relationship between them and how we ought to live, still more if they are to determine action, they cannot simply be physical descriptions. If they were, they could not justify the comprehensive programmatic prescriptions characteristic of ideologies. They must themselves be 'prescriptive' descriptions.

4.2.2 An institutional fact is one kind of prescriptive description (see 2.3.4 above). Particular institutional facts are not, however, descriptions of the nature of the world. Nor is the most general of institutional facts – that to be a member of a community is to be a moral agent (see 2.2.2 and 2.3.4 above) – such a description. This fact includes two sets of prescriptions: those of common morality and those of the particular morality of an individual community, because to be a member of a community is always to be a member of an individual community. But what the latter are depends upon the way of life of that community with its particular values and institutions: that is, upon particular institutional facts. The prescriptive descriptions of ideologies therefore cannot be institutional facts. The detailed prescriptions of the latter differ from one community to another. They do not and cannot constitute the comprehensive programmatic prescriptions characteristic of an ideology.

We have come across another kind of prescriptive description in connection with religion. Any description of the religious belief in the dependence of the natural upon the supernatural necessarily includes a prescription about complying with whatever instructions for living come from the supernatural (see 4.1.1 above). Part of what it is to be dependent upon the supernatural is to have an obligation to comply. But religious belief is extra-rational. A description of the content of religious belief is a description of what is believed by those who have made the leap of faith and there can be no obligation to make that leap. It is not a description of 'the nature of the world', of 'what is the case'. It is not, that is to say, a description which can be literally true (see 4.1.3 above). But this is what ideological descriptions profess to be. It follows that the prescriptive descriptions characteristic of ideologies cannot be of the same kind as those characteristic of religion. What then are they? How can a description of 'the nature of the world', of 'what is the case', be prescriptive?

A clue lies in the humanistic side of agnosticism. This consists of a description which includes a challenge. Human beings are alone in the mysterious universe. It is up to them to give human life whatever significance it is to have (see 4.1.3 above). The clue lies in interpreting an ideology as a comprehensive response to the challenge. It endorses the agnostic description of 'what is the case' and prescribes what it asserts to be the best way of making the most of human life. But, although there is a core of truth in this interpretation, it is only a partial answer. An ideology must do more than merely endorse the agnostic description of 'what is the case', because, while that description includes the challenge, it does not prescribe any comprehensive response. As a description, it is only implicitly prescriptive. It implies that the challenge should be responded to, but that is all. An ideology must contain an explicitly prescriptive description of a kind which will determine action in the form of its comprehensive response. It must therefore supplement the agnostic description with a prescriptive description of a suitably selected aspect of human life which it presents as focusing upon what is of decisive importance, both for how things are and for how they can be made better. The content of its prescriptive description of this aspect differentiates it from other ideologies which may have selected the same or a similar aspect, and gives it a distinct identity.

4.2.3   What has just been said is true of what today are commonly referred to as 'ideologies'. Or, to put it another way, there are a number of comprehensive social and political doctrines in the world today of which it is true, and it is these which are commonly called 'ideologies'. Two which stand out as both intellectually sophisticated and influential are Marxism and libertarian capitalism. Each selects the economic aspect of human life, but their prescriptive descriptions of it are very different. For libertarian capitalism, it is free-market transactions which are of decisive importance, not only because they maximise the production and distribution of wealth according to consumer demand, but also because they foster the virtues of self-reliance and personal initiative. For the full benefit of free-market transactions to be reaped, however, the role of government must be limited to the protection of person and property, the enforcement of contracts and the prevention of any form of 'restraint of trade'. The political prescription of libertarian capitalism is the 'nightwatchman state'.[10] According to Marxism, what is of decisive importance is class exploitation and class conflict, which are generated by the division of labour and the private ownership of the means of production. Law and government protect this ownership and perpetuate the poverty and degradation of the exploited classes. The remedy lies in abolishing private ownership by overthrowing the legal order which protects it, and putting an end to class conflict by creating a classless society in which the full human potential of everyone can be realised. The political prescription of Marxism is revolution.[11]

There is of course much more in both libertarian capitalism and Marxism than is contained in the foregoing brief accounts. But any fuller statements would include them, and they are sufficient for my present contention. This is that a distinguishing characteristic of those comprehensive social and political doctrines commonly called ideologies is a prescriptive description of a selected aspect of human life which is presented as the justification for their programmatic prescriptions. What has been said here about libertarian capitalism and Marxism is enough to show that they both possess this characteristic. A brief mention may be made of some other, less influential doctrines which also possess this characteristic and which are commonly called ideologies. One is anarchism.[12] The characteristic it selects for prescriptive description is autonomy, the human capacity for independent choice and decision. Authority in general and government in particular violate autonomy. Hence the anarchist prescription that we should try to do without them or, failing that, have as little of them as possible. Another such doctrine is nationalism. The selected aspect here is some version of cultural, ethnic or racial identity, which is described as being frustrated by alien political rule. Hence its prescription of national self-determination through political independence. There are also non-Marxist versions of socialism which select various aspects of free-market transactions and describe them as cruel, unjust or in some other way iniquitous. Their prescriptions vary with the character of their indictments: co-operation instead of competition, public instead of private ownership, central planning instead of 'market forces', syndicalism instead of private enterprise.[13]

4.2.4   There is another characteristic feature of every ideology. This is the demand for the complete commitment of its adherents to its programmatic prescriptions, and, as part of that commitment, the uncritical acceptance of its prescriptive description of its selected aspect of human life. Or again, to put it another way, this is a characteristic possessed by those social and political doctrines commonly called 'ideologies'. It is what makes them 'comprehensive' doctrines. An ideology is a doctrinal 'package'. It demands to be accepted as such. Its adherents cannot, while remaining adherents, question its foundations. The only reply they can make to such questioning is to reaffirm their commitment. This may be what A. D. Lindsay had in mind when he commented upon Marx, 'There is some truth in what he said. It is not very profitable to ask how much.'[14] For non-Marxists to put this question to Marxists is necessarily unprofitable. They cannot, while remaining committed Marxists, take it seriously. They are like religious believers who accept the first answer to the question about religious diversity. Lindsay's first point, however, stands. There is some truth in what Marxism says about class conflict and exploitation. But then there is also some truth in what libertarian capitalism says about free-market transactions. There must be some truth in any ideology. It prescriptively describes a selected aspect of human life. If there were no truth in what it says about that aspect, it could have no credibility and would be a non-starter as a comprehensive social and political doctrine. Its programmatic prescriptions would be dismissed as irrelevant and it would have no adherents.

   There are circumstances in which many people find an ideology credible. Its prescriptive description appears to them to highlight and illuminate familiar features of their own situation, and its programmatic prescriptions suggest to them a way of dealing with it. This may well be how Marxism appears to many of the poor in Latin America today. It was probably how nationalism appeared to many members of the indigenous populations of Third World countries living under colonial regimes after the Second World War, and how, in the form of Zionism, it appeared to many Jews after the 'Holocaust'. But the contingent fact that, in particular circumstances, many people find an ideology credible does not vindicate that ideology. Its claim to be the best way of making the most of human life and its demand for complete commitment are not thereby justified. The claim is based upon a selected aspect of human life. Even if, in particular circumstances, this aspect is arguably important, that cannot show that the ideology's programmatic prescriptions are the best way of making the most of human life. It shows at most that, in those circumstances, there may be something to be said for action along the lines of the prescriptions. In other circumstances, where a different aspect is arguably more important, such action is unlikely to do any good and may well make things worse. The demand requires the surrender of independent thought and judgement. It entails uncritical acceptance of the programmatic prescriptions, irrespective of whether or not in the circumstances, they are appropriate.

Underlying every ideology is the unjustified presumption that there is one best way of making the most of human life. There is no warrant for this presumption in agnostic humanism. This says that it is up to human beings to make the most of human life and implies that the challenge should be responded to. But it says nothing about what the response should be. There is certainly a variety of ways in which life can be enhanced and enriched. But what can be done to improve its quality must necessarily depend upon the circumstances of time and place. Moreover, it must not be assumed that all good things are compatible. On this last point, some words of Sir Isaiah Berlin are worth recalling. After pointing out that, because all truths are necessarily compatible, it does not necessarily follow that all human values must be as well, he argues

> The belief that some single formula can be found whereby all the diverse ends of men can be harmoniously realised, is demonstrably false. If, as I believe, the ends of men are many and not all of them are in principle compatible with each other, the possibility of conflict and tragedy can never wholly be eliminated from human life either personal or social. The necessity of choosing between absolute claims is then an inescapable characteristic of the human condition.[15]

Belief in a single formula is characteristically ideological. An ideology's programmatic prescriptions disregard the incompatibility between different human values, and deprive people of freedom to choose.

4.2.5   There are certain resemblances between ideology and religion. There must be a definitive statement of an ideology's prescriptive description and of its programmatic prescriptions. There can be different sects of the same ideology, divided by different versions or rival interpretations of its definitive statement. No religion can be literally true and no religion can be rationally justified. But there is nothing in the case of ideology corresponding to the amended second answer in the case of religion. Because religious belief is extra-rational, there is no obligation either to believe or not to believe. But religious belief is self-justifying in the sense that those able and willing to make the leap of faith are justified in making it. Ideological commitment, however, cannot be self-justifying, because it is commitment to a claim which cannot be justified: the claim of an ideology that its programmatic prescriptions are the best way of making the most of human life. Those who make such a commitment therefore either do not fully understand what they are doing, or are being irrational: that is, they are doing what they know to be unjustified, not for the sake of some ulterior purpose but simply for the sake of doing it. Not that a genuine commitment can be made for an ulterior purpose. In such a case, what purports to be a commitment is really action for the sake of expediency or prudence. By the same token, those who create and expound ideologies cannot fully understand what they are doing. If they did, they could not do it. They could only produce propaganda for some social and political objective which, for reasons of self-interest or, perhaps, moral reasons, such as the interest of their community, they already supported. As the creators of ideologies, they are like religious innovators who accept the first answer and believe in the literal truth of what they preach and teach.

The rise and spread of ideologies is a modern phenomenon. It is roughly contemporaneous with those developments which, it was suggested in the last section, explain why in the case of religion many people today have turned from the first to the second answer: improved communications, greater contact between peoples, widespread literacy – all of these being made possible by the growth of scientific knowledge and of modern industry and commerce. These developments have helped many people to understand the challenge in agnostic humanism: that it is up to human beings to make the most of human life. An ideology is a comprehensive response, albeit an unjustified one, to that challenge. As we have seen, there are circumstances in which many people find a particular ideology credible. All this makes the rise and spread of ideologies intelligible. There is another respect in which there may well be a resemblance between religion and ideology. It was pointed out in the last section that, while, outside the communist world, most people today still profess some form of religious commitment, only a minority take it seriously. The same is probably true of ideology. Communist countries are offically committed to some version of Marxism. But it is likely that, outside the ranks of the Communist Party, if not within it, few people in communist countries are more than nominal adherents of Marxism. Most people 'go along with it' for the sake of a quiet life but are not 'true believers'.[16] This may well be true of ideologies generally. By no means all those who in particular circumstances find an ideology credible are fully committed to it. They go along with it because, and so long as, circumstances are such that it holds out a practical prospect of bettering their lot. The 'true believers' are largely confined to the activists who organise and lead movements in the name of that ideology.

4.2.6   We can now return to the suggestion at the beginning of this section that it is ideological rather than religious diversity which is the key factor today in moral diversity. This rests upon two assumptions. The first is that, just as there is religious morality, so there can also be ideological morality – an ideology's programmatic prescriptions taking the place of a religion's instructions for living. The second assumption is that, whereas in the past there were religious communities – for instance, Christian, Muslim and Buddhist communities – what we have today are ideological communities: that is, communist, capitalist, non-Marxist socialist and nationalist communities, the last being communities based on a particular cultural, ethnic or racial identity. Of these two assumptions, the first is logically prior to the second. Unless the first is true, the second cannot be. An objection to the first is that the demand for ideological commitment cannot be justified. Those who make such a commitment either do not fully understand what they are doing or are being irrational. But those who, when making a religious commitment, accept the first answer, about religious diversity also do not fully understand what they are doing. They mistakenly believe in the literal truth of their religion's definitive statement. This mistake does not mean that they are not genuinely committed and do not have an obligation to comply with their religion's instructions for living. It means only that they are not justified in requiring, in the name of their religion, compliance from those who have not made the same commitment, although they can be justified in requiring them to comply on social grounds (see 4.1.3 above). Now this applies to ideology no less than to religion, which means that ideological morality is conceivable. Those who make an ideological commitment mistakenly believe their ideology's claim that its programmatic prescriptions are the best way to make the most of human life. This does not mean that they are not genuinely committed and do not have an obligation to comply with those instructions. It means only that they are not justified in requiring, in the name of their ideology, compliance from those who have not made the same commitment. But here too they can be justified on social grounds.

Given that ideological morality is quite conceivable, we can now consider the second assumption. It is certainly plausible in the case of communist countries which are officially committed to Marxism. The same holds of newly independent Third World countries, which are officially committed to nationalism in their own image and often to some version of socialism, Marxist or otherwise. But it is less plausible in the case of Western countries. Free-market transactions have come to play a prominent part in their ways of life, and the obligations connected with these transactions are part of their particular moralities. But this does not mean that Western countries are officially committed to libertarian capitalist ideology and that its programmatic prescriptions are part of their particular moralities. Western countries are not officially committed to any ideology. Among their members, there are 'true believers' both in libertarian capitalism and in various versions of socialism. But these are a small minority. However, the number of 'true believers' is small in both communist and Third World countries and this casts doubt on the second assumption in their cases. The most that can be said is that communist prescriptions have entered into the particular moralities of communist countries, and nationalist and other socialist prescriptions into those of Third World countries. This is because deliberate attempts have been made in both cases to mould institutions according to these prescriptions. But these attempts have been made by 'true believers', who are a minority. Whether the majority acknowledge an obligation, as distinct from judging it prudent to comply with these prescriptions, is at least open to question. Perhaps many of them, like *de facto* agnostics in religion, acknowledge a nominal obligation which they do not take very seriously.

The second assumption, then, must be drastically modified. It is far too sweeping to say that today we have ideological communities in place of the religious communities of the past. Some communities today are officially committed to certain ideologies but others are not. Of those which are officially committed, certain ideological prescriptions may have entered their particular moralities, but how seriously they are taken is open to question. It follows that the suggestion that ideological rather than religious diversity is today the key factor in moral diversity is unacceptable. Ideological diversity plays some part in it, but how much is a matter for empirical inquiry. So also is the nature and extent of moral diversity itself. That it is considerable there can be no doubt. There are obvious cultural, political and economic differences between Western, communist and Third World countries. These are reflected in the principles, rules and virtues, together with their attendant obligations, which constitute their respective particular moralities. The same holds of perhaps more subtle differences between the different countries of each group: Western, communist and Third World. These too are reflected in their respective particular moralities. Despite the decline in its importance, religion is likely to be a significant factor in both sets of differences, perhaps primarily through its cultural influence. Over and above common morality, the particular moralities of some countries, especially those which historically have much in common, will have features in common. Here too, religion is still significant. But this again is a matter for detailed empirical inquiry. Finally, such inquiry may well show that, with the increasing understanding, especially in the West, of the challenge of agnostic humanism, humanist ideas and values are increasingly penetrating the particular moralities of many modern communities.

5 Morality and the 'Categorical Imperative'

5.1 EXPOSITION AND CRITICISM OF THE 'CATEGORICAL IMPERATIVE'

5.1.1 As we have seen (see 2.1.2), according to Kant obligations are categorical imperatives: that is, imperatives from which people cannot release themselves except by complying with them. Particular obligations, however, are particular cases of a universal obligation which Kant calls the 'Categorical Imperative'. It is universal in the straightforward sense of applying to all human beings always and everywhere. He sums it up in the formula, 'Act always according to maxims which at the same time can be adopted as universal laws.'[1] The 'can' in this formula is a logical 'can'. A maxim can be adopted as a universal law only if it is logically possible for everyone always to obey it and logically impossible for everyone always to disobey it. This is the criterion of 'universalisability'. If a maxim can be universalised, there is an obligation always to obey it. If it cannot, if it is logically impossible for everyone always to obey it, there is an obligation to refrain from acting according to it. This negative side of the Categorical Imperative may be rendered as, 'What cannot at all times be done by everyone, ought never at any time to be done by anyone.' There are, however, maxims to which universalisability is logically inapplicable. Consider, 'Always take a cold bath first thing in the morning', and its logical contrary, 'Never take a cold bath first thing in the morning.' It is logically possible for either the maxim or its logical contrary, but not both, always to be obeyed. Because this is so, there cannot be an obligation to obey either of them. With respect to each, there can only be a hypothetical imperative. For Kant, that is to say, imperatives are hypothetical when universalisability is logically inapplicable to them.

According to Kant, universalisability is the criterion of morality. If an action falls under a maxim which can be universalised, there is an obligation to do it. If it falls under a maxim which cannot be universalised, there is an obligation to refrain from doing it. An example is theft. The maxim 'Be a thief' cannot be universalised. If all were to become thieves, the institution of property would break down because no one would obey its central constitutive rule, the prohibition of theft. But without property there could be no theft, because there would be nothing to steal. Hence, because it is logically impossible for everyone to be a thief, no one ought to be one. Refraining from theft is therefore an obligation. What is true of theft is true of deceitful promising and of lying. If everyone always made deceitful promises, the practice of promising would break down, and, if everyone always told lies, there could be no communication. Without *bona fide* promising there can be no deceitful promising, and without communication lying is impossible. Hence there is an obligation to refrain from both. But their logical contraries can be universalised. Hence there is an obligation always to make *bona fide* promises and always to tell the truth.

Now, if universalisability is the criterion of morality, it follows that constitutive rules must be moral rules and that regulative rules cannot be. This is because of their respective logical characteristics.[2] Constitutive rules are necessarily universalisable. The actions they govern are logically dependent upon the rules in the sense that without the rules there could be no such action. It must therefore be logically possible for everyone always to obey them and logically impossible for everyone always to break them. If everyone always broke the rules of chess, there could be no such game and no chess moves. But universalisability is logically inapplicable to regulative rules. The actions they govern are logically independent of them in the sense that they can be done in the absence of the rules. It is therefore logically possible for everyone either always to obey them or always to break them: either always to keep to the speed limit or always to break it. There is, however, something wrong with this. Keeping to the speed limit is a moral as well as a legal obligation, because exceeding it is socially irresponsible and there is a moral obligation to be socially responsible. Some regulative rules are therefore moral rules: that is, rules which there is a moral obligation to obey. There is a moral obligation to obey the rules of the game, but not because they are universalisable. Rather it is because there is a moral obligation not to cheat. Cheating is both unfair and dishonourable and there is a moral obligation both to act fairly and to act honourably. This is not to deny that some constitutive rules are moral rules: for instance, truth-telling and promise-keeping. But what makes them moral is not the logical characteristic of universalisability. It is that they are necessary for social life as such. Other constitutive rules – for instance, those of grammar and syntax – are not moral.

5.1.2   If universalisability were the criterion of morality, there could be no such thing as a 'white lie'. But, while lying cannot be universalised, there can be occasions when telling a lie is the lesser evil: for instance, in order to save an innocent life.[3] There can therefore be occasions when there is an obligation to act according to a maxim which cannot be universalised – from which it follows that universalisability cannot be the criterion of morality. One reason why Kant failed to see this is that he equated 'maxims' with 'rules', and failed to appreciate the difference between a rule and a principle. He therefore did not realise that a principle can justify breaking a rule (see 1.2.4 above). It may nevertheless be thought that the discussion of amoral egoism in Chapter 2 shows that universalisability is somehow involved in morality. The amoral egoist is a free rider (see 2.3.3 above). He takes the benefits of social life without meeting his share of its costs. The maxim 'Be a free rider' cannot be universalised. If everyone became a free rider, the costs of social life would not be met at all and it would break down. But, if it broke down, no one could take its benefits because there would not be any. It is therefore logically impossible for everyone to become a free rider.

This is of course correct, but it was not how amoral egoism was shown to be rationally indefensible. That was by invoking the practical-reason principle, which requires that like cases should always be treated alike and that there should be differential treatment only where there are relevant differences. The amoral egoist says that all except himself should be amoral. He accords to himself a status which he denies to everyone else in the absence of any relevant differences. What is right for him is not right for them, although he and they are alike in all relevant respects. It is therefore not necessary to invoke Kant's universalisability criterion to show that amoral egoism is rationally indefensible. That criterion does not allow for special circumstances and relevant differences. It coincides with the practical-reason principle in the case of amoral egoism, because in that case there are no special circumstances and relevant differences. The practical-reason principle lays down requirements for rational procedure in all action, instrumental no less than moral. It is not, therefore, a moral principle. It enables action to be informed by an understanding of what is rational, not of what is moral. In moral contexts, such action presupposes an understanding of morality, but that understanding must come from moral principles. The practical-reason principle can clarify thought about moral matters: for instance, by showing that amoral egoism is rationally indefensible. But, as we have seen, showing that presupposes an understanding not only of what morality is, but also of why there has to be morality at all (see 2.3.3 above).

Because it presupposes this understanding and cannot itself provide it, the practical-reason principle cannot be the criterion of morality. It is not an alternative to Kant's universalisability principle. To think that there is a single criterion of morality which can be expressed in a formula applicable to all actions is an error. We have seen that Kent fell into it, at least in part, through his failure to distinguish between rules and principles. But, apart from that, the idea is an error because it takes no account of moral diversity and assumes that morality is always and everywhere the same. This is indeed true of common morality. Its principles are necessary for social life as such. But they cannot be compressed into a single formula. To think that they can would be to repeat

Kant's mistake of not distinguishing between principles and rules. It would also be to ignore the relation between common morality and the particular morality of an individual community with its own way of life, institutions and values. The latter is the context within which the principles of the former must be interpreted. Beneficence and justice are principles of common morality. But which good is the greater and which evil the lesser, as well as what counts as good and what as evil, depend upon an individual community's particular morality. What is just, what in detail is due to each and from whom, depends upon the terms upon which the members of the community are living together and upon the social order which these terms constitute.

5.2 KANT'S HUMANITY PRINCIPLE AS THE BASIS FOR A UNIVERSAL MINIMUM MORAL STANDARD

5.2.1 We have not yet finished with the Categorical Imperative. Kant gives another statement of it: 'Treat humanity, whether in your own person or in that of another, always as an end withal and never merely as a means.'[4] For him, this is entailed by the universalisability criterion. If human beings are always to act only on maxims which can be universalised, they must treat humanity always as an end and never merely as a means. Hence there is a universal obligation so to treat humanity. But what is important about this statement of the Categorical Imperative is not that it is entailed by the universalisability criterion (although, as we shall see, it is); rather it is the substantive moral principle which it contains and which for brevity I shall call the 'humanity principle'. It needs to be investigated. To treat a human being merely as a means is to treat him as lacking all intrinsic value. If he has any value at all, it is only extrinsic or instrumental. To treat him always as an end is always to treat him as having intrinsic value, irrespective of any extrinsic value he may happen to have. But what is it to treat him as always having intrinsic value? Clearly, never to treat him merely as a means: this is the negative side of the humanity principle. But what on the positive side does this principle require?

According to Kant, it requires that a human being must always be respected as an autonomous agent: that is, as a person capable of formulating and pursuing purposes of his own. But, while this may be true, it needs explanation, and for that something must be said about the notion of intrinsic value. Nothing can have value unless someone values it. This is obvious in the case of extrinsic value. Something which has extrinsic value is useful, and it must necessarily be useful potentially, if not actually, for something and to someone. Something which has intrinsic value need not be useful for anything to anyone. It has value in itself: that is, its existence is worthwhile for its own sake. But there must be someone for whom it has value in itself – some person, or at least some sentient subject, to whom its existence is worthwhile for its own sake.[5] Now, every human being who is not in a state of pathological depression has intrinsic value for himself. This is so irrespective of whether he is happy. He may be the victim of hardship and have to suffer many privations, but, for all that, his own existence is to him worthwhile for its own sake. If it were not, he would not try to maintain himself, endeavouring as best he can to provide for his needs. In exercising his capacity for formulating and pursuing purposes of his own, he implicitly acknowledges his intrinsic value for himself. This capacity is a distinctively human characteristic and is possessed in some measure by every human being who is not mentally defective.

This means that Kant's account of the positive side of the humanity principle is correct so far as it goes. To respect a human being as an autonomous agent is to treat him as having intrinsic value for himself. He need not have intrinsic value for other people. They can be indifferent to him or actively dislike him. For the humanity principle, their personal feelings about him are irrelevant. Its requirement is that he always be treated as having intrinsic value for himself. That means respecting him as an autonomous agent and therefore refraining from interfering with him in the formulation and pursuit of purposes of his own, provided that he shows the same forbearance in all his dealings with other people. According to Kant, to show this respect to all human beings is a categorical imperative because it is entailed by the universalisability criterion. It is logically possible for everyone always to respect everyone, including themselves, as autonomous agents, and logically impossible for everyone always to act to the contrary of this maxim. For each to treat all, including himself, always merely as a means and never as an autonomous agent would be for each always to treat all, including himself, as a slave. But there can be slaves only if there are slave-owners and a slave-owner logically cannot be one of his own slaves. *Qua* slave-owner, he must respect himself as an autonomous agent in order to be able to treat others as slaves: that is, merely as means to his ends. Hence it is logically impossible for every human being always to treat every human being, including himself, merely as a means. It follows that to respect the personal autonomy of every human being, including oneself, is a universal obligation. This obligation, however, entails a restriction upon the exercise of the human capacity for autonomy. No one must adopt as his own any purpose which cannot be universalised. If it cannot be adopted and pursued by everyone, it must not be adopted and pursued by anyone.

5.2.2 We have, however, seen that there is no obligation to act only on maxims which can be universalised. Kant's case therefore fails. There may be a universal obligation to act upon the humanity principle, but not for his reasons.

Now, a limited version of the principle on its negative side is implicit in common morality. For any member of a community to be treated by any of his fellow members merely as a means is to deny that he is a member at all. It contravenes the principle of fellowship, because to treat him merely as a means is to show no concern for his well-being. It contravenes the principle of justice because it denies that anything is due to him. Worst of all, it contravenes respect for life, because to treat him merely as a means is to treat his life as expendable. It may be a member's duty to sacrifice his life in defence of his community. But to call upon him to perform this duty is to treat him as a moral agent, not merely as a means. But should the negative side of the humanity principle be confined to the fellow members of the same community? What about the requirements of the practical-reason principle? Is the difference between fellow countrymen and foreigners a relevant difference – that is, a difference which justifies any of the former treating any of the latter merely as a means?

There are obvious differences, of which fellow countrymen are well aware, between foreigners and themselves. Foreigners live in other communites, speak 'foreign' languages and have different cultural traditions with different institutions and values. But, whether or not fellow countrymen take account of it, there are respects in which foreigners and themselves are the same.[6] Foreigners too are human beings. They have intrinsic value for themselves and possess the distinctively human characteristic of being able to formulate and pursue purposes of their own. If fellow countrymen treat foreigners merely as a means they are ignoring the respects in which they and foreigners are the same. Foreigners are not fellow countrymen, but they are fellow human beings. To treat them merely as a means is to deny this. It is not to treat like cases alike but to treat them differently in the absence of relevant differences. The practical-reason principle entails that, because the negative side of the humanity principle is implicit in common morality, and therefore in the terms upon which in every human community the members are living together, there is at least one universal moral obligation. This is to act in all dealings with other human beings, with foreigners as well as fellow countrymen, with heathens and infidels as well as co-religionists, always upon the negative side of the humanity principle. The same obligation applies also to dealings with all those who, while living in a community, do not have the status of members: to slaves, serfs and 'untouchables'. Although not fellow members, they too are fellow human beings.

Historically, the negative side of the humanity principle has often been contravened. The institution of slavery is one instance. The Nazi policy of genocide, less than two generations ago, is another. But the fact that the humanity principle has often been contravened does not invalidate it. Historically, many contraventions have been owing to ignorance: to the belief that, while all human beings are human, some are less human than others. Various theories have contributed to this belief, not least Aristotle's doctrine of 'natural' slavery.[7] But modern knowledge, especially in anthropology, shows the belief to be false. There can never be any justification for treating any human being merely as a means. If any community's particular morality permits, and especially if it requires, such treatment, it is in that respect morally defective. The significance of the humanity principle is that on its negative side it sets a universal minimum moral standard to which, on rational grounds, every particular morality should conform.

5.2.3   But acting on the negative side of the humanity principle entails acting on its positive side. If a human being is not to be treated merely as a means, he must be treated as having intrinsic value, at least for himself. This requires respecting him as an autonomous agent. But the account which has so far been given of that requirement is incomplete. It has been limited to the prohibition 'Do not interfere with anyone's personal autonomy so long as he does not interfere with anyone else's', which is still negative. It says nothing about how positively a human being must be dealt with, in order to be respected as an autonomous agent. The short answer is that he must be dealt with according to the principles of common morality. We already know that these principles are necessary for social life as such, and also in any form of human association (see 3.2.2). Not to deal with a human being according to them is to deny that it is possible to live with him on any terms at all, and also that it is possible to enter into any kind of association with him. Both denials are false. Every human being who is not severely mentally handicapped is capable of social living and of associating with other people. He develops his capacity for personal autonomy within the framework of social life, learning to adapt his own purposes to meet its requirements and to associate with other people for the sake of shared purposes. To deal with him according to the principles of common morality and thereby to respect him as an autonomous agent is to deal with him according to principles with which, through his social experience, he is already familiar.

Another way of coming to the same conclusion is this: if a human being is not to be treated merely as a means, there are certain ways in which he must be treated and others in which he must not. Not only must he not be wantonly killed: his life must never be unnecessarily endangered. His freedom of action must never be arbitrarily interfered with. He must never be gratuitously insulted or humiliated. He should never be subjected to unprovoked violence. He must always be dealt with both fairly and honourably, and his suffering, so far as possible, must be relieved. Now, respect for life, freedom from arbitrary interference and civility are principles of common morality (see 3.1.2 and 3.3.2

above). So are fairness, honourable conduct and fellowship. The treatment which must be accorded to a human being if he is not to be treated merely as a means is what they require. Hence only if a human being is always dealt with according to the principles of common morality can he be treated as having intrinsic value for himself and respect be shown for his personal autonomy. All this, however, presupposes an understanding: first of the humanity principle and of the implications for it of the practical-reason principle; second, of what common morality is, and therefore of its necessity both for social life as such and for all forms of human association.

Kant's preoccupation with universalisability prevented him from acquiring this understanding. He therefore failed to appreciate the full significance of the humanity principle which he himself had formulated. This is that common morality must be applicable to all dealings between human beings. That is the positive side of the universal minimum moral standard which, on its negative side, requires that no human being must ever be treated merely as a means. The universal applicability of common morality has important implications for the idea of human rights. But, before these can be explored, the idea of rights must itself be investigated. More also needs to be said about the universal applicability of common morality and about the contextual interpretation of its principles in relation to the ways of life and particular moralities of individual communities. But that too can be deferred until we have investigated the idea of rights.

Part II
Rights

6 The Idea of Rights (i)

6.1 ANALYSIS AND EXPOSITION OF THE CONCEPT OF A RIGHT

6.1.1   What is it to have a right? What are the sources of rights? Why should there be rights at all? An investigation into the idea of rights must answer these questions. In this chapter I shall be concerned with the first, in the next with the other two. The key notion in the concept of a right is 'entitlement'. To say that you have a right to something is to say that you are entitled to it: for instance, to vote, to receive an old-age pension, to hold your own opinion, to enjoy domestic privacy. To say that rights are entitlements is, of course, only to substitute one word for another. But the substitution is helpful in elucidating the concept of a right. It focuses attention on the source of rights. If you are entitled to something, either you, or someone else on your behalf, must be able to answer the question, 'What entitles you to it?' This presupposes that there are ways of becoming entitled to things and three immediately come to mind. They are law, custom and morality. But more on them and how entitlements come about later. First let us make use of the notion of entitlement to elucidate the concept of a right.

If you are entitled to something, for you to be denied it by the action or the failure to act of someone else is wrong. It is also wrong for other people to penalise you or to make you suffer for having it. This follows from the meaning of 'entitlement'. If it is not wrong for other people to deny you something, not wrong for them to penalise you or to make you suffer for having it, then it cannot be something to which you are entitled. It is therefore appropriate for 'entitlements' to be called 'rights'. If you are entitled to something, it is right for you to have it. But this is subject to an important qualification which we shall come to in a moment. The role of other people is crucial in having a right. No wrong is done to you if you are denied what you are entitled to not by the action or failure to act of other people but by a natural event. If illness keeps you from a meeting which you are entitled to attend, that is unfortunate, but no one is to blame. No right of yours has been violated. Not so if someone forcibly prevents you from attending. He is violating one of your rights and thereby doing wrong to you. This shows that what there can be rights to is limited to what can be affected by actions and forbearances for which people are responsible. No one can have a right to have fine weather on holiday, or to have a talented son. These are cases of good fortune, not of entitlement.

It follows from all this that, for any right, it must be possible to say what action or failure to act would constitute a violation of it. If no such action or inaction is conceivable, there cannot be a right. A distinction drawn by Professor Raphael is helpful here. According to him, rights are of two kinds: rights of action and rights of recipience.[1] To have a right of action is to be entitled to do something or to act in a certain way. To have a right of recipience is to be entitled to receive something, or to be treated in a certain way. A right of recipience is violated when someone from whom you are entitled to receive something refuses to provide it, or when someone fails to accord you the treatment to which you are entitled: for instance, if you are refused your old-age pension, or treated with discourtesy. There is also a violation if you are made to suffer for demanding what you are entitled to receive, or abused and threatened for protesting against being denied the treatment to which you are entitled. A right of action is violated when someone stops you doing what you are entitled to do, or threatens you with dire consequences if you do it: for instance, if someone forcibly prevents you voting, or tries to intimidate you into remaining silent when you are entitled to speak.

It is widely held that, for every right, there must be some correlative obligation. What has been said about rights being limited to what can be affected by action and inaction for which people are responsible suggests that this is true. But some amplification is necessary. There is a general obligation to refrain from doing wrong. To violate anyone's rights is wrong. Everyone is therefore under a general obligation to refrain from doing anything which would violate anyone else's rights. It follows that at least one obligation is correlative to every right. This is an obligation upon everyone to refrain from doing anything which would violate the right. It is the only obligation which is necessarily correlative to every right of action. If you have a right to do something, everyone else must have an obligation not to stop you doing it, not to interfere with you while you are doing it, and not to penalise you or make you suffer for having done it. The same obligation is correlative to rights of recipience. Everyone is under an obligation not to harass, abuse, penalise or injure anyone for either demanding or receiving what he is entitled to. But, in addition to this general obligation of forbearance, there are specific positive obligations which are correlative to rights of recipience. If you are entitled to receive something, there must be someone who is under an obligation to provide it. If you are entitled to certain treatment, there must be others with an obligation to accord it to you.

6.1.2   It is, however, also wrong for anyone to do anything which prevents anyone else from meeting an obligation or which impedes or interferes with his meeting it. Equally, it is wrong for anyone to be penalised or made to suffer for meeting an obligation. The general obligation of forbearance which is correlative to every right is also correlative to every other obligation. The general principle behind this is that it is wrong for what is right to be penalised, obstructed, threatened or prevented. Hence, because it is right for people to have what they are entitled to, it is wrong for them to be denied it or penalised for having it. Equally, because it is right for people to meet their obligations, it is wrong for them to be prevented from or penalised for meeting them.[2] But, if it is right both for people to have what they are entitled to and for them to meet their obligations, where does the difference between having a right and being under an obligation lie? A *prima facie* difference is this. When you are under an obligation, you must meet it unless a more pressing obligation supervenes, in which case you must meet the latter. Subject to this qualification, you do not have a choice about whether or not to meet an obligation. Not so in the case of a right. When you have a right, you are not obliged to exercise it. You have a choice. To be entitled to do something is also to be entitled to refrain from doing it, and to be entitled to receive something is also to be entitled to decline it, or to acquiesce without protest if it is refused. There is, however, a difficulty about taking choice with respect to their exercise to be a universal characteristic of rights as such. There are at least some cases where what are *prima facie* rights of recipience admit no choice about their exercise. But more about that in a moment. First, more needs to be said about obligation and the absence of choice.

To say that there is no choice about whether or not to meet an obligation is not to deny that it is physically possible not to meet it. In most countries the law imposes an obligation upon car-owners to insure their cars. It is physically possible for a man to drive his car without insuring it, but if he does so he does wrong. The obligation legally excludes choice but cannot physically exclude it (see 1.3.3 and 2.1.2 above). No human law can do that. By the same token, if I have made a promise, I am under a moral obligation to keep it. It is physically possible for me to break it but that would be wrong. The obligation morally excludes choice but cannot physically exclude it. No action can be either right or wrong unless it is one which it is physically possible for the agent either to do or not to do. Choice is normatively excluded in the sense that a right action is one which must be done and a wrong action one which must not be done. To choose to do a wrong action or not to do a right action, while physically possible, is wrong. That to have a right is to have a choice is straightforward in the case of rights of action. If I have a right, as distinct from being under an obligation, to attend a meeting, I am entitled to choose whether or not to attend. Choice is normatively provided for, as well as being physically possible. This is also true of most rights of recipience. If I have made you a promise, not only am I under an obligation to keep it, but you have a right to demand that I should. But your right entitles you, if you choose, to release me from my obligation. It does not oblige you to insist that I do what I promised.

6.1.3   But this is not so in all cases. The right of children to be looked after by their parents is a right of recipience from which choice is normatively excluded. Children are not entitled to decline parental care and protection. Even if they do not want it, they must put up with it. It may be thought that this right, like other children's rights, must be exercised for them by adults. If, through illness, poverty or incompetence, parents are failing to look after their children, close relatives or social workers must make other arrangements. But this is beside the point. Children have no choice, morally or legally, about accepting the arrangements made for them. They must be looked after, either by their parents or by other competent adults. It follows that, if to have a right is to have a choice about whether or not to exercise it, then strictly speaking children do not have a right to be looked after. They have an obligation to submit to it. But this is at variance with ordinary language. We do not say that children have an obligation to accept parental care and protection, but that they are entitled – that is, have a right – to it. The case of animals is similar. Owners, users and breeders of animals are under an obligation to treat them humanely. It is often said that animals are entitled to such treatment, which is in effect to say that they have a right to it. But no one says nor would it make sense to say that animals are entitled to decline such treatment, or that they have a choice about whether or not to accept it.

To accommodate such cases, a distinction must be drawn between 'elective' and 'non-elective' rights: a distinction which cuts across that between rights of action and of recipience. Elective rights normatively confer choice. Every right of action is an elective right because the right-holder is entitled not only to do but also to refrain from doing what he has a right to do. The same holds for every right of recipience which entitles the right-holder not only to receive but also to decline what he has a right to receive, or to acquiesce in not receiving it without protest. Non-elective rights normatively exclude choice. They are those rights of recipience which entitle the right-holder to receive something but do not entitle him to decline it. This, however, gives rise to a problem. What is the difference between non-elective rights and obligations? If the non-elective right-holder has no choice but to accept what he has a right to receive, is this not to say that he has an obligation to accept it? There is, however, a difference and it is this: non-elective rights are essentially passive in character. There is nothing which the right-holder is required to do. He is simply the beneficiary of certain treatment which others are under an obligation to accord to him. Because they are under an obligation to accord it to him, he can properly be said to be entitled to it – that is, to have a right to it.

This certainly fits the case of animals. While they are the beneficiaries of the humane treatment which owners, users and breeders are under an obligation to accord to them, there can be no question of their being under an obligation to accept it. As animals, they lack the capacity for responsible action and cannot have any obligations at all. The case of children is more complicated. In the course of growing up, they gradually acquire the capacity for responsible action. At a relatively early age, it has developed sufficiently for them to incur an obligation to obey their parents. After they have incurred it, they must meet it if their parents are to be able to meet their obligation to them. Unless children do what they are told, their parents cannot look after them. This suggests that, because there is something which children are required to do, their non-elective right is after all no different from an obligation. This is not, however, the case. What children have a right to is not to be told what to do but to be looked after. Their obedience cannot guarantee that their parents will care for and protect them. It is only a necessary, not a sufficient, condition for them to receive what they are entitled to. The obligation of parents is not to order their children about, but to give thought to and to provide for their well-being. While their authority over their children is necessary to enable them to meet this obligation, it is distinct from it. They may abuse their authority, ordering their children about to suit their own convenience and neglecting their needs. It follows that the right of children to parental care and protection is distinct from their obligation to obey their parents. It is a non-elective right properly so-called because it does not as such require them to do anything, although a necessary condition for them to have what it entitles them to is that they should meet their obligation to obey their parents.

6.1.4   The distinction between elective and non-elective rights is conceptual, not linguistic. In ordinary language, the term 'a right' is used to cover both cases. The distinction clarifies the position about responsibility for the exercise of rights. Elective rights confer choice, and the right-holder is therefore responsible for their exercise. Non-elective rights do not confer choice, and the right-holder cannot be responsible for their exercise. There can be occasions when it would be wrong for a man to do what he has a right to do: for instance, to attend a meeting at which he has a right to be present when illness in his family makes it necessary for him to stay at home. If a right of action can be exercised only at the cost of failing to meet an obligation, it is wrong to exercise the right. This applies also to elective rights of recipience. It would be wrong for a man to insist that a promise made to him be kept if keeping it involved serious difficulties for the promisor and failure to keep it only minor inconvenience to him. In such a case, the principle of beneficence requires him to release the promisor from his obligation. Hence the need for a qualification to what was

said earlier about the appropriateness of calling entitlements 'rights' (see 6.1.1).
It is normally right for the holder of an elective right to have what he is entitled
to; but not in cases when exercising his right means failing to meet an
obligation. This qualification does not, however, apply to non-elective rights. It
is always right for children to be looked after, either by their parents or by
guardians, and always wrong when they are not. The same is true of animals
and humane treatment.

But, while there can be occasions on which it is wrong for the holder of an
elective right to exercise it, there can be others on which it is wrong for him not
to do so. This is expressed in ordinary language by saying that there is both a
right and a duty to do something. Given the argument presented here, this
sounds paradoxical. Elective rights confer choice; obligations normatively
exclude it. How can there be both a choice and not a choice to do something?
The statement is, however, elliptical, not paradoxical. Suppose I say that I have
both a right and a duty to speak at a meeting: a right because I am a member of
the body concerned and am thereby entitled to attend and to speak at its
meetings; a duty because there is a matter on the agenda which affects the
welfare of certain people and I have promised to be their spokesman. I must
therefore speak if I am to meet my obligation. On this occasion, my obligation
normatively excludes the choice conferred on me by my elective right – but
only with respect to the relevant item on the agenda. On the other items I retain
my right to speak or not as I choose. If I did not have the right to attend and
speak, I could not be a spokesman and could not have incurred the obligation.
Having the right is a necessary condition for having the obligation. All this is
encapsulated in my initial statement, which is why it is elliptical. As is often the
case with ordinary language, analysis is required to elicit the full import of what
is being said.

6.2   HOHFELD ON THE CONCEPT OF A RIGHT

6.2.1 The distinction between rights of action and rights of recipience is
between two kinds of rights. According to Wesley Hohfeld, however, there are
not two but four kinds of right; or rather, according to him, the term 'a right' is
used in the law to cover four things which are conceptually distinct. Since its
appearance more than sixty years ago, Hohfeld's *Fundamental Legal Conceptions*
has become a classic in the philosophy of legal rights. According to at least one
contemporary writer, the significance of his work is not confined to legal rights
but extends to moral rights, including human rights.[3] The last section was
concerned with the concept of a right: that is, with what it is to have a right,
whether its source is law, custom or morality. It would be foolish to neglect

what can be learned from Hohfeld's work and in this section I shall briefly consider it. I shall try to show that, while his starting-point and focus of interest are rather different from mine, his conceptual analysis is nevertheless logically compatible with that of the last section. Its significance for the understanding of human rights will be taken up in later chapters.

Hohfeld calls the four things which the term 'a right' covers 'claims', 'privileges' or 'liberties', 'powers' and 'immunities'. All are legal 'advantages'. Although he does not say so, one thing which they have in common is that they are all entitlements: that is, advantages which the law entitles their possessors to have. Henceforth I shall refer to them respectively as 'claim rights', 'liberty rights', 'power rights' and 'immunity rights'. Examples of claim rights are the right of an old-age pensioner to a pension, and of a promisee to have a promise kept.[4] Examples of liberty rights are the right of a man to spend his leisure as he pleases, and to grow a beard if he wants to. A power right entitles the right-holder to require other people to do certain things at his discretion. Examples are the right of a landlord to alter the rent paid by his tenants, and the right of a policeman to question eye-witnesses at the scene of a crime. An immunity right entitles the right-holder to be exempt from something: an MP to be exempt from the law of libel for what he says in Parliament, a conscientious objector to be exempt from military service.

Hohfeld's analysis preserves while amplifying the action–recipience distinction. Claim rights and immunity rights are respectively rights of positive and of negative recipience. A claim right entitles the right-holder to certain treatment. An immunity right exempts him from certain treatment: that is, entitles him not to be treated in that way. In the language of John Stuart Mill, liberty rights are rights of 'self-regarding' action while power rights are rights of 'other-regarding' action.[5] While a liberty right entitles the right-holder to please himself about what he does, it does not entitle him to determine the action of other people. A power right entitles him to determine the action of certain other people who stand in a specific relationship to him. Henceforth, if further amplification is unnecessary, I shall confine myself to the action–recipience distinction. But, whenever such amplification is required or is helpful, I shall make use of Hohfeld's analysis. The exposition of that analysis is, however, not yet complete and there are certain matters arising from it which need consideration.

Hohfeld goes on to distinguish between 'opposites' and 'correlates' of the four legal advantages. Both are disadvantages but for different people. The opposite of a legal right is the legal disadvantage which a person who does not have the right is under. Because he does not have the right in question, he is not entitled to the advantage it confers. The opposite of a claim right is what Hohfeld calls a 'no right'. If you are not an old-age pensioner, you have no right to a pension. If a promise was made not to you but to someone else, you have no right to what was promised. The opposite of a liberty right is a duty. If you have a duty to do something, you do not have the right – that is, lack the liberty – to refrain from doing it. You also lack the liberty to do – that is, do not have the right to do – anything which is incompatible with doing your duty. If you have a duty to do something in your spare time, you are not at liberty to spend it as you please. If you are a soldier in the British army, you do not have the right to grow a beard, because army regulations impose upon you a duty to shave every day.[6] The opposite of a power right is a disability. If you do not have a particular power right, you are disabled from requiring others to do what those who have the right are entitled to require them to do. If you are not the landlord, you have no power to raise the rent. If you are not a policeman, you are not entitled to require an answer to your questions. The opposite of an immunity right is a liability. If you do not have a particular immunity right, you are liable to whatever it is from which the right exempts those who have it. If you are not an MP, you are liable to the law of libel without qualification. If you are not a conscientious objector, you are liable to be conscripted.

What Hohfeld calls 'correlates' overlap, but are not identical with, the obligations correlative to rights discussed in the last section. According to him, the advantage conferred by a legal right upon one party entails a disadvantage for another party. This disadvantage is the legal correlate of the right. The correlate of a claim right is a duty. If you have a right to an old-age pension, there must be an agency with a duty to pay it to you. You can have the right to a sum of money from me only if I owe it to you and therefore have a duty to pay. The correlate of a liberty right is a no right. If I have the right to spend Saturday afternoon as I please, no one can have a claim right upon me to do something on Saturday afternoon. I can have the right to grow a beard only if no one has the right that I should shave every day. The correlate of a power right is a liability. The landlord has the right to determine the rent and his tenants are liable to pay whatever he demands. Eye-witnesses are liable to be questioned by the police. The correlate of an immunity right is a disability. Everyone is disabled from suing – that is, is denied the right to sue – an MP for what he says in Parliament; the military authorities are disabled from conscripting – that is, are denied the right to conscript – a conscientious objector.

6.2.2   In Hohfeld's analysis, the correlate of one kind of right is the opposite of another. It follows that, if a first party has a right of one kind, a second party must lack a right of another. The correlate of a claim right is a duty; a duty is the opposite of a liberty right. Hence a first party's claim right entails a second party's lack of a liberty right. The correlate of a liberty right is a no right; a no right is the opposite of a claim right. Hence a first party's liberty right entails a second party's lack of a claim right. The correlate of a power right is a liability; a liability is the opposite of an immunity right. Hence a first party's power right entails a second party's lack of an immunity right. The correlate of an immunity right is a disability; a disability is the opposite of a power right. Hence a first party's immunity right entails a second party's lack of a power right. This can be restated in terms of the action–recipience distinction. A first party's right of recipience entails a second party's lack of a right of action: in the case of a claim right, a liberty right; in the case of an immunity right, a power right. Conversely, a first party's right of action entails a second party's lack of a right of recipience: in the case of a liberty right, a claim right; in the case of a power right, an immunity right[7] (see 6.1.1).

Hohfeld does not explain why this is so. It can, however, be shown to be entailed by the relation between rights and obligations. Two aspects of that relation are relevant. The first is that for every right there must be some correlative obligation which others are under. The second is that obligations take precedence over rights in the sense that, if someone is under an obligation, he cannot have a right to anything which would prevent him from meeting that obligation. Or, to put it the other way round, he can have a right to something only if it does not prevent him from meeting an obligation he is under. Take first claim rights and liberty rights. A claim right is a right of recipience. Every right of recipience entails a specific obligation upon someone else. In the case of a claim right, someone else has a duty — that is, is under a specific obligation — to meet the claim. Whoever is under this obligation is not at liberty — that is, has no right of action in the form of a liberty right — to do something which would prevent him from meeting his obligation. A man who has made a promise has no right to accept an invitation which would prevent him from keeping it. An official whose duty it is to pay out pensions has no right to refuse to pay a *bona fide* claimant. Liberty rights are rights of action. Every right of action entails a general obligation of forbearance. Everyone must refrain from stopping anyone from doing what he has a right to do, from interfering with him while he is doing it, and from penalising him for having done it. This general obligation of forbearance entails that no one can have a right of recipience in the form of a claim right against the holder of a liberty right which requires him to do something incompatible with the exercise of his liberty right. My right to spend Saturday afternoon as I please entails a general obligation upon other people to leave me alone, and, *a fortiori*, that no one has a claim right upon me to do something during that time. The same is true of my right to grow a beard. If I choose to exercise it, others must put up with the result. No one has the right to require me to be clean-shaven.

Turning to power rights and immunity rights: those liable to the decisions of the holder of a power right have an obligation to comply with his decisions.

They therefore cannot have any right which is incompatible with meeting this obligation. A tenant has no right of recipience in the form of an immunity right to be exempt from the increased rent. As a tenant, he is liable to the landlord's decision and has an obligation to pay. Nor has an eye-witness a right to be exempt from police questioning. He is liable to the power right which the police are entitled to exercise, and has an obligation to answer their questions. An immunity right is a right of recipience and the obligation correlative to it is to respect the immunity it confers. To be under this obligation is to lack a right of action in the form of a power right to make the holder of the immunity right liable for what his immunity right exempts him from. The military authorities are under an obligation to respect the conscientious objector's exemption from military service, and have no right to conscript him. Everyone is under an obligation to respect an MP's right to immunity from libel actions for what he says in Parliament, and therefore no one has the right to sue him for it. They lack, that is to say, a right of action in the form of a power right to sue for libel.

6.2.3   According to Hohfeld, rights are advantages and their opposites and correlates are disadvantages. The term 'advantage' can be used in two senses – one competitive, the other not. An advantage in the competitive sense is possible only in a situation in which individuals or groups are contending for something. In such a situation, one party's advantage is necessarily another's disadvantage. A competitive advantage is always an advantage over a rival, who is thereby at a corresponding disadvantage. In a battle, the occupation of high ground gives one side a tactical advantage over the other. In its non-competitive sense, an advantage is simply a benefit: that is, something which in an identifiable way is for someone's good without on that account being to anyone else's detriment. A new drug is an advantage to sufferers from a chronic condition which it alleviates. It entails no corresponding disadvantage to anyone else. Now, if a right is an advantage in the competitive sense, it follows that one party's right entails a lack of the same right by another party. Otherwise having the right would not give the right-holder an advantage over anyone. But this is incompatible with Hohfeld's analysis. According to him, one party's right entails a second party's lack – not of the same right, but of a right of a different kind. One party's right of recipience entails a second party's lack of a right of action and *vice versa*. Hohfeld must have meant 'advantage' in the non-competitive sense.

    Hohfeld apart, the idea that a right is, as such, a competitive advantage, or, more accurately, an entitlement to a competitive advantage, is untenable. It would mean that there could be no universal rights: that is, no rights which everyone had and no one lacked. This is because there would be no one over whom to have an advantage. Universal suffrage would be a logical impossibility. The right to vote would have to be restricted to the members of a particular class so as to give them a competitive advantage over the unenfranchised. But universal suffrage is not only logically possible — that is, conceivable without self-contradiction: in certain countries it is a fact. It therefore cannot be the case that a right is, as such, an entitlement to a competitive advantage. By no means all rights can be universal. Many are necessarily restricted by the logic of what they are rights to. This is true of certain immunity rights, as our examples show. If everyone was exempt from the law of libel, there could be no such law. If everyone was exempt from military service, there could be no conscription.[7] Exemption from the law of libel is not conferred upon an MP to give him an advantage over anyone. Nor is this why exemption from military service is conferred upon conscientious objectors. The reason in the one case has to do with an MP's political role; in the other, with a conscientious objector's moral convictions. Whether any right can as such be an entitlement to a competitive advantage is questionable. It would be an entitlement to be better off at the expense of someone else being worse off, and it is not clear upon what grounds such an entitlement could be justified.

The idea that rights are advantages in the non-competitive sense is unexceptionable. It means that a right is an entitlement to a benefit: that is, to something which in an identifiable way is for the right-holder's good. A claim right entitles the right-holder to the benefit of having his claim met: for instance, the payment of an old-age pension or the keeping of a promise.[8] A liberty right entitles the right-holder to the benefit of acting according to his own choice: to the satisfaction of doing what he likes in his spare time, or of growing a beard. A power right entitles the right-holder to the benefit of being able to require other people to do certain things at his discretion: a landlord to require his tenants to pay more rent, a policeman to require eye-witnesses to answer his questions. An immunity right entitles the right-holder to the benefit of exemption from something: in the case of an MP, the benefit of being able to speak freely in Parliament; in the case of a conscientious objector, that of being able to follow the dictates of his conscience. But the expected benefit may not always materialise: raising the rent may mean that the landlord loses his tenants; the newly bearded man may be disappointed with the change in his appearance. A right can only entitle its holder to a presumptive benefit: that is, to something which can reasonably be presumed to be for his good.

6.2.4   According to Hohfeld, the opposite of a right is a disadvantage. This is misleading, because it suggests that a right is an entitlement of a competitive advantage, and that, as we have seen, is untenable. Because a right is an entitlement to a presumptive benefit, its opposite must be a non-entitlement to the same presumptive benefit. It is a disadvantage only in the non-competitive sense: that of lacking the entitlement to a presumptive benefit. This must have been what Hohfeld meant. Thus the opposite of a claim right is a no right. A man under sixty-five has no right to an old-age pension: that is, is not entitled to the presumptive benefit of receiving it. The opposite of a liberty right is a duty. To have a duty to shave every day, is not to be entitled to the presumptive benefit of growing a beard. The opposite of a power right is a disability. A man who is not a policeman is not entitled to the presumptive benefit of interrogating eye-witnesses. The opposite of an immunity right is a liability. A man liable to conscription is not entitled to the presumptive benefit of exemption from military service.

The correlate of a right, according to Hohfeld, is also a disadvantage. But it too can only be a non-competitive disadvantage, which again is what Hohfeld must have meant. The correlate of one right is the opposite of another, and we have seen why this must be so. The obligation correlative to a particular right entails that whoever is under that obligation cannot have a right to something which prevents him from meeting the obligation. The correlate of one right can therefore always be stated as the lack of another: the latter being the right to something which prevents the obligation correlative to the first right from being met. To state a correlate in this way is to state it as the non-entitlement to a presumptive benefit: in other words, as a disadvantage in the non-competitive sense. This is how Hohfeld states the correlates of liberty rights and immunity rights. The correlate of a liberty right is a no right: that is, a non-entitlement to the presumptive benefit of having a claim met. The correlate of an immunity right is a disability: a non-entitlement to the presumptive benefit of being able to require other people to do certain things at your discretion. But it is not how he states the correlates of claim rights and power rights. They are stated simply as the specific obligations correlative to rights of these kinds: duties in the case of claim rights, and liabilities in the case of power rights. Strictly speaking, it is questionable whether correlates in the form of specific correlative obligations can be described as non-competitive disadvantages. But they certainly entail them: in the case of claim rights, non-entitlement to the presumptive benefits of certain liberty rights, and, in the case of power rights, non-entitlement to the presumptive benefits of certain immunity rights.

6.2.5   Why was Hohfeld not consistent about this? Why did he state the correlates of claim rights and power rights in one way, and those of liberty rights and immunity rights in another? A possible answer is this: he was concerned with legal rights and with the task of the courts in identifying and protecting them. For a court, the important question is what must be done or, as the case may be, not done if a right is to be respected and not violated. It is therefore with the correlates of legal rights that a court is specially concerned. In the case of claim rights and power rights, it is what must be done which is important. Hence a court is concerned with their correlates in the form of duties and liabilities. But, in the case of liberty rights and immunity rights, it is what must not be done which matters. Hence it is with their correlates in the form of rights which people do not have that a court is concerned: with claims which they are not entitled to make and powers which they are not entitled to exercise. Be that as it may, there is nothing in Hohfeld's analysis which is incompatible with that of the last section. He includes, by implication, the distinction between elective and non-elective rights. Liberty rights, power rights and immunity rights are elective. A man can give up his free Saturday afternoon and work. He can refrain from raising his tenants' rent. Although eligible through his religious affiliation to be a conscientious objector, he may waive his immunity and accept conscription. But a claim right can be either elective or non-elective. A child's right to parental care and protection is a non-elective claim right.

But Hohfeld's analysis is not only compatible with the last section: it is a valuable addition to it in two ways. One is by introducing further distinctions which amplify the distinction between rights of action and of recipience. Claim rights are rights of positive recipience, immunity rights of negative recipience. Liberty rights are rights of self-regarding action, while power rights are rights of other-regarding action. The other contribution of Hohfeld's analysis is in calling attention to the complexity which the simple term 'a right' may sometimes conceal. Take the case of the right to vote. At first sight, it is a straightforward liberty right. The right-holder is entitled to vote and everyone else has an obligation not to interfere with him. But this entails that he has a claim right upon the police to protect him from interference and they have a duty to meet this claim. Where the ballot is secret, he is entitled to the privacy of the polling-booth. Hence he has a further claim right upon the officials at the polling-station to provide him with this privacy and they have a duty to provide it. What seems initially to be a single right turns out to be a cluster, and Hohfeld's analysis makes this intelligible.

7 The Idea of Rights (ii): On the Sources and Significance of Social Rights

7.1 POSITIVE LAW AND MORALITY AS SOURCES OF RIGHTS

7.1.1   No one can have a right solely in virtue of his individual identity. John Doe cannot be entitled to anything simply as John Doe. What then can entitle him? The short answer is, rules and principles. For there to be a right to something, there must be rules or principles which specify certain conditions and declare that all those and only those who satisfy them are entitled to it. To have the right to vote in a British general election, John Doe must satisfy the conditions specified in the rules of British electoral law: for instance, he must have British nationality, have reached the age of eighteen, not be a peer of the realm, a convicted felon or a certified lunatic. To have the right to have a promise kept, he must be a promisee, what this is being specified in the rules of the practice of promising: that is, he must be someone to whom another person has made a *bona fide* promise at a given time and place. Law, custom and morality have already been mentioned as sources of rights (see 6.1.1). What makes them sources is that they contain rules and principles.[1] But, if they are to be the sources of John Doe's rights, he must already be subject to them. What subjects him to them in the first place?

Law and custom are social institutions. Every system of positive law is the positive law of some community, and the same is true of every body of custom. Morality is social in the sense that without it there can be no social life at all: hence common morality. But social life can take different forms: hence particular morality. To be a member of a community is to be a moral agent with obligations as a member (see 2.2.2 and 2.3.3 above). As a person, John Doe is necessarily a member of a community. It follows that what subjects him to the law, custom and morality which are the sources of his rights, is that he is a member of the particular community whose law, custom and morality they are. Every community consists of a group of people living together upon terms which enable each to know what is due from him to other members and what is due from them to him (see 2.3.1 above). John Doe's obligations are what is due from him, his rights what is due to him, as a member. But, if there are any human rights, not all rights are social. There must be some which people have simply as human beings, irrespective of their membership of particular communities. However, more about that in the next chapter. Not all rights may be social but most certainly are: for instance, the rights which people have as citizens, neighbours, friends, parents, workers, colleagues, clients and customers.

7.1.2   Rules which confer rights must be constitutive, not regulative: that is, they must be rules which are logically prior to the cases which they cover.[2] Regulative rules can impose obligations but they cannot confer rights. This is because the actions they regulate are logically independent of them. It is possible for people to do them or not to do them in the absence of any rules prescribing or forbidding them. This is not so in the case of right-conferring rules. It is not possible for people to be entitled to do something or to receive something in the absence of either rules or principles which confer the entitlement and prescribe the obligations correlative to it. In this respect, having a right is like having authority. A man cannot have authority over other people unless there are constitutive rules which confer it upon him and prescribe obedience to it. As with authority, so with entitlement: when it is conferred by rules, these must necessarily be constitutive. The difference between authority-conferring rules and entitlement-conferring rules is that the former must be secondary rules. The latter may be secondary or primary, depending upon the kind of right which is conferred.

Secondary rules are not about what is to be done but about who decides. Hohfeldian power rights entitle the right-holder to decide. They entitle a policeman to decide whether to question eye-witnesses and, if so, what questions they are to answer. They entitle a landlord to decide whether to raise the rent and, if so, by how much. They must therefore be conferred by secondary rules. But secondary rules are not needed to confer claim rights. They are rights to have things done and can be conferred by primary rules. The right to have a promise kept is conferred upon the promisee, and the obligation correlative to it to keep the promise is imposed upon the promisor by the primary rules which constitute the practice of promising. The same is true of immunity rights. They entitle the right-holder to be exempt from something: an MP from libel actions for what he says in Parliament, a conscientious objector from conscription. Rules which confer immunity rights are primary. They are about what is to be done and, more especially, what is not to be done. But they must be constitutive because without them there could be no entitlement to immunity.

It may be thought that liberty rights are an exception: that they can be conferred by regulative rules. The rule setting a speed limit of 30 miles per hour in built-up areas is regulative. What it regulates, the speed of vehicles in built-up areas, is logically independent of it. Drivers can keep below 30 miles per hour in such areas whether or not there is a rule requiring them to do so. It may be contended that the rule confers a liberty right upon drivers. It entitles them to drive at any speed compatible with safety, provided that they keep below the prescribed limit. This is not so. The rule does not confer a new right. It regulates the exercise of an existing one. This is the right of drivers to drive at any speed compatible with safety. It is a liberty right limited by the obligation not to be a danger to anyone else. What the rule does is to clarify and give precision to this obligation. Driving at more than 30 miles per hour in built-up areas is dangerous to other people. Drivers still have the right to drive at any speed compatible with safety, but, according to the rule, more than 30 miles per hour in built-up areas is incompatible with safety.

Rights which are conferred by rules must not be confused with rights which are presupposed by rules. Constitutive rules which confer certain rights can also presuppose others. These latter rights are logically prior to the former and cannot be conferred by the rules which confer the former. An example is the practice of promising. Its constitutive rules confer the right to have promises kept but they also presuppose liberty rights. A *bona fide* promise cannot be made under duress. Nor, with one exception, can anyone have an obligation to make a promise. On any given occasion, it is up to a person to decide whether or not to make a promise. He has a liberty right either to promise to do something or not to promise, as he sees fit. The exception is where someone is already under an obligation and can meet it only by making a promise: for instance, a doctor who in order to fulfil his professional duty to a patient must promise to visit him. Nor, subject to the same qualification, has anyone an obligation to accept a promise. A man faced with the offer of a promise is free – that is, has a liberty right – either to accept or to refuse it. But if he is already under an obligation to do something and needs another person's help, the situation is different. If, out of goodwill and without having to suffer much inconvenience, the latter promises to help him, he has an obligation to accept.

7.1.3   Hohfeldian liberty rights are legal rights. In his analysis, however, Hohfeld did not distinguish between particular liberty rights and the general right to legal liberty. In effect, he concentrated on the former and took the latter for granted. Particular liberty rights can be defined and conferred by legal rules: for instance, the right to vote and the right to marry. The general right to legal liberty is conferred by, or, more accurately, is contained in, the principle of 'freedom under the law'. This is one of three interrelated specific principles which together make up the general principle of 'the rule of law'. The other two are 'the supremacy of law' and 'equality before the law'. We have already encountered 'equality before the law' as an example of a legal principle. It too contains a right: the right to the equal protection of the law (see 1.3.1 above). Any community which maintains a system of positive law is morally committed to the rule of law, which means that its members are morally committed to the three specific principles. To the extent that these principles are not implemented, or are more honoured in the breach than in the observance, the community has something less than a system of positive law properly so-called. The commitment is necessarily a moral one. Positive law must make identifiable breaches of it punishable offences. But it cannot create the commitment *ab initio*. It presupposes that most people acknowledge the commitment and are able and for the most part willing to meet it without compulsion. Hence, as we have already seen (in 1.3.3), the logical priority of morality to law.

Action informed by understanding is needed to maintain a system of positive law, and the three principles provide the basis for it. Their essentials are the following. According to the supremacy of law, legal obligations are paramount. The law does not acknowledge any authority within the community superior to itself.[3] All activities, all forms of voluntary association, must conform to what is permitted by law. If there is a conflict between legal and other demands, such as those of family life, of friendship, of work, or simply of self-interest, legal demands must take precedence. The other two principles are corollaries of the supremacy of law. According to equality before the law, no one is above the law. All within the community are equally subject to legal demands, including the government. When the law is changed it must be done in the legally prescribed manner. The same applies to the enforcement of the law. The methods by which it is done must be legally authorised. But not only is no one above the law: no one is below it. All members of the community are equally entitled to — that is, have an equal right to — the protection of the law, and to whatever facilities it affords. According to freedom under the law, nothing is compulsory which is not legally required by law. Where the law is silent, all are free — that is, have a general liberty right — to act according to their own choice and decisions. This general liberty right entitles everyone not to have his freedom of action interfered with except when the law authorises it.

The relation between a set of principles and the activity of which they are the principles is a logical one. To engage in the activity is to act upon its principles (see 1.2.4 above). It follows that, if a community is to maintain a system of positive law, all its members must have the right to the equal protection of the law, and the general right to legal liberty. To live under such a system is to have these rights. The right to the equal protection of the law is primarily a claim right, although it entails ancillary power rights in matters of detail. The obligations correlative to the claim right are mainly upon those concerned with law enforcement: judges, the police, government officials and the legal profession.[4] But there is also an obligation upon the government of the community to maintain the courts, the judiciary, the police and the penal system and itself always to act lawfully. Correlative to the general right to legal liberty is the general obligation of forbearance. No one must interfere with anyone else's freedom of action under the law. But there is also a special obligation upon those responsible for law enforcement to protect the right. Both rights are elective. A person is entitled to seek legal protection from, and legal redress for, violations of them. But he is not obliged to do so. If he thinks that making a fuss is not worth the trouble, he can choose to suffer petty bureaucratic inequity or a minor infraction of his liberty without resorting to legal remedies. But, before waiving his right, he ought to consider the responsibility which he shares with all fellow members for maintaining the supremacy of law within the community. He should acquiesce in violations of his rights only if doing so does not threaten that supremacy. If it does, he has a moral obligation to assert his rights and seek legal protection and redress despite the trouble and inconvenience.

The commitment to the rule of law is part not of common morality but of the particular morality of any community which maintains a system of positive law. While there can be no social life in the absence of morality, there can be without positive law. Why should there be positive law at all? Two reasons can briefly be mentioned here. The first is security. The safety of person and property is better achieved through positive law than by leaving it to 'private enterprises'. There is a general obligation to respect security arising out of the obligations of common morality: notably from the requirement of respect for life, fellowship, honourable conduct and civility. But people do not always act morally, and security is too important a matter to be left to personal moral conduct. The presumption is that most people will respect security without being required to do so by law. But, for those who are unable or unwilling to meet this moral obligation, positive law is there with its sanctions. The second reason for positive law is that it enables a community to organise and regulate its affairs. It is a method of social co-operation for bringing about conditions which are in a community's interest and which either could not be brought about at all without it, or could be brought about only partially and imperfectly.

7.1.4   The three specific principles are moral principles of positive law: moral because the commitment to the rule of law is a moral one. They are part of the particular morality of any community which maintains a system of positive law. But equality before the law and freedom under the law are applications of two principles of common morality to the institution of positive law. These are justice in the particular form of 'fair treatment', and freedom from arbitrary interference (see 3.1.3 above). Fair treatment is treatment according to proportionate equality. Where there is a system of positive law, this entails equality before the law. So far as the scope of the law is concerned, there are no relevant differences. All must be equally subject to it and equally protected by it. Freedom from arbitrary interference requires that no one's freedom of action should be arbitrarily interfered with. Where there is a system of positive law, legally authorised interference is morally justified. It follows that the ultimate source of the right to the equal protection of the law is the moral principle of justice as 'fair treatment', and the ultimate source of the right to freedom under the law is the moral principle of freedom from arbitrary interference. The principle of justice in its general form of 'to each his due' is, however, of special importance. It is the necessary foundation of all rights.

To see why, let us go back to John Doe. His obligations as a member of a community are what is due from him to other members, his rights what is due to him from them. Justice requires that each should receive what is due to him and should render what is due from him. Justice is therefore the principle that all rights must be respected. Injustice is done to John Doe whenever any of his rights is violated: that is, whenever, owing to an avoidable act of commission or omission, he does not receive what is due to him. Justice in its particular form of fair treatment contains the right to such treatment. This is entailed by justice in its general form. We have seen (in 3.2.1) that one thing which is due to every member of every community is to be treated according to 'proportionate equality'. John Doe therefore has a claim right to this treatment. He also has whatever rights are contained in the other principles of common morality. Two of these principles are worth touching on briefly here because they contain rights which every member of every community must have if he is to have any rights at all, and so be a member properly so-called. One is respect for life: the other, which has just been referred to, freedom from arbitrary interference. Respect for life contains the right to life and its necessity is obvious (see 3.1.2 above). Wanton killing is the denial of rights as such. If John Doe is to have any rights at all and so have the status of a member of a community, he must at least have the right to life. Similar considerations apply to freedom from arbitrary interference. If John Doe's freedom of action can be arbitrarily interfered with, he can be prevented from exercising the particular rights of action and recipience which he has as a member of a community. He must have the right to freedom from arbitrary interference as a necessary condition for the exercise of his other rights.

John Doe's other rights depend upon his particular status in his community, this being defined by its terms of membership. These are embodied in its particular morality; in its positive law, if it has any; in its institutions and customs. The rules and principles they contain set out in detail the rights and obligations of the community's members. Moral diversity means that these will not be the same in all communities. According to the moral principles of family life in traditional Hindu society, a father has a power right to arrange his daughter's marriage. Not so in contemporary Western society, where the moral principles of family life are different. According to these, a father has no power right to make matrimonial plans for his daughter at any time in her life. She has an immunity right exempting her from any such plans and, once she is grown up, a liberty right to accept or refuse any offer of marriage. The principles of representative government give citizens liberty rights to form and to join political parties, and publicly to criticise the government of the day. The principles of absolute monarchy contain no such rights. Those who live under such a government are subjects, not citizens. The most they can have in the way of political rights is a claim right to petition the monarch for the redress of grievances.

7.2   CUSTOM AS A SOURCE OF RIGHTS

7.2.1   So much for positive law and morality as sources of social rights. What about custom? First something must be said about the concept of 'custom'. The term 'custom' is both descriptive and prescriptive. It describes what is invariably done in a specified social context and prescribes that it should continue to be done. An example is tipping. The statement 'Tipping is a custom in modern Western society' is at once the statement of a generalisation and the statement of a rule. The generalisation is that people invariably tip waiters, porters, taxi-drivers and the like; the rule, that they should continue to tip them. The rule is logically dependent upon the generalisation. Unless people are already invariably doing something, there cannot be a rule telling them to continue to do it. But why should they continue to do it? What is the reason for the rule? The short answer is that they should continue to do it because it is what is already invariably done. The reason for the rule is the generalisation upon which it is logically dependent. The key idea in the concept of custom is that of continuing to do what is invariably done because it is invariably done. This is not, however, a complete answer. But, before amplifying it, something must be said about customs as institutional facts. Particular customs are particular institutional facts (see 2.3.4 and 4.2.2. above). However, there is a difference between them and institutional facts about roles, offices and social positions.

7.2.2   An institutional fact is a prescriptive description. So is a custom in the sense that it both describes and prescribes. But, as we have just seen, in the case of a custom the prescription is logically dependent upon the description, the rule upon the generalisation. In the case of institutional facts about roles, offices and positions, this relation is reversed. The description is logically dependent upon the prescription. The statement 'John Doe is a Roman Catholic priest', if it is true, is the statement of an institutional fact. It describes an individual man as being under certain obligations, those of a Roman Catholic priest. But this description is logically dependent upon there being such obligations. If there are not, it cannot be true that John Doe is under them. One of the obligations he is under is to obey the rule 'Never betray the secrets of the confessional.'[5] This is not a customary rule. It does not say, 'Never betray the secrets of the confessional because Roman Catholic priests invariably keep them.' Rather it says, 'Never betray them because keeping them is part of what it is to be a priest.' This is a constitutive rule of the practice of confession, a practice which is of central importance in the Roman Catholic Church. Part of what it is to be a priest is to officiate in this practice.

The difference between this example and a custom is that, in the case of a custom, the prescription is a regulative rule. Customary rules are necessarily regulative not constitutive, and it is not difficult to see why. The acts which a regulative rule prescribes or forbids are logically independent of it. They are acts which it is possible to do or not to do, whether or not there is a rule about them. It is possible for people to drive at more or less than 30 miles per hour in a built-up area, whether or not the law makes 30 miles per hour the speed limit. The opposite is true of a constitutive rule. The acts which it prescribes or forbids are logically dependent upon it. They are acts of a kind which it is impossible either to do or not to do in the absence of the rule. In the absence of the rule 'Never betray the secrets of the confessional', there could be no such practice as confession, and therefore no possibility of either keeping or betraying its secrets. A customary rule says, 'Continue to do in this social context what is invariably done.' Hence its logical dependence upon a generalisation. But the acts which are the subject of the generalisation must be of a kind which it is possible to do in the absence of the rule. Only if it is both possible to do them and they are in fact already being done, although they might not have been, can they continue to be done. Tipping must be both possible and widespread before there can be a rule prescribing that it should continue to be done. Hence the acts which a customary rule prescribes are logically independent of it, and a customary rule is therefore a regulative rule.

It does not follow that, because customary rules are regulative, customs are not institutional facts. But, before enlarging on the special case of customs, more must be said about institutional facts as such. It is constitutive rules which make them 'institutional', but regulative rules can also enter into them. It is an institutional fact in Britain today that there is a legal speed limit of 30 miles per hour in built-up areas. What makes this fact 'institutional' is that the speed limit is legal. The institution concerned is positive law. A constitutive rule of positive law is the secondary rule that all positive laws must be obeyed – what counts as a positive law being defined by other secondary rules, which confer legislative and judicial authority. The institutional fact about the speed limit is the fact that in Britain drivers have a legal obligation not to exceed 30 miles per hour in built-up areas. They have this obligation because there is a system of positive law in Britain, because, like everyone else in the country, they have an obligation to obey all British laws, and because it happens to be the case that among these is the law about the speed limit. What makes this institutional fact 'institutional' is the constitutive rules of positive law. Without the secondary rule that all positive laws must be obeyed there could be no legal obligation to obey the speed-limit law. Without the secondary rules conferring legislative and judicial authority, there could be no positive law and therefore no law about the speed limit.

7.2.3   The statement of an institutional fact, like that of a brute fact, is the statement of a contingent truth. Its contradictory is not self-contradictory. It states what 'in fact' is the case, but it is logically possible that it might not have been. It is a contingent truth that in Britain the legal speed limit in built-up areas is 30 miles per hour. There might have been no legal speed limit at all, or it might have been 25 miles per hour. It is a contingent truth that John Doe is a Roman Catholic priest. He might have been a stockbroker or an airline pilot. But, if it is true that in Britain the legal speed limit is 30 miles per hour, then it is necessarily true that drivers in Britain have an obligation not to exceed that speed in built-up areas. If it is true that John Doe is a Roman Catholic priest, then it is necessarily true that he has an obligation never to betray the secrets of the confessional. It is a characteristic of all statements of institutional facts that, while they state contingent truths, they also state necessary prescriptive truths. The latter are entailed by the constitutive rules of the institution concerned. Statements of brute facts lack this characteristic. They state contingent truths but not necessary prescriptive truths.[6] This is because they say nothing about institutions and therefore contain no reference to the prescriptions of constitutive rules (see 7.2.1 above).

The statement of a custom is the statement of a contingent truth. It might not have been the case that tipping is a custom in modern Western society. But, as the statement of an institutional fact, it must refer to custom as an institution. That means that it must include not only a generalisation and a regulative rule, but at least implicitly a constitutive rule of the institution of custom which entails the regulative rule as a necessary prescription. Compare the institutional fact of a custom with the institutional fact of the legal speed limit. The statement of that fact includes implicitly the secondary rule that all positive laws must be obeyed, and it is this constitutive rule which entails the obligation to obey the legal regulative rule setting the speed limit. What is the corresponding constitutive rule in the case of the institution of custom? The answer lies in the key idea in the concept of custom: the idea of continuing to do what is invariably done because it is invariably done. This is more than the descriptive idea of socially imitative behaviour. It is a prescriptive idea in the form of a secondary rule which runs, 'Whatever is invariably done in any specified social context, should continue to be done in that context.' It is this secondary rule which constitutes the institution of custom. A familiar version of it is the proverbial maxim 'When in Rome, do as the Romans do.'

Pursuing the comparison with law, what makes a regulative rule a positive law in Britain is

(a) that it has either been enacted by Parliament or declared by the courts;
(b) that whatever is thus enacted or declared must be obeyed.

What in Britain or anywhere else, makes a regulative rule a customary rule is

(c) that what it prescribes is invariably done in a specified social context;
(d) that what is invariably done in any social context should continue to be done.

(a) and (c) are contingent truths. It is, but might not have been, the case that Parliament enacted the speed-limit law, and that people invariably tip waiters, porters and taxi-drivers. (b) and (d) are the secondary rules which make the positive law and the customary rule necessary prescriptions. The constitutive rules of the institution of positive law cannot answer the question 'Why should there be positive law at all?' But a brief answer has already been indicated (see 7.1.3). Positive law provides protection and facilitates social co-operation. We have so far only an incomplete answer to the corresponding question about custom. What is invariably done should continue to be done because it is what is invariably done (see 7.2.1 above). This must now be amplified.

7.2.4 The purpose served by the institution of custom is social conservation. To conserve something is to keep it substantially unchanged. Social conservation is the maintenance of a community's way of life substantially in its existing form. Custom contributes to this by preserving unchanged certain ways of acting in social contexts. No community can afford to neglect social conservation. It can assimilate change only if, while change is going on, it can maintain at least part of its way of life substantially in its existing form. According to Dostoyevsky, 'man is an animal who can get used to anything'.[7] But it takes time to get used to something. If everything changed at once, all would be unfamiliar. Past experience would be irrelevant and people would be at a loss to know what to do. The need for time to get used to change limits what a revolutionary government can accomplish in the short run. If it attempts too much too soon, day-to-day life will break down, because people will be unable to understand what is happening and what is expected of them. Hence even a revolutionary government, if it is wise, will not neglect social conservation.

An objection is that not only custom but rule-governed action as such preserves unchanged certain ways of acting in social contexts and thereby contributes to social conservation. Primary rules do this by prescribing or forbidding acts of the same kind on occasions of the same kind; secondary rules, by prescribing obedience to the same authority in situations of the same kind. It is true that non-customary rule-governed action contributes incidentally to social conservation, but that is not the principal purpose it serves. In the case of constitutive rules, this is to make possible the activities they constitute: in the case of regulative rules, either to facilitate the activities they regulate or to benefit those affected by them. The point of the rules of chess is to make possible the playing of chess; of the laws of property, to make possible ownership and the use and exchange of what is owned. The point of traffic laws is to expedite the movement of traffic and to promote road safety; of the rules of hygiene, to promote health. The contribution of customary rules to social conservation is not incidental. It is the point of them. 'Do it because it is what is invariably done.' They also serve other purposes. Tipping shows appreciation for personal services. Rules of polite behaviour facilitate social intercourse. But these are subsidiary to the purpose they serve as customs: that of contributing to social conservation by preserving unchanged certain ways of acting in social contexts.

A community's members have an obligation to maintain and promote whatever is in its interest (see 2.3.1 above). Social conservation is in its interest and the institution of custom contributes to it. They therefore have an obligation, subject to a qualification, to obey the constitutive rule of the institution of custom. This is an obligation of common morality because it is a requirement of social responsibility. Hence the reason why growing up in a community involves learning to do what is invariably done in particular social contexts. But social adaptation is also in the interest of a community. If it is to survive, its members must be able to respond to new circumstances; for instance, to the social and economic repercussions of technological and industrial innovation. They must also be able to respond to the social and moral implications of new knowledge and increased understanding. While it takes time to get used to something, people must be able and willing to get used to changes which in practice are irreversible. They must not be slaves to custom. If what is invariably done in a particular social context becomes an obstacle to dealing with new problems or to taking advantage of new opportunities, it is time to stop doing it. Until recently in Western society, it was customary in middle-class marriage for the husband to be the bread-winner and the wife the home-maker. Not so today. Frequently they both work and sometimes the roles are reversed so that the wife can pursue a career. As a result of increased expectations by women and greater opportunities for them in the professions, commerce and industry, what used to be customary is so no longer.

Social conservation must be reconciled with social adaptation. Hence the need for a qualification to the obligation to obey the constitutive rule of custom. This is *ceteris paribus*: 'Do what is invariably done, other things being equal.' Other things are not equal if doing what is invariably done conflicts with the requirements of social adaptation, requirements which, no less than those of social conservation, fall under the principle of social responsibility. Social conservation does not require all a community's customs to be preserved intact indefinitely. Nor does it require this of any one particular custom. What it does require is that enough of a community's customs should be maintained to provide a stable framework for the assimilation of change. How much is 'enough', however, is not a question to which there can be a precise answer. There can only be an initial presumption in favour of the customary: 'Go on doing what is invariably done unless or until there is a good reason to stop doing it.' It is up to those who would depart from a custom to make good their case. No case has to be made for observing it. It is sufficient that it is customary. The case for departing from it must be based on the requirements of social adaptation: that the custom inhibits an adequate response to new circumstances, or to the social and moral implications of new knowledge and increased understanding. Such cases can often be made out, despite the intitial presumption in favour of the customary, but each must be judged on its merits.

When times have changed and there is a good case against a particular custom, it is unlikely to survive for long. As understanding of the case spreads, observance will decline and the custom will be eroded. How a new custom comes into being is a more complicated question. Here it must suffice to point out four distinct stages. The first is that a few people start regularly doing the same thing in the same social context. The second is, that this 'catches on' and becomes widespread. The third is that it lasts, so that it becomes what is invariably done in that context. The fourth is that this is generally acknowledged and, through being acknowledged, becomes a rule. With the fourth stage, a new custom is born. There is no necessary transition from the first to the second stage, or from the second to the third. By no means everything that a few people start doing regularly 'catches on'. The fact that something is widespread does not guarantee that it will last. It may only be a passing fashion. The transition from the third to the fourth stage marks the generation of a rule from a generalisation. The institution of custom predisposes the members of a community to generate such rules. It fosters in them, that is to say, a disposition to accommodate into their existing body of custom any way of acting which has come to be what is invariably done in a particular social context. The origins of the institution of custom must be sought in the origins of human social living.[8] Like language, property and the practice of promising, it emerged with the emergence of human social life out of the animal life of our pre-human ancestors.

7.2.5   What has been said here about the concept of custom and about custom as an institution is far from being a complete account.[9] But it is sufficient to show how custom is a source of rights. Rules which confer rights must be constitutive, not regulative (see 7.1.2 above). Particular customary rules are regulative and therefore cannot confer rights. What makes custom a source of rights is that it is an institution. Its constitutive rule imposes upon each member of a community an obligation to observe existing customs, and confers upon each a correlative right to have them observed. It is in virtue of this general claim right that a waiter is entitled to a tip from a diner. It is not simply that he has served him, but this together with the fact that tipping is customary, which entitles him. For the same reason the diner has an obligation to tip him: that is, not simply because he has been served by the waiter but because tipping is customary. It may be thought that particular customary rights must be claim rights because the general right from which they derive is a claim right. But this is not so. Consider the case of a customary 'right of way' – for instance, to use a path across privately owned land. This is a liberty right, as analysis shows.

The path has been used by the public for generations without objection by successive landowners. What began as a favour has come in the course of time to be 'what is invariably done' and so a custom. The generalisation is, 'The public have always been allowed to use the path', and the rule, 'The public must continue to be allowed to use it.' Because there is an obligation to observe whatever is customary, the present landowner has an obligation to observe this particular custom. For the same reason, members of the public have a claim right upon him to observe it. But their claim right also gives them a liberty right to use the path. This is because the landowner's obligation to observe the custom entails that he has no right to stop them. Because the custom entitles them to use the path and because they have a claim right upon him to observe the custom, and therefore not to stop them, they have a particular liberty right to use it. Whether a particular customary right is a claim right or a liberty right, or, for that matter, a power right or an immunity right, depends upon the particular custom. What makes it a 'right', however, is not simply the particular custom, but the general claim right to have whatever is customarily observed.

We have seen (in 7.1.4) that the principle of justice is the moral foundation of all rights. The general claim right conferred by the constitutive rule of the institution of custom is no exception. What is due from every member of a community includes observance of existing customs. This is because of the requirements of social conservation. But these requirements must be reconciled with those of social adaptation. Hence the *ceteris paribus* qualification to the constitutive rule (see 7.2.4 above). If, for the sake of that reconciliation, a customary right has to be overridden, there is no injustice. Since continued respect for that particular right is contrary to the community's interest, it cannot be due to the members. Other things are not equal, so it falls outside the scope of their general claim right. If the land-owner sells the land for industrial development, that will be the end of the 'right of way'. But, if this development creates much needed local employment, it is in the interest of the local community. The loss of the 'right of way' is an inconvenience but not an injustice. Finally, returning to the comparison between law and custom: law can deliberately create new rights but custom cannot. Thus, while custom is limited to contributing to social conservation, law can contribute both to that and to social adaptation. As we have seen, no community can exist without custom. But a community which has positive law as well as custom is in a better position to respond to new circumstances and to reconcile effectively the demands of conservation with those of adaptation.

7.3 ON THE SIGNIFICANCE AND LIMITATIONS OF RIGHTS

7.3.1 Two of the three questions raised at the beginning of the last chapter have now been answered: 'What is it to have a right?' and 'What are the sources of rights?', although the answer to the latter has been confined to social rights. The third remains: 'Why should there be rights at all?' The answer is implicit in the answers already given, especially to the second question. Making it explicit, however, brings to light further issues about which something must be said. There is also some unfinished business connected with the first two questions. We have seen that no one can be a member of a community unless there are both things which are due from him to fellow members and things which are due to him from them (see 2.3.1 and 7.1.1 above). His rights (what he is entitled to as a member) consist of all that is due to him; his obligations, of all that is due from him. A community consists of its members in the sense that, unless there are members, there cannot be a community. Since to be a member is *inter alia* to have rights, without rights there can be no community. Having rights is part of human social living in any form, so there have to be rights if there is to be any human social life at all.

An objection to this is that a community is conceivable in which all the members have obligations but none has any rights: for instance, a community dedicated to the service of a religious or ideological ideal. Its members are totally committed to the service of the ideal and are always 'on duty'. But, even in such a community, certain things must be due to every member as well as from him. He must be entitled to what he needs to enable him to meet his particular obligations. That means claim rights to enough food, clothing and shelter, and a liberty right to enough rest and leisure, to enable him to keep himself fit for duty. We have seen that the right to life and the right to freedom from arbitrary interference are necessary if there are to be any rights at all.[10] In the present case, it is the duty of each member if necessary to sacrifice his life for the common cause. But he must have the right not to be wantonly killed if he is to make any contribution to that cause. He must have the right to freedom from arbitrary interference if he is not to be prevented from meeting his particular obligations, and from exercising the other rights which he must have in order to be able to meet them. The rights to life and to freedom are contained in the principles of common morality. Because this morality is part of community life as such, it follows that, even in the present case, the members must have all the rights contained in its principles. Justice gives to all members the right to be treated fairly, fellowship the right to relief from distress. Honourable conduct gives them the right to be treated honourably, civility the right to civil treatment. The principle of child welfare gives to all children, who when they grow up will become members, the right to care and protection (see 6.1.3 above, on the cases of children and animals).

A community in which all the members had obligations and none any rights is logically impossible and therefore inconceivable. To be a member is necessarily to have rights as well as obligations. It is part of the status of membership. What many of these rights are, depends upon the individual community: its way of life, particular morality, terms of membership, institutions and values. But certain rights, those whose source is common morality, are possessed by every member in every community. Rights entail correlative obligations upon other people: in the case of rights of action, the general obligation of forbearance; in the case of rights of recipience, this general negative obligation together with specific positive obligations (see 6.1.1 above). Many of a member's obligations are correlative to his fellow members' rights. In demanding from them respect for his own rights as a member, he commits himself to acknowledging, and so far as possible meeting, the obligations correlative to their rights whenever he is required to do so. This commitment is entailed by the practical-reason principle. While the members of a community do not all have the same rights, they are alike in all having rights. If a member demands respect for his rights from his fellow members while refusing to respect theirs, he is not treating like cases alike. In exempting himself from what he demands from them, he is treating himself differently from them when, in all relevant respects, he and they are alike.[11]

7.3.2 There are situations in which the rights of different people can conflict. In most cases, although not in all, this manifests itself in a conflict between the obligations correlative to each right which someone is under. He cannot meet them both, which means that he must necessarily fail to respect one of the rights. Take the case of a man who has promised his colleagues that he will attend an important meeting on their behalf, but on his way is stopped at the scene of an accident and asked to help a woman who has been seriously injured in it. His colleagues have a claim right to what he promised them, the victim a claim right to his help. He must choose between keeping his promise at the expense of the victim's right to his help, and helping her at the expense of his colleagues' right to what he has promised them. Beneficence almost certainly requires him to help the victim. If so, it requires his colleagues to waive their right and acquiesce without complaint in not having their right respected. A journalist's right to free inquiry can conflict with a citizen's right to privacy – a conflict between a liberty right and an immunity right. This is not a case in which a person is faced with conflicting obligations correlative to different rights. The obligation correlative to each right is upon the holder of the other right. The journalist has an obligation not to invade privacy, the citizen an obligation not to obstruct free inquiry. If, in the circumstances, freedom of inquiry is more important than privacy, the citizen has an obligation to waive his right to privacy. If the opposite is the case, the journalist has an obligation not to exercise his right to free inquiry.

In the first example, the source of the conflicting rights is common morality. The right of the victim to aid is contained in the principle of fellowship. The right to have a promise kept is conferred by the constitutive rules of the practice of promising, and obedience to these rules is a requirement of honourable conduct. What gives rise to the conflict is not any inherent incompatibility between fellowship and honourable conduct, but the physical limitations of finitude. A man cannot physically be in two places at once, but, owing to unforeseen events, this is morally required of him. In the second example, the sources of the conflicting rights are two principles of the particular morality of a community dedicated to liberal-democratic values. One is freedom of speech and inquiry, the other personal privacy. There is an inherent incompatibility between these two principles which, in a situation to which they are both applicable, can give rise to a conflict between their respective requirements.

Consider now a third example. An official conducting a public investigation into a security matter has a power right to question a journalist, who is under an obligation correlative to this right to answer his questions. But the journalist also has an obligation not to betray a confidential source of information. The official's power right to question may conflict with an informant's claim right to confidentiality. The journalist must then choose betwen answering the official's questions at the expense of his informant's claim right, and keeping faith with the latter at the expense of the official's power right. The source of these conflicting rights is again common morality. The informant's claim right is conferred by the practice of promising, and respect for it is a requirement of honourable conduct. The official's power right is conferred by law, but is also contained in the principle of social responsibility, a principle which also requires the jouralist to co-operate in the public investigation. This suggests that the conflict can readily be resolved. Honourable conduct cannot require socially irresponsible conduct and the informant ought to waive his claim right to confidentiality. But there is a deeper issue involved.

This is between the requirements of security and those of freedom of speech and inquiry, because respect for the confidentiality of informants is a requirement of the latter. The deeper issue is between a principle of common morality – social responsibility – and a principle of the particular morality of a community dedicated to liberal-democratic values; freedom of speech and inquiry. It manifests itself in a conflict between the official's power right and the journalist's liberty right contained in the principle of freedom of speech and inquiry. This is another case in which the obligation correlative to each right is upon the holder of the other right: in the case of the official, his obligation to respect the journalist's liberty right; in the case of the journalist, his obligation to respect the official's power right. Either the journalist's liberty right or the official's power right must be waived. Which it ought to be depends upon whether, in the particular circumstances of the case, the requirements of security or of freedom of speech and inquiry should take precedence. Is the interest of the community best served by giving precedence to security at the expense of a condition important for freedom of speech and inquiry, or by frustrating the security investigation? In the circumstances of the case, is the safety of the community more important than one of the values for which it stands and which makes it the kind of community it is, or should safety be risked for the sake of that value? The key question is clearly the seriousness of the security matter under investigation. How great is the risk to safety involved in protecting freedom of speech and inquiry? These are matters of judgement.

Returning to the first two examples, the limitations of finitude are imposed by unalterable physical conditions. Hence conflicts between rights arising from those limitations can never be eliminated from social life. The problem of an inherent incompatibility between different principles of a particular morality is not imposed by unalterable physical conditions. But it may be worth facing for the sake of the values served by each principle. A community can benefit both from freedom of speech and inquiry and from personal privacy, if its members are prepared to waive their right to one of them when their respective requirements come into conflict. It is an error arising from a false analogy between truth and value to think that all values must always and everywhere be compatible. Truths are necessarily compatible in the sense that no true statement can contradict another. Not so values. There is no pre-established harmony which guarantees that what gives value to one aspect of human life can never conflict with what gives value to another. The possibility of having to choose between conflicting values can never be eliminated from human life.[12] The third example shows that such choices are inescapable in determining where the interest of a community lies, because that involves making judgements of priorities: the needs of security over freedom of speech and inquiry, or *vice versa*.

7.3.3   All this entails that conflicting rights are elective rights, since one of them has to be waived. Non-elective rights by definition cannot be waived (see 6.1.3 above). They are passive rights of recipience and it is clear from Hohfeld's analysis that they must be claim rights: for instance, the right of children to be looked after, and of animals to humane treatment. Their passive character, which means that the right-holders are helpless when they are violated, strongly suggests that failure to respect them can never be the lesser evil. This is generally acknowledged in the case of children. That their right to be looked after should always have priority is uncontroversial. But it is far from being acknowledged in the case of animals. Their right to humane treatment is usually given a lower priority than the needs of medical research and the commercial interests of food-producers.[13] The exercise of elective rights calls for principle-governed action. Right-holders must know when they ought to waive them and they must therefore be capable of meeting the requirements of moral principles.

Our three examples have focused upon conflicts between moral rights. But, in the third, the official's power right, while contained in the principle of social responsibility, is also a legal right. A public investigation must be authorised and established by law. The principle of the supremacy of law requires that legal rights should take precedence over moral and customary rights (see 7.1.3 above). So far as the law is concerned, there is therefore no conflict. The official's power right must simply be respected. The journalist's moral obligation to keep faith with his informant, and the latter's moral claim right to confidentiality have no legal standing. The same goes for the journalist's liberty right, because of his obligation to answer the official's questions. Unlike moral rights, legal rights cannot conflict, because positive law does not allow them to. All legal rights are subject to judicial definition and interpretation, and it is for the courts to decide what a particular legal right entitles the right-holder to.

There can of course be disputes about legal right: for instance, between two parties about what they are respectively entitled to under the terms of a will, or about the compensation to which one party is entitled from another because of the latter's negligence. But such disputes must be settled by a court on the basis of existing law. A judicial decision in favour of one party and against another removes the possibility of a conflict between their respective legal rights.

7.3.4   Positive law is not limited to modifying existing rights by judicial definition and interpretation. New rights can be created by legislation: that is, by formally enacting rules which confer them and prescribe their correlative obligations.[14] Legislation can also abolish or alter existing rights by abolishing or altering the rules which confer them. But, in all legislation, the rules must be formulated with sufficient precision to enable a court to decide, in particular cases, whether the prescribed obligations have been met. A new right may simply extend an existing right to people who have not hitherto had it: for example, the extension of the right to vote to people previously unenfranchised. It may be a right which no one has hitherto had and which is conferred upon a limited group: the right to an old-age pension, for instance. Or, again, it may be one which no one has had and which is conferred upon everyone, such as the right to free medical treatment. A legal right which is abolished may be one which hitherto everyone had. When, in Britain, the wearing of seat belts was made compulsory, all lost their liberty right to decide for themselves whether or not to wear them. The right lost may be one which was possessed only by a limited group: for example, the right of university graduates to an extra vote. We have seen, in connection with Hohfeld (see 6.2.4), that a right is an entitlement to a presumptive benefit. To create new legal rights, to abolish or alter existing ones, is deliberately to change the presumptive benefits to which the members of a community are legally entitled. What justifies such changes?

The general answer is that they are justified if they are necessary to remove discrepancies between the legal rights which the members of a community actually have and those which they ought to have. The latter are the legal rights which in the conditions of that particular community, will best serve the purposes of positive law, security and social co-operation (see 7.1.3 above). The rights to life, to freedom from arbitrary interference and to property are essential for security and must be secured to all members in a community with a system of positive law. They are part of what is involved in having such a system. The same is true of the right to have contracts kept. What the law can do for social co-operation depends upon a community's way of life, its particular morality, its institutions and values, and, not least, its economy. If it is dedicated to liberal-democratic values, the law must confer political rights upon all its adult members. If it has a modern industrial economy, fellowship requires legal provision for social welfare and welfare rights. We have seen that social adaptation is in the interest of any community (see 7.2.4 above). If it is to survive, its members must respond to new circumstances and to the moral and social implications of new knowledge and better understanding. It is through responding that they become aware of discrepancies: for instance, that existing welfare rights are inadequate, that there are no good reasons for denying political rights to women or for giving extra votes to university graduates or to businessmen.

Justice is the moral foundation of rights and it requires that, when discrepancies are identified, they should be removed. To acquiesce in them is to acquiesce in injustice. There is injustice both when the law fails to confer upon people rights which they ought to have, and when it confers upon them rights which they ought not to have. In the one case they are being denied what is due to them, in the other being given what is not due to them. But some qualifications are necessary. Not everything which is socially desirable is something to which there can be a legal right. That adequate medical services should be available to all members of a community is socially desirable, but in a Third World country lack of both human and medical resources may mean that for the foreseeable future this is an unattainable ideal. In a community with a modern industrial economy, full employment, or, more accurately, the absence of involuntary unemployment, is socially desirable, but there cannot be a legal right to a job, if that means a right for all to have work of the kind they want provided where and when they want it. The obligation correlative to such a right is one which, for physical and economic reasons, neither a government nor any socially authorised agency can possibly meet. There can be a legal right to work in the sense of a right to take any job you can get and to initiate commercial and industrial enterprises within the limits of the law, but, notoriously, such a right cannot guarantee full employment. Something which members of a community ought to have can be a legal right only if it is possible for them to have it in existing conditions. That means that it must be possible not only to specify what the correlative obligations are, but also for them to be met in existing conditions.

This is not all. There must be widespread agreement about what in detail particular discrepancies are, and that cannot be counted upon. People vary in their responses to social change and to new knowledge. They are often reluctant to accept reforms which affect what they are used to: for instance, new rights for women which enlarge their career opportunities but which affect men's ideas about their status and role in society. Proposals for new legal rights may be controversial. There may be widespread agreement that existing health-care arrangements are inadequate but disagreement about the merits of a proposed comprehensive health service with a legal right for all to free medical treatment. These considerations do not affect the requirement of justice that, when discrepancies are identified, they should be removed. But they show that identifying them is not always a straightforward matter. Where there are representative political institutions, demands for new legal rights can be pressed through constitutional political action and the issues they raise can be publicly discussed. But much of mankind do not live under such institutions. They must be lucky enough to have enlightened rulers if discrepancies are to be identified and removed. Still less can anything be expected in a community which is deeply and painfully divided along racial, religious, linguistic or economic lines. If people are unable to agree about the terms upon which they are to live together, they are unlikely to agree about the legal rights which they ought to have. In such a community, the ideas of the most powerful of the polarised groups will be imposed upon the rest. All this shows that new legal rights cannot be panaceas for serious social ills. They can facilitate social co-operation in relatively uncontentious matters. But too much must not be expected of them.

7.3.5   This chapter has been concerned with the social rights of individuals: that is, of persons as members of communities and of associations within them. Nothing has been said about the corporate rights which associations themselves have within communities: for instance, commercial companies, trade unions, clubs, charitable foundations, churches and universities. With one exception, however, they do not give rise to any fresh conceptual issues. As corporate persons, these associations have legal, moral and customary rights in the same way as do individual persons. They can make agreements and acquire claim rights. They have liberty rights to pursue their own particular purposes subject to legal and moral requirements not being transgressed. Some of them become landlords and have power rights over their tenants. Some of them have immunity rights: for instance, the right of charitable foundations to be exempt from taxation, and of trade unions to be exempt from liability for losses incurred by employers during strikes. Their rights are exercised by agents who act on their behalf and who are responsible to their members: for instance, boards of directors, trade-union officials, management committees and trustees. The exception concerns the power rights which associations have over their members. Here the analogy between 'corporate' and 'individual' persons breaks down. But this is a matter best considered in connection with self-sufficient communities and their power rights over their members.

The typical form of self-sufficient community today is the nation state. In international law, nation states are corporate persons with rights and obligations *vis à vis* one another. Of these the most important are the immunity right of every state to non-interference in its internal affairs, and, correlative to this right, the obligation upon every state not to interfere. But discussion of international law, of international rights and obligations and of the idea of an international community which both presuppose must be deferred until Chapter 9.[15] We have seen that under the principle of social responsibility, every member of a community has an obligation to give precedence to the interest of the community over his personal self-interest. This entails a correlative power right of the community to impose obligations upon its members for the sake of its interest, which, it will be remembered (see 2.3.1 and 2.3.3), is also their interest as members. The situation is fundamentally the same in the case of associations, except that, where membership is voluntary, a member can always resign if he finds the obligations of membership too demanding.[16] In the case of a nation state, this correlative power right is vested in the government as part of its authority over the members. The concept of authority includes but is wider than that of a power right. But further discussion of authority and of liberty rights and immunity rights which set limits to it, as in a constitutional 'Bill of Rights', must also be deferred until Chapter 9. What has been said in this and the previous chapter about the idea of rights is sufficient to enable us to take up the topic of human rights.

8 The Idea of Rights (iii): Human Rights

8.1 EXPOSITION OF HUMAN RIGHTS AS UNIVERSAL MINIMUM MORAL RIGHTS: FIRST STAGE

8.1.1 Human rights must necessarily be universal moral rights. But there can be such rights only if there is a universal morality which is their source (see Introduction). We saw in Chapter 5 that there are rational grounds for the universal applicability of common morality. They lie in Kant's humanity principle together with the practical-reason principle (see 5.2.2–3 above). These yield a universal minimum moral standard which on its negative side requires that no human being should ever be treated merely as a means; on its positive side, that, in all their dealings, all human beings must always observe the principles of common morality. Hence we have in common morality a morality which is universal, not only in the sense of being part of the actual morality of every community, but in the sense of being applicable to all human beings irrespective of who they are and what communities and associations they belong to. As the principles of community life as such, the principles of common morality are neutral about moral diversity. They entail no commitment to any particular way of life, any particular morality, any particular institutions, beliefs or values. But we have also seen that their universal applicability modifies this neutrality in an important respect. Any particular morality which requires or merely permits the treatment of any human being merely as a means and thereby violates the universal standard is for that reason morally defective (see 5.2.3 above).

People do not normally have dealings with one another simply as fellow human beings. That happens only in emergencies when the preservation of life is the paramount consideration: for instance, in natural disasters such as earthquakes, floods and famines; following accidents such as air crashes, shipwrecks and fires; or in the aftermath of wars and revolutions. They normally have dealings with one another in established social contexts with their particular institutions and roles: as neighbours, friends, colleagues and citizens; as husbands and wives, parents and children, teachers and pupils, employers and workers, customers and salesmen, doctors and patients, lawyers and clients, to mention only some familiar examples in contemporary Western society. The same is true of dealings with foreigners. They are typically encountered as tourists, diplomats, visiting businessmen, athletes, artists, musicians and the like.

All this, however, does not affect the universal applicability of the principles of common morality. Like all principles, they have to be contextually interpreted. But they must be interpreted not simply as the principles of community life as such, but as applying to all human beings. That interpretation must be with reference to the values, roles and institutions of particular social contexts. But these must meet the requirements of the humanity principle. Wherever they do not, wherever they deny the applicability of any of the principles of common morality to any human being, there are rational grounds for moral criticism and for reform based on that criticism: for instance, in the case of the institution of slavery.

In the last chapter the question was asked, 'Why should there be rights at all?' The answer was that without rights there can be no human communities. Having rights is part of what it is to be a member of any community, whatever its particular form (see 5.2.3 above). But this is not a complete answer because it is limited to social rights. It takes no account of requirements of universal morality: that is, of the universal minimum moral standard on both its negative and positive sides. To treat a human being merely as a means is to deny that anything at all is due to him, which is to deny that he has any rights. If he is to be treated not merely as a means but as a person having intrinsic value for himself, he must have rights. This gives us a more complete answer. Not only do there have to be rights if there are to be any communities: there have to be rights which every human being has, if the requirements of the universal minimum moral standard are to be met. This does not, however, tell us what these rights are. For that we must go to the principles of common morality, because the universal standard on its positive side requires that in all their dealings all human beings must observe them. It is they which contain the rights which every human being must have: that is, universal moral rights or human rights properly so-called. In the last chapter, a brief indication was given of what the rights contained in the principles of common morality are. But that was in connection with social rights, the principles being taken simply as the principles of community life as such. They must now be taken as applying to all human beings, not merely to the fellow members of the same community, and the rights which they contain when so taken must be examined in detail. Their contextual interpretation and its implications for these rights must also be considered. They do not, however, all contain rights – beneficence, as we shall now see, being a principle which does not.

8.1.2   The principle of beneficence requires that, between good and evil, good must always be chosen; between goods, the greater good; and, between evils, the lesser evil. Together with the practical-reason principle, it is the foundation of all rational action, moral, prudential and instrumental. While the detailed identification of good and evil is a matter of contextual interpretation, there is an absolute moral obligation to meet the abstract requirements of beneficence in every moral context, irrespective of time, place and circumstances. It is the only moral principle of which this is true. The reason is that its requirements can never justifiably be overridden by those of any other moral principle, because it is itself the principle upon which all such overriding must ultimately be justified. It cannot contain an elective right because that would mean that on a particular occasion the right-holder would be entitled to waive it and release someone else from his obligation to act beneficently. Since this obligation is absolute, no one can be entitled to release anyone else from it. It cannot contain a non-elective right because there would be nothing specific to which the right-holder was entitled. As the right to have all other rights respected it is otiose, adding nothing to what any other right entitles the right-holder to. All moral wrongs, including every violation of every other right, would be a violation of it. The violation of a child's right to be looked after is a moral wrong and contravenes the principle of beneficence. But what is violated is not a putative right of the child to beneficent treatment, but his right to be looked after, because this violation is a moral wrong and like every moral wrong which is not, under the circumstances, the lesser evil, it contravenes the principle of beneficence.

8.1.3   The principle of respect for human life has two main requirements: first, that no human being should ever be wantonly killed; second, that no human life should ever be unnecessarily endangered. Wanton killing is morally unjustified killing. But what counts as a moral justification for taking human life is not always and everywhere the same: hence the need for contextual interpretation with special reference to the particular morality of the community concerned. Duelling, abortion and euthanasia are cases of wanton killing according to some moral codes but not according to others. The need for contextual interpretation is obvious in the case of unnecessary danger. Here, however, it is prudential considerations arising out of particular circumstances which are of special relevance. The principle clearly contains the right to life. Every human being is entitled not to be wantonly killed and not to have his life unnecessarily endangered. The correlative obligation is to refrain from treating any human being in either of these ways. In terms of Raphael, the right is one of negative recipience. According to Hohfeld, it consists of two immunity rights: immunity from wanton killing and immunity from unnecessary exposure to danger.

Wantonly to kill a fellow human being is not to treat him as a fellow human being at all. Unnecessarily to endanger his life is to treat him as expendable and, therefore again, not as a fellow human being. Hence the right is a human right properly so-called since having it is part of what constitutes the status of 'fellow human being'. The right to life is an elective right because it is possible for the right-holder to waive it. He can accept being murdered so as to allow others to escape. He can volunteer for a dangerous enterprise which no one in authority has a power right to order him to undertake, for the sake of what will be gained if it is successful. Whether the right entitles the right-holder to take his own life for personal reasons depends how suicide is regarded in the particular morality concerned. In some it is morally excluded; in others, morally permitted.

The right-holder exercises his right to life by resisting attempts wantonly to kill him and by refusing to do anything which would unnecessarily endanger his life. In thus exercising it, the right entitles him to take whatever steps he can for his own self-preservation, provided that he does not violate the right to life of any innocent party. This means that, as the right to self-preservation, the right to life is a right of action as well as of negative recipience. In Hohfeldian terms it is a power right, because those who threaten it are thereby liable to suffer the consequences of whatever defensive measures the right-holder takes in exercising it. There is also an important implication of moral diversity. As we have seen with reference to duelling, abortion and euthanasia, what counts as wanton killing is not always and everywhere the same. Hence what counts as a violation of the right to life according to one moral code is not necessarily so according to another. This conflicts with widely held ideas about human rights and more will be said about it later. There are, however, cases which count as wanton killing always and everywhere because contravening the universal minimum moral standard on its negative side: that is, treating a person merely as a means and not as a fellow human being at all. Examples are killing for private gain, for social expediency or for sadistic pleasure. If such killing is licensed by a particular morality because the victim is 'racially inferior', an 'enemy of the people', or belongs to a class whose members are socially expendable, such as 'untouchables', then so much the worse for that particular morality. By not branding such killing as wanton and permitting it, it shows itself to be morally defective.

8.1.4   There is a difference between violating someone's right to life and denying that he has the right at all. It cannot be violated unless he has it, and an act which violates it is as such morally wrong. But, if he does not have the right to life, killing him is not as such morally wrong, although it may be pointless or inexpedient. It may be objected that the difference is unimportant. When someone is about to be killed, it does not matter to him whether his killer is violating his right to life or denying that he has it. All that concerns him is that his life is about to be taken. No doubt this is true, but it does not mean that the difference is unimportant. It is necessary to understand what is happening when human life is taken. For instance, it helps to clarify what is at issue in the controversy over abortion. Those who oppose abortion on moral grounds hold that the foetus's right to life is violated. Those who hold that abortion is morally permissible, deny that the foetus has the right to life at all. According to them, rights cannot be acquired until birth. In the case of euthanasia, those who oppose it hold that it is a violation of the right to life. Those who support it may hold that it is suicide by proxy. But they may hold that, with the irreversible termination of the capacity for thought and action and so for all significant human experience, the right to life is no longer possessed.

Supporters of abortion are not committed to denying that there is a universal moral right to life. Nor are supporters of euthanasia. The disagreement in the one case is about when the right is acquired; in the other, about when it ceases. Such disagreements arise from differences in particular moralities, none of which necessarily conflicts with universal morality. In the controversy over capital punishment, the question is whether a murderer in violating his victim's right to life morally forfeits his own. More will have to be said later (in 8.3.4) both about capital punishment in particular and about punishment in general. Here it is sufficient to point out that to be in favour of capital punishment for murder is not to deny that there is a universal moral right to life. The murderer cannot forfeit his right to life unless he already has it. Upon what grounds, if any, a universal moral right can be morally forfeited is again something about which more must be said later (see 8.3.5). But there can be, and historically have been, particular moralities which deny that there is a universal moral right to life. According to Nazi morality, Aryan Germans had the right to life but Jews and other 'inferior' races did not. The wanton killing of an Aryan German was murder. The officially planned killing of millions of Jews was not murder but 'eugenic extermination'. This terrible example highlights the implications of denying that certain human beings have the right to life. The denial deprives them of all moral status. They do not count as fellow human beings and can be killed with impunity. This is what makes the right to life a human right. It is one which a person must have if he is to count as a fellow human being. This, as we shall see, is true of all human rights properly so-called.

8.1.5   In the case of the principle of justice, some recapitulation may be helpful. In the last chapter (see 7.1.5) we saw that the principle in the form of 'to each his due' is the moral foundation of social rights. It requires that the rights of every member, whatever they are, must be respected. Because the principles of common morality are the principles of community life as such, the rights which they contain are rights which in every community every member has. Apart from these, the other rights of the members depend upon the particular status which each has within the community, this being defined by its terms of membership. Such rights are specified in detail in the community's system of positive law (if it has one), in its customs and in its particular morality. Moral diversity means diversity in the detailed rights which the members of different communities have. But in a community with a system of positive law there are two rights which every member necessarily has: the right to the equal protection of the law and the right to freedom under the law. This is because having these rights is part of what it is to live under a system of positive law. In a community with a system of positive law, there is therefore a legal right to justice in the sense of a right to the equal protection of the law. It is violated whenever equal protection is not accorded; for instance, through maladministration or police or judicial corruption. But this is a right to legal justice and a community can exist without a system of positive law. Where there is such a system, it may infringe the universal minimum moral standard: for instance, by legally maintaining slavery. Moreover, people who are not subject to the same system of positive law, or not subject to any at all, can have dealings with one another. Hence, important though it is, a right to legal justice is not in itself a human right, although, as we shall see (in 9.2.1–2), as the interpretation of the right to fair treatment in the context of positive law, it is the legal and political embodiment of a human right.

To make justice in the form of 'to each his due' universally applicable is to make it the moral foundation not only of social rights but of human rights. But this logically excludes it from itself being a human right. It cannot itself be part of that of which it is the moral foundation. Suppose there were such a right, what would it be a right to? In terms of 'to each his due', it could only be the right to have all rights respected. But, whether elective or non-elective, such a right is vacuous. There is nothing specific to which it entitles the right-holder. It entitles him to whatever he is entitled to, which is not itself a distinct entitlement. This in no way, however, diminishes the importance of justice as the moral foundation of human rights. The universal minimum moral standard on its positive side extends the principles of common morality to all human beings. Hence every human being, irrespective of nationality, religion, sex, colour or wealth, has all the rights contained in these principles. They are his due and justice requires that he have them. He is treated justly when they are respected, unjustly when they are not. But, while all this is true, it leaves out something important. We saw in Chapter 3 that one thing which is due to every member of a community is fair treatment. It is a distinctive requirement of justice which is not called for by any of the other principles of common morality. This means that the right to justice in its particular form is the right to something specific. As a human right, it entitles every human being to be treated fairly.

8.1.6   We saw in Chapter 3 that 'fairness' is 'proportionate equality'. There is fair treatment when this principle is properly applied, unfair treatment when it is not. The right to fair treatment is the right to have it properly applied whenever and wherever it is applicable. As a human right, it entitles not only the members of the same community but all human beings to fair treatment. It is a right of positive recipience – in Hohfeldian terms, a claim right. Its correlative obligation is to apply the principle properly. This is an obligation which all are under who are involved in making allocations, in apportioning praise or blame, in making assessments or in competitions, whether as officials or as competitors. What in particular they have to do to meet this obligation depends upon the details of the context: upon what is being allocated and who are eligible, upon what it is for which praise or blame are being apportioned, upon what is being assessed, and upon the nature of the competition. The right is violated whenever its correlative obligation is not met: whenever equals are treated unequally, unequals equally or, if unequally, then not in proportion to their comparative inequality.

Failure to meet the obligation may be because of favouritism or prejudice: in allocating, giving more to one's friends irrespective of comparative need; in assessing professional competence giving weight to irrelevant factors such as sex, religion or colour. But it may simply be owing to ignorance: blaming someone more than he deserves because of being unaware of mitigating circumstances; not noticing a foul which enables the offending player to gain an 'unfair advantage'. Not all violations of the right to fair treatment are equally serious. The right-holder exercises his right by insisting on receiving fair treatment: by demanding that his particular needs receive proper consideration; by protesting against being blamed more than he deserves; by drawing attention to relevant factors which have been ignored in assessing his performance; by protesting against conditions which make competition unfair. The right is elective and can be waived. It entitles the right-holder to put up with unfair treatment if making a fuss is not worth the trouble: to acquiesce in receiving less than his fair share, in not being given all the credit he deserves, in being assessed below his true worth, in the biased decision of a referee.

As with the right to life, there is a difference between violation and denial. Someone whose right to fair treatment is violated has the possibility of redress. Not so someone to whom the right is denied. In the latter case, because no one has an obligation to treat him fairly, he can have no redress: no grounds for complaint when the share allotted to him is less than proportionate to his comparative need, when he is blamed more than he deserves, when relevant factors to his credit are ignored in assessing him, when he is cheated by competitors. He is totally dependent for his treatment upon other people's caprice. If some of them choose to treat him fairly – that is, according to the requirements of proportionate equality – that is his good fortune. But it is not his right and, if they choose not to do so, he must simply put up with it. This highlights the importance of fair treatment as a human right. To be totally dependent for one's treatment upon the caprice of other people is not to share with them the status of fellow human being. It is to be a slave, or at best a domestic pet. If a human being's interests are not to be ignored, he must be entitled to stand up for them, and this the right to fair treatment entitles him to do. It does not of course entitle him to whatever he judges to be in his self-interest. But it does entitle him to fair treatment whenever and wherever his interests are involved: that is, in all distributive, adjudicative, critical and competitive contexts.

8.2 EXPOSITION OF HUMAN RIGHTS AS UNIVERSAL MINIMUM MORAL RIGHTS: SECOND STAGE

8.2.1   Two human rights have now been shown to be contained in the first group of principles of common morality: the right to life and the right to justice in the form of fair treatment. These are separate rights and the first is logically prior to the second. To deny someone's right to life is *ipso facto* to deny his right to fair treatment, because, if it is morally permissible to kill him, he cannot be morally entitled to be treated fairly. But the right to life can be recognised while the right to fair treatment is denied. Something like this was the case in many forms of the institution of slavery. We have seen (in 3.3.1) that the second group of principles of common morality are all derivatives of justice in its general form of 'to each his due'. Meeting their specific requirements wherever and whenever they arise is due from every human being. The rights which they contain are therefore further human rights. As we shall see, with one exception each of them contains such rights. The exception is social responsibility.

8.2.2   As a principle of community life, social responsibility requires every member of a community to play his part in maintaining and promoting the community's interest. When they come into conflict, he must always give precedence to the community's interest over his personal self-interest. Each member is responsible to the corporate membership of the community for meeting these requirements. This applies also in the case of an association. Its members have the same responsibility for its interest. It follows that the only right contained in the principle is one which is possessed by the community or association as a corporate group. This is a Hohfeldian power right. For the sake of maintaining and promoting its interest, the community through agents acting on its behalf is morally entitled to organise and regulate the activities of its members. The liability which the members have as the correlate of this power right is to have their activities organised and regulated to the extent that this is necessary. There are moral limits to what the community can do in exercising this power right. Its members' right to justice must be respected, which means that burdens and sacrifices necessary for the community's interest must be allocated fairly. The principle of social responsibility also sets limits to the members' liberty rights. Their obligation to meet its requirements means that they can never have a liberty right to do anything which conflicts with that obligation.

We shall return to corporate rights in the next chapter. The point here is that, because social responsibility confers no rights upon the individual members of a community but only obligations, it cannot confer any rights upon individual human beings. There is, however, a related matter which needs to be considered. Social responsibility is a principle of community life and therefore of common morality. But it is applicable only where there is a genuine community or association. Can it then be part of universal morality? Only if there is an intelligible sense in which humanity constitutes a genuine community. Reference was made in the last chapter (see 7.3.5) to the idea of an international community which is presupposed by international law. Today we have in the United Nations a practical expression of that idea. But there is an objection to equating an international community such as the United Nations with a single community of humanity. This is that the members are nation states, which in practice means national governments. Individual human beings are members only in virtue of their membership of individual nation states. This means that any human beings who, because of race, colour or creed, or for any other reason, are denied membership of the nation states in which they live, or who do not live in any nation state at all, are thereby denied membership of the international community. National governments, as members of that community, are morally committed to the principles of common morality in their dealings with one another but not in their dealings with all human beings.

The UN Universal Declaration of Human Rights is not an adequate safeguard. As we saw in the Introduction the rights which it lists are liberal-democratic rights, not human rights properly so-called. Most of humanity have never experienced liberal democracy and are unlikely to do so in the foreseeable future. But the objection is nevertheless not decisive. Humanity today consists of more than 4000 million human beings. It can therefore constitute a genuine community only as some form of international community: that is, as a universal community of communities. The objection shows only that the United Nations today is a far from perfect embodiment of such a community. This is not, however, because of any inherent defect in the structure and organisation of the United Nations. Rather it is because of moral defects in some member nations and because of a less than complete commitment by many of them to the United Nations as an international community. This is another topic to which we shall have to return in the next chapter. Two things, however, are worth mentioning here in connection with it. One concerns human rights, the other social responsibility.

Human rights properly so-called – that is, the rights contained in the principles of common morality – are, because they are contained in those principles, part of the universal minimum moral standard on its positive side. Any national community in which any of them is denied to any human being is for that reason morally defective. So is any form of international community in which that national community is included. It necessarily falls short of constituting a genuine universal human community. The difference between denying that human rights are possessed and violating them is here crucial. It is the fact that they are denied to certain human beings, not that they are violated, which is incompatible with the existence of a genuine universal human community. This is because those human beings to whom they are denied are thereby excluded from membership. While the violation of any human right is always morally wrong, there is at least the possibility of redress. The victims of the violation are not being denied the status of fellow human beings. Something else about which more will be said later is this: the principles of common morality and therefore the rights they contain require contextual interpretation. This means that what counts as a violation of a human right in one context may not in another. But, when it is denied that certain people possess human rights at all, the possibility of contextual interpretation so far as those people are concerned cannot even arise.

The principle of social responsibility is applicable to any form of international community. The interest of such a community is in maintaining conditions which will enable every member nation not merely to survive but so far as possible to prosper. The principle therefore requires all national governments to co-operate in promoting that interest, and to subordinate the pursuit of national self-interest to the requirements of such co-operation. These requirements also apply to associations within the international community: for instance, multinational corporations, industrial organisations such as the Organisation of Petroleum Exporting Countries, the European Economic Community, and alliances and combinations among national governments. The global impact of modern technology means that, if humanity is to survive, let alone prosper, an international community is essential. Modern technology has brought all parts of the world into contact and generated world-wide commercial and industrial interdependence. But it has also enabled sophisticated weapons of mass destruction to be manufactured and prepared for instant use. Two matters which are obviously in the interest of an international community today are the preservation of world peace and the conservation of the natural environment. Others include checking the growth of the world's human population and the reduction of poverty. Although the United Nations is a very imperfect embodiment of a universal human community, it at least provides a context for the application of social responsibility as a principle of universal morality. Such a principle, together with that of beneficence, requires national governments to interpret their responsibilities as members of the United Nations in ways which will make it a better embodiment of a universal human community.

8.2.3   As a principle of community life, fellowship requires every member not to be indifferent to the lot of any other member and to give whatever help he can when it is needed. It therefore confers upon every member in distress a Hohfeldian claim right to aid from his fellow members. How in particular the requirements of the principle can best be met, and what in detail the right entitles members to, are matters of contextual interpretation. Today, in Western nations, there is organised provision for the relief of distress through social services and specific welfare rights. But these do not release members from an obligation to take individual action when necessary. Nor in such cases do they affect the right of a member to have the action taken. The right, however, is elective. The right-holder is entitled to refuse it and, in circumstances when providing it endangers other people's lives, may well have an obligation to do so. Universal morality extends fellowship to all human beings. Any human being in distress has the right to aid, and any human being in a position to provide it has an obligation to do so. Today there are a number of organised attempts to relieve human distress. The United Nations, through such agencies as the Relief and Rehabilitation Administration (UNRRA) and United Nations International Children's Emergency Fund (UNICEF), the foreign-aid programmes of several Western governments, the International Red Cross and Oxfam are instances. But, here too, the existence of these and other organisations does not release individual human beings from their obligation to do what they personally can to help. Nor does it affect the right of any human being in distress to aid from anyone in a position to give it.

Because human distress is so acute and widespread, it may be thought that there is little that individual human beings can do about it on their own. The only effective way is through organisations, both governmental and voluntary. But an individual cry for help must be answered at once. By the time an organisation can go into action, it may be too late. If a drowning man is to be rescued, immediate action is necessary. The human right to aid entitles a person in distress to be given it irrespective of who he is. A drowning man must, if possible, be rescued, whatever his nationality or religion. Here again there is a difference between denying that there is a right to aid and violating it. It is violated when those who could help refrain from doing so: perhaps because of possible danger to themselves, because they 'do not want to get involved', or simply because it is inconvenient. It is denied when the obligation to help is not acknowledged: 'His own people should look after him', 'He is not one of us', 'He is only a native.' Probably few people today would openly excuse themselves in these or similar terms. But time was when there was no such reticence and such excuses were made in all sincerity. Giving practical effect to the human right to aid involves problems. The human right to fair treatment must be respected both in distributing the aid and in allocating the costs of providing it. Conflicting claims arising from the distress of fellow countrymen and of foreigners must somehow be reconciled. Such problems do not, however, invalidate the right to aid. They only serve as a warning against unrealistic expectations about the extent to which human distress can be relieved.

8.2.4   As a moral principle of community life, 'freedom from arbitrary interference' contains the right of every member to such freedom. This consists of three Hohfeldian rights: an immunity right, a general liberty right and a power right. The immunity right entitles the right-holder to immunity from all arbitrary interference. The liberty right entitles him to do anything which he has no obligation not to do, and to refrain from doing anything which he has not an obligation to do, provided that neither his action nor his forbearance prevent him from meeting any other obligation which he is under. Interference with the exercise of this liberty right is arbitrary unless it is morally justified. To be morally justified, it must be interference which is necessary to prevent the right-holder from doing what he is entitled to do or to make him do what he is not entitled to refrain from doing. In other words, he is entitled not to be interfered with so long as, either by commission or by omission, he does nothing wrong. Interference is also morally justified if it is necessary to prevent the right-holder from unintentionally harming himself: that is, doing something which, if he had been aware of the outcome, he would not have chosen to do. Such interference is directly justified by the principle of 'fellowship', ultimately by 'beneficence'. The power right entitles the right-holder to resist arbitrary interference, but the means used must not be excessive. If someone unjustifiably blocks his path, he is entitled to push him out of the way but not to kill him. Nor must the means used harm any innocent parties. The liability which is the correlate of the power right is upon those who arbitrarily interfere. They are liable to bear the consequences of the right-holder's resistance.

The obligation correlative to both the immunity right and the liberty right is to refrain from all interferences with the right-holder's freedom of action unless such interference is morally justified. In the case of the power right, it is to refrain from interfering with the right-holder's resistance to arbitrary interference. This is an obligation which the fellow members of his community are under as third parties. But in addition they have an obligation to do what they can to help him resist it. This obligation, however, is correlative not to the right-holder's right to resist arbitrary interference but to his right to aid. Like that right, it is contained in the principle of 'fellowship'. The liberty right is clearly elective. Anything which the right-holder is not under an obligation to do or to refrain from doing is left to his discretion. He is entitled to act or not, as he sees fit. The power right is also elective. The right-holder is entitled to resist arbitrary interference but he is not under an obligation to do so. Prudence suggests compliance with, rather than resistance to, the wishes of a gunman and the right entitles him to take the prudent course. As a corollary of the power right, the immunity right is also elective. The right-holder is entitled to acquiesce in the violation of his immunity right: that is, to put up with arbitrary interference without protest.

In the contextual interpretation of the liberty right, moral diversity is crucially important. The right-holder is entitled not to be interfered with, so long as he does nothing wrong. But what counts as 'wrong' depends upon a community's particular morality. What in orthodox Islamic society is wrong for a married woman to do may not be wrong in contemporary Western society: for instance, consorting in public with men. 'Freedom' as a principle of community life and therefore of common morality must not be equated with 'freedom' as a principle of the particular morality of a modern Western nation. In the latter case it incorporates liberal-democratic values, but not in the former. As a principle of community life, it requires that every member should be free to go about his business. But it has nothing to say about what his business is. That depends upon an individual community's way of life with its particular morality, institutions and values. What the liberty right entitles the right-holder to do, therefore, depends upon the social context. This is also true of the power right. What the right-holder is entitled to resist depends upon what counts as arbitrary interference. Also, what kind of resistance he is entitled to make depends in part upon his community, its legal system if it has one, its police and its internal security arrangements.

Universal morality extends the right to freedom from arbitrary interference, and therefore the immunity right, the liberty right and the power right, to all human beings. But, subject to an important qualification, its universal extension does not affect its contextual interpretation. Civility as a principle of community life and, as we shall see, of universal morality requires observance of the maxim 'When in Rome, do as the Romans do.' This means that foreigners no less than members have an obligation to respect the restrictions upon liberty prescribed by a community's particular morality, and its laws and customs. The qualification arises from the requirements of the universal minimum moral standard. There can be no obligation to respect restrictions upon liberty which breach that standard by denying the right to freedom to certain human beings. The institution of slavery is the most obvious example of the denial of this right. What the visitor to a slave-owning community is morally required to do is another matter. He certainly has an obligation not to condone the institution and no obligation to respect it. But more about this later (see 9.4.2).

As with other human rights, there is a difference between violating the right to freedom and denying that it is possessed at all. The immunity right and the liberty right are necessarily violated when interference is morally unjustified: when the violator is doing what he has an obligation to refrain from doing and therefore no right to do. The victim is entitled by his power right to resist arbitrary interference. Any interference with that resistance by third parties is itself arbitrary. Someone to whom the right to freedom is denied is in a worse position. There is nothing which he is entitled to do, and he is not entitled to resist any interference with his freedom of action. He has neither the liberty right nor the power right. Unless he is a slave, his status is comparable to that of a wild animal who is at the mercy of hunters and predators. As a slave, he is the property of his master. An unprovoked assault upon him by a third party is a violation of his master's property right, not of his right to freedom, because he has no such right. As a principle of universal morality, freedom from arbitrary interference is applicable to all encounters in 'state of nature' situations: for instance, on the high seas, in 'outer space', and in any terrestrial unexplored or uninhabited regions, such as jungles, deserts and mountains. Travellers are entitled to proceed on their way without interference, provided that they do not themselves arbitrarily interfere with anyone whom they encounter. The right to freedom from arbitrary interference is also of great importance in relations between groups of human beings, and especially in international relations. But, again, more about that later (see 9.4.2).

8.2.5 The principle of honourable conduct requires all members of a community in all their mutual transactions always to be truthful, to keep their word and to refrain from deception. They are required at all times to be honest in word and deed. The principle contains a Hohfeldian claim right to such treatment. But the elective character of the right is important. While the right-holder is entitled to be told the truth about any matter which concerns him, he does not have to insist on knowing everything about it. A patient has the right to know that, in his doctor's opinion, his disease is fatal, but he is not obliged to exercise his right and insist on knowing the worst. His doctor has an obligation not to deceive him, but this does not mean that he must impart the grim news if his patient does not want to hear it. The requirements of civility and beneficence must be borne in mind in meeting the obligation. The context affects the scope of the right. In business or diplomacy, what one is entitled to be told is different from what it is in personal relations. But contextual interpretation does not affect the significance of the right to be treated honourably. A man to whom it is denied cannot trust anyone. He can be lied to, deceived and cheated with impunity. No one has an obligation to keep faith with him. But to be treated thus is incompatible with being treated as a fellow human being. Hence universal morality requires that the right to honourable treatment be extended to all human beings, to all strangers and foreigners, no less than to neighbours and fellow countrymen.

'Civility' requires all members of a community and of any form of association always to show courtesy in their mutual dealings. Not only must they refrain from unprovoked violence, but they must show respect for one another's feelings, which means both refraining from insulting and humiliating and from unnecessarily frightening, shocking and distressing one another. At all times they must be considerate. The qualification 'unnecessarily', however, is important. There is no incivility when plain speaking for the sake of justice, social responsibility or honourable conduct frightens, shocks or distresses those to whom it is addressed. As a principle of common morality, civility contains a Hohfeldian claim for the right-holder to be treated civilly on all occasions. But the right's elective character means that incivility may be tolerated. The right-holder is entitled to acquiesce in rude, insulting or insensitive behaviour if he thinks that it is not worth making a fuss. The context makes a difference to the requirements of civility. What according to one set of values is acceptable behaviour according to another is rudeness: for instance, different conventions of polite behaviour towards men and women. A person to whom the right is denied is denied effective participation in any form of human association. He can be insulted, humiliated, scorned, mocked and bullied with impunity. He can be treated as less than a fellow human being, which is why universal morality requires civility and the right it contains to be extended to all human beings. The right must be interpreted in terms of local conventions of good manners and polite behaviour, provided that these meet the requirements, negative and positive, of universal morality. Where they do not, there is no incivility in plain speaking. On the appropriate occasion, 'honourable conduct' requires speaking out against injustice regardless of the distress or embarrassment it causes.

8.2.6   As a principle of community life, child care requires that all children of members must be looked after until they have grown up and can look after themselves. It also requires all associations to pursue their activities in ways which do not infringe this requirement. The principle confers a non-elective Hohfeldian claim right upon the children to be looked after. The obligation correlative to this right is in the first instance invariably upon the parents. But there is a residual obligation upon the community, in the case of orphans or when parents fail to meet their obligation, to see that arrangements are made to provide children with the care to which they are entitled. What, in detail, the right entitles children to depends upon the social context. When one becomes 'of age', what being looked after involves, and what arrangements there are for the care of orphans and for children whose parents have neglected and abused them are matters which vary from one community to another. But this diversity in detail does not affect the fundamental significance of the right. A child to whom it is denied is denied the prospect of adult life in any community, which is incompatible with treating him as a fellow human being. Hence universal morality extends the principle and the right to all children, irrespective of nationality, ethnic origin, religion or any other differentiating characteristic. This means that, where the correlative obligation is not met by parents or by a particular national community, it falls upon the international community. This is acknowledged today both by the United Nations and by voluntary international organisations.

8.3   IMPLICATIONS AND AMPLIFICATIONS: FIRST STAGE

8.3.1   Summarising this chapter so far, universal morality is the source of seven main rights and it is these which are human rights properly so-called. They are the rights to life, to justice in the form of fair treatment, to aid, to freedom in the negative sense of freedom from arbitrary interference, to honourable treatment, to civility and, in the case of children, to care. Of these, the first two, life and justice, are contained in the first group of the principles of common morality. The other five are contained in the second group. In terms of the action–recipience distinction, the right to freedom is a general right of action because it entitles the right-holder to do anything which is not morally wrong. The other six are all rights of recipience: that is, rights which are correlative to obligations which, by the principles of universal morality, every human being has to treat all human beings in certain ways. They are therefore rights to be treated in these ways. But the action–recipience distinction is insufficiently discriminating and must be supplemented by Hohfeld's conceptions in order to bring out what each right entitles the right-holder to. Thus the right to life consists of two immunity rights and a power right, while the right to justice consists of a claim right. The right to aid is primarily a claim right. But it can also be regarded as a power right, because all human beings are liable to be called upon to relieve human distress, and any human being in distress is entitled to call upon them. The right to freedom consists of an immunity right, a general liberty right and a power right. The rights to honourable treatment and to civility are claim rights to the kinds of treatment which fall under these heads. But they also include immunity rights: in the one case, immunity from any form of dishonesty; in the other, from discourtesy, insults and any form of unnecessary distress. The right of children to care is a claim right. This last is a non-elective right while all the others are elective. Thus, while there are seven main rights, some of these turn out on examination to involve several distinct rights. One merit of Hohfeld's analysis is that it enables this to be shown.

8.3.2   In the case of the human right to freedom, however, Hohfeld's analysis needs supplementing. This is because the right to freedom consists of a general liberty right as well as an immunity right and a power right. According to Hohfeld, the opposite of a liberty right is a duty or obligation. This is straightforward in the case of a particular liberty right. If I have an obligation to do something, I cannot have a right to do something which prevents me from meeting that obligation. Nor is there any problem in the case of slavery. A slave has no general liberty right. He is subject at all times to the will of his master. He has a general obligation always to obey his master and therefore to do only what the latter permits and never what he forbids. Where Hohfeld's account needs supplementing is in the case of those, such as the Jews in Nazi Germany, who lack even the minimal moral status of slavery. They have no moral status at all and therefore neither rights nor obligations. They lack the general liberty right as well as the immunity right and the power right not because, like slaves, they have a general obligation, but because they have no moral status at all. They are not entitled to do anything and no one has any obligation to refrain from interfering with them. This means that, in their case, no interference is arbitrary. Anyone and everyone can interfere with them at will. This is why, as we have seen, like wild animals they are at the mercy of hunters and predators.

Hohfeld did not consider the case of people to whom all liberty rights were completely denied. As we have seen, he was concerned with particular liberty rights as a legal conception. This does not, however, detract from the contribution of his analysis to understanding what the denial of human rights to particular human beings entails. We saw in Chapter 6 that one party's claim right excludes another party's liberty right and *vice versa*. The same holds of power rights and immunity rights. One party's power right excludes another's immunity right and *vice versa*. This applies to universal rights. If there are certain rights which everyone has, there must be others which no one can have. No one can have a right to anything which violates any universal right. What this entails in terms of Hohfeld's analysis for the seven main human rights may briefly be summarised as follows.

The universal right to life entails that no one can have either a liberty right or a power right entitling him either wantonly to kill any human being or unnecessarily to endanger any human life. Nor can anyone who does either of these things, or who aids and abets those who do them, have an immunity right from defensive action by those threatened. As a universal claim right, the right to justice entails that no one can have a liberty right to do anything which is unfair to any human being. As a universal immunity right, it entails that no one can have a power right to treat unfairly any one liable to his decisions. As a universal claim right, the right to aid entails that no one in a position to help can have a liberty right entitling him to disregard a cry for help. As a universal power right, it entails that no one can have an immunity right entitling him not to be liable to be called on for help. As a universal immunity right, the right to freedom entails that no one can have a power right entitling him to direct the conduct of anyone over whom he has no jurisdiction. As a universal liberty right, it entails that no one can have a claim right upon anyone to do anything unless the latter already has an obligation to do it. As a universal power right, it entails that no one who arbitrarily interferes with other people's freedom of action can have a right to immunity from counter-measures by them. As universal claim rights, honourable treatment and civility entail that no one can have a liberty right to do anything dishonourable or to act uncivilly. As universal immunity rights, they limit the scope of all power rights. No one can be entitled to treat anyone over whom he has jurisdiction either dishonourably or uncivilly. As a universal claim right, the right of children to care entails that no one can have a liberty right to do anything which deprives any child of the care of adults. As a universal power right, it entails that no adult can have an immunity right exempting him from being liable to contribute to such care.

8.3.3   In the last chapter we saw (in 7.3.2) that different rights can conflict with one another. Three sources of conflict were identified:

(1) the limitations of finitude;
(2) an inherent incompatibility between different values in a particular morality;
(3) an incompatibility between the requirements of a community's interest and respect for some of its members' rights.

Now (2) does not arise in the case of human rights. Their source is universal morality, not a particular morality. Universal morality consists of the principles of common morality extended to all human beings. The principles of common morality are the principles of community life as such, and that is a single, albeit an abstract, value. We have already seen (in 8.2.5) that the right to civility entitles the right-holder not to be unnecessarily frightened, shocked and distressed. If telling the painful truth is necessary, there is no incivility. There is no inherent conflict between the requirements of honourable conduct and of civility. But the limitations of finitude are inescapable. So, therefore, are conflicts between human rights arising from them. The example discussed in the last chapter was of just such a conflict. It was between the right to aid and the right to have a promise kept, the latter being a particular case of the right to honourable treatment. But both parties, the accident victim'and the promisees, are entitled to fair treatment. On the assumption that the victim's need is greater, proportionate equality requires that she should be attended to immediately. The promisees' right to fair treatment cannot entitle them to have their claim right met at the expense of the victim's suffering and possible death. On the contrary, their obligation to be fair requires them to waive their right to have their promise kept. The victim's right to fair treatment justifies her in exercising her right to aid.

Proportionate equality, together with the right to fair treatment which it contains, is the moral basis for resolving conflicts between human rights arising from the limitations of finitude. This is because, owing to these limitations, human rights are competing for respect and proportionate equality is applicable in all competitive contexts. Thus, when there is not enough room in the lifeboat, not everyone's right to life can be respected. But everyone has the right to a fair chance, and, when lots are drawn for the available places, the lottery must be fairly conducted. This suggests that the right to fair treatment is the primary human right. It at least can always be respected when other human rights come into conflict. The suggestion appears to be endorsed by (3): an incompatibility between a community's interest and respect for some of the rights of its members. Whatever the sacrifices required by that interest, every member at least has the right to be treated fairly in allocating them. Military service in defence of the community means that some of its members will have to lose their lives. But the terms of war service, and the provision of pensions for the disabled and war widows can and should be fair.

But there can be occasions when the requirements of a community's interest make some unfair treatment unavoidable: for instance, a 'state of emergency' in which detention without trial is a necessary security measure. After the emergency is over, it may be possible, and if so is certainly right, for compensation to be given to innocent people who have been detained. But that does not alter the fact that their right to fair treatment has been violated, albeit as the lesser evil. There has been a conflict between the community's power right to take measures necessary for its security and the claim right to fair treatment of certain of its members. 'States of emergency' are in their nature exceptional. But the fact that they can sometimes be justified means that not even the most fundamental of human rights can always be respected. All this points to the importance for constitutional checks upon a community's exercise of its power right, and, more generally, to the political significance of human rights (see 9.2.1 below). Law and government, the institutions within a community which can most effectively protect them, can also be a danger to them – but more about that in the next chapter.

8.3.4   It was pointed out in the last chapter (see 7.3.1) that, in demanding from the fellow members of his community respect for his own rights, a member commits himself to acknowledging and, so far as possible, meeting the obligations correlative to their rights. This commitment is entailed by the practical-reason principle. A member who demands respect for his rights from his fellow members while not respecting theirs is not treating like cases alike. In exempting himself from what he demands from them he is treating himself differently when in the relevant respect he is not different. Now this holds also of universal moral rights. Anyone who demands respect for his human rights while not respecting those of another human being is not treating like cases alike. He is exempting himself from what he demands from others when, as fellow human beings, he and they are alike in the relevant respect. It may be thought that such a person morally forfeits his own human rights. Because he has not respected those of someone else, he cannot be morally justified in demanding respect for his own. But matters are not so straightforward.

Particular social rights can be morally forfeited. A motorist, after many convictions for drunken driving, loses his licence and is disqualified from driving. He has morally forfeited his right to drive by not accepting the discipline required of all drivers. He has not treated like cases alike because, although the same as other drivers in the relevant respect, he has exempted himself from what applies to them all. A man is expelled from a club because he has repeatedly broken its rules and disregarded the rights of his fellow members. By his conduct, he has morally forfeited his membership and his rights as a member. He too has not treated like cases alike, because, although a member, he has exempted himself from what applies equally to all members. In these cases, however, it is particular social rights which are morally forfeited. Both the drunken driver and the erstwhile clubman continue to be members of their national community and retain all their other rights as members. Can a person morally forfeit his membership of his native community and his rights as a member? The logic of the club example suggests that the answer is yes. Someone who is disloyal to his tribe or his country morally forfeits his membership together with his rights as a member. But what about human rights? Can they be morally forfeited?

8.3.5   In support of the contention that they can, consider the following argument. A murderer cannot morally object to being wantonly killed, because he would only be suffering the same fate as his victim. He is not morally justified in demanding respect for his own right to life because, by failing to honour the commitment implicit in that demand, he has morally forfeited the right. With one exception, this applies to all human rights. Anyone who intentionally violates any of them morally forfeits the right which he has violated. The exception is the right of children to be loóked after. Because chldren are not responsible moral agents, they cannot make any commitment when they, or, more accurately, adults on their behalf, demand respect for their right to be looked after. Now this argument rests upon two assumptions. The first is that everyone is morally liable to the same treatment as he accords to others. The second, which is entailed by the first, is that everyone has a moral power right to treat anyone else in the same way as the latter has treated him. Are these assumptions justified? In particular, can there be such a right? It would include the right to vengeance. The right-holder would be entitled to avenge himself upon those who had harmed him, by inflicting upon them the same kind and degree of harm.

The *lex talionis* enshrined the right to vengeance in the form of 'an eye for an eye and a tooth for a tooth'. Properly so, it may be thought, because the right is part of the victim's right to fair treatment. By the principle of proportionate equality, the wrong-doer must suffer the same fate as his victim: that is, undergo suffering the same in kind and equal in degree to that which he has inflicted. But is this true? Does proportionate equality require vengeance? Now, it is unfair, because it is a case of equals being treated unequally, when a man who has wrongly harmed someone 'gets away with it'. Although culpable, he is treated as if he were innocent. He receives the equal treatment due to moral equals when he is morally unequal. Fairness requires that he should take the blame for what he has done and be accorded the treatment appropriate to wrong-doers. But what sort of treatment is that? The only general answer is treatment which will enable the wrong-doer to atone for what he has done. To atone for a wrong is to do whatever can be done to make amends for it, including, to the extent that this is possible, compensating any victims for the harm they have suffered from the wrong.

But what about punishment? Is it not part of the treatment appropriate for wrong-doing? Yes, when the wrong is a legal offence and punishment is legally prescribed. But is not punishment vicarious vengeance? The wrong-doer is made to suffer by agents of the law acting on behalf of his victim for the harm he has done. No, because not all legal offences, although cases of wrong-doing, in fact cause harm: for instance, a drunken driver who is apprehended before he causes an accident. The wrong-doer is punished not because he has done harm, but because he has broken the law. This prompts questions about the nature and purpose of, and justification for, punishment. They cannot, however, be pursued here. I shall assume that punishment is morally justified because it is necessary to uphold the supremacy of law. Granted this assumption, it follows that punishment is one form of the treatment appropriate for wrong-doing. It is a way of enabling one class of wrong-doers, legal offenders, to atone for the wrong they have done. What proportionate equality requires is treatment which will enable wrong-doers to atone for their wrong-doing. Although the desire for it is understandable, vengeance is morally wrong because it contravenes beneficence. That principle requires that the better alternative should always be chosen. Vengeance is always the worse alternative because it simply compounds one evil by another, adding the suffering of the wrong-doer to the suffering of his victim. The better alternative is that required by proportionate equality, treatment which enables the wrong-doer to atone.

Because vengeance is wrong, a right to vengeance would be a right to return wrong with wrong. But, proverbially, 'Two wrongs do not make a right', and there cannot be a right to do wrong. Hence there cannot be a right to vengeance. Nor, because it would include such a right, can there be a moral power right entitling the right-holder to treat others in the same way as they have treated him. It follows that the first assumption, that everyone is morally liable to the same treatment that they have accorded to others, is unjustified. The fact that a man has tortured or bullied others cannot make him morally liable to be tortured and bullied himself. But, by the principle of proportionate equality, he is morally liable to treatment which will enable him to atone for these evils. All this entails that, because it rests upon unjustified assumptions, the argument in support of the contention that human rights can be morally forfeited is unacceptable. The contention is false. Human rights cannot be morally forfeited. Someone who intentionally violates another's human right is still morally justified in demanding respect for the same right in his own case. But, because he has failed to honour the commitment implicit in that demand, he is morally liable to atone for that failure.

Thus a murderer can morally object to being wantonly killed but not to being punished. If the legally prescribed penalty for murder is death, he cannot morally object to being executed. His execution is a case not of wanton killing but of capital punishment.[1] Punishment in the form of imprisonment drastically curtails the wrong-doer's liberty. But, because it is not arbitrary, it is not a violation of his right to freedom. This points to a fundamental limitation upon the morally permissible forms of punishment. They must not violate any of the wrong-doer's human rights – those to honourable treatment and civility being specially important because being especially at risk. None of this affects the moral forfeiture of particular social rights. Neither the drunken driver in losing his licence nor the erstwhile clubman in losing his rights as a member suffers any violation of human rights. Their moral status as human beings is unaffected.

But is depriving a man of membership of his native community compatible with respecting his human rights? Yes, provided that one of two conditions is satisfied. The first is that he has committed an offence, such as treason, the punishment for which is either death or life imprisonment without possibility of remission. The second that he is exiled to a country willing to take him in.

8.4 IMPLICATIONS AND AMPLIFICATIONS: SECOND STAGE

8.4.1   There is at least some common ground between the account of human rights presented here and the traditional doctrine of 'natural rights'. According to that doctrine, natural rights are inalienable. According to my account, human rights cannot be morally forfeited. This comes to the same thing. To say that a right is inalienable is to say that, no matter what he does, the right-holder cannot lose it, which means, among other things, that he can never morally forfeit it. This has implications for the denial–violation distinction. Because human rights are universal and can never be morally forfeited, the denial that some human beings possess them is necessarily false. Institutions and practices based upon and supported by appeals to such denials always, in fact, violate human rights. Because such institutions and practices are not only possible but historically not uncommon, the distinction is necessary in order to understand them and the character of the violations they perpetrate. In every version of the traditional doctrine, the rights asserted to be natural include the right to life and the right to freedom. Both are included in my list of seven main human rights. But in my account the right to freedom is the right to freedom from arbitrary interference, and what counts as 'arbitrary' is a matter of contextual interpretation. These qualifications are missing in the traditional doctrine. The only restriction upon the right to freedom is what is necessary to respect the natural rights of others. Neither the distinction between rules and principles nor the significance of moral diversity is properly appreciated in any of its versions.

In most versions, the ownership of private property, together with its voluntary transfer by sale and gift, is a natural right. But not so in my account. Private property is not one of the seven main human rights. I have indeed contended (see 2.3.1) that some form of the institution of property is necessary for social life as such; but it can take different forms in different communities, which it takes depending upon a community's way of life, its economy and particular morality. To assert that 'private' property is necessary for social life as such is to deny that a commune or kibbutz, in which property is communally owned, is a possible form of social life. But there is no justification for this denial. In such a commune, clothing, tooth brushes and other personal items could be issued to individual members from communal stores in much the same way and upon similar terms as they are issued to soldiers in the army.[2] There are therefore no grounds for regarding 'private' property as a human right. But, in any community, the human right to civility requires respect for whatever property rights are recognised within it, provided that the universal minimum moral standard is not contravened. Thus, in a slave-owning community, respect for property rights does not entail an obligation to respect the rights of slave-owners over their slaves (see 8.2.5 above). Subject to this qualification, robbery in any community is a violation not only of a specific property right but also of the human right to civility. If, as is likely, it involves force or the threat of force, the human right to freedom from arbitrary interference is also violated. Theft involving deception is not only a violation of civility, but also, for obvious reasons, of the human right to honourable treatment.

In the American Declaration of Independence, Thomas Jefferson cited as one among certain inalienable rights with which all men had been endowed by their Creator a right to the pursuit of happiness. According to him, this was one of several 'self-evident truths'. Such a right is not, however, contained in any of the principles of universal morality. Historically, many Christian communities have been dedicated to the attainment of salvation, and to the worship and glorification of God, rather than to the pursuit of happiness. What according to Jefferson are self-evident truths in fact are statements of certain beliefs and values of eighteenth-century deism. He has presented as part of universal morality what belongs to a particular morality. The human right to freedom from arbitrary interference can be contextually interpreted to include a right to pursue happiness. But it can also be, and historically has been, interpreted in ways which exclude such a right. This comment upon Jefferson is applicable to all versions of the traditional doctrine of natural rights. Among the rights which they assert to be universal are some which have been drawn from a particular morality: for instance, the right to private property. As we have just seen, this is owing to a failure to appreciate the significance of moral diversity and also the distinction between principles and rules. This is also true of 'Natural Law', which is the logical foundation of any version of natural rights. In Natural Law theory, the necessity of morality for social life as such is understood, but not all the implications of the distinction between common and particular morality.

8.4.2   We have seen that the contextual interpretation of human rights means that what is a violation of a human right in one community is not necessarily so in another. This is illustrated by the institution of purdah. It greatly restricts the activities of the women subject to it. But these restrictions are prescribed by Islamic morality. In an Islamic community, they are not arbitrary and do not constitute a violation of the human right to freedom. But in contemporary Western society they would be arbitrary because having no justification in the prevailing post-Christian liberal morality. To attempt to impose them in Western Europe or North America would be a violation of the human right to freedom. Does this entail moral relativism? Moral relativism is a theory about moral diversity. According to it, differences in moral codes reflect cultural differences: that is, differences in ways of life and in their associated beliefs and values. Moral decisions, judgements and criticisms must necessarily be made in terms of the principles and rules of a particular moral code.[3] They are therefore relative to the culture which is the foundation of that code. It follows that moral codes cannot themselves be criticised on moral grounds. There is no rational basis for judging that Christian morality is morally superior to Islamic morality, or liberal morality to communist morality. They are simply different.

The answer is that what has been said here about moral diversity and the contextual interpretation of human rights entails a *qualified and limited version of moral relativism*. It is a *qualified* version because universal morality sets a minimum moral standard which every particular morality is morally required to meet. If a particular morality fails to meet this standard – for instance, by permitting slavery and thereby falsely denying human rights to certain human beings – it is for that reason morally defective and morally inferior to every morality which satisfies the morally required minimum. But the account is still a version of *relativism*, because universal morality only sets a minimum standard. It cannot be the rational basis for the moral criticism of moralities which satisfy the minimum and do not deny human rights to any human beings. They are simply different moralities about which universal morality has nothing to say. This version of relativism is *limited* because it does not exclude a non-moral rational basis for the criticism of moralities which satisfy the moral minimum. That there is such a basis can be shown by recalling what was said in Chapter 4 about religion and ideology.

We saw there that religious belief is extra-rational. It requires a 'leap of faith' and to refrain from making the leap is not irrational. Reason cannot go beyond agnostic humanism. It follows that a community in which no religious commitment is required and in which religious diversity is permitted is more enlightened than one in which all are required to subscribe to the tenets of a particular religion. The first is more enlightened because its way of life embodies a better understanding of the nature and significance of religion than does that of the second. This does not mean that the first community is morally superior to the second. It means only that, with respect to religion, its particular morality is more enlightened. All this is equally true of ideology. We have seen that there is no justification for the characteristic ideological demand for total commitment. A community whose way of life is centred round a single monolithic ideology and requires total commitment from all its members to that ideology's programmatic prescriptions is less enlightened than one which does not require ideological uniformity and permits, or at least tolerates, the expression of different opinions on political and social matters. Assuming that in both communities the universal minimum moral standard is met, the second is not morally superior to the first. But, on the subject of political and social opinions, the particular morality of the second is more enlightened than that of the first.

8.4.3 All this applies to the contextual interpretation of human rights. From what has just been said, it follows that the interpretation of the right to freedom is more enlightened when it includes the right to religious freedom than when it does not; more enlightened when it includes the right to hear and express different social and political opinions than when it does not. The interpretation of the right to aid is more enlightened when it entitles those in need to help from public social services than when it does not, so forcing the needy to rely upon private charity. The first interpretation is more enlightened because it shows a better understanding of human vulnerability and human dignity. The interpretation of the right to fair treatment is more enlightened when it entitles women to the same educational and career opportunities as men than when it entitles men to more and better opportunities. The first interpretation is more enlightened because it recognises that intelligence and talent are not related to sex. But what is the situation when certain people become aware of a more enlightened interpretation of a particular human right than that which currently prevails in their community? Suppose that certain women in a community in which men enjoy superior educational and career opportunities become dissatisfied and demand to have the same opportunities. Their demand presupposes a more enlightened interpretation of the right to fair treatment than that which is endorsed by their community's particular morality. Can it be morally acceptable to their fellow members?

Not if the different educational and career opportunities for men and women are contained in the instructions for living of a single religion which is the foundation of their community's particular morality. The demand cannot be morally acceptable, because it is incompatible with these instructions and therefore with their community's particular morality. The same is true when the different opportunities are laid down in the programmatic prescriptions of a single ideology to which the community is officially dedicated. The demand cannot be morally acceptable because it is contrary to these prescriptions and therefore to the community's officially approved moral code. It will be morally acceptable in a community whose way of life and particular morality incorporate the standpoint of agnostic humanism. According to that standpoint it is up to human beings to make the most of human life (see 4.1.3 above). The community is therefore morally committed to reforming any of its institutions and practices which can be shown to prevent its members from making the most of human life. The more enlightened the interpretation of human rights in such a community, the better the prospects of its members for making the most of human life. In our present example, women are likely to be able to contribute more if they have the same educational and career opportunities as men. Hence, in such a community, any demand which presupposes a more enlightened interpretation of a human right than that which currently prevails will be morally acceptable. Those who make it have a moral claim right not only to a fair hearing but, so far as practically possible, to have their demand met.

It follows that the critical scrutiny of existing institutions and practices must also be morally acceptable. The community's commitment to reforming any of them when the need for it has been shown entails that the members must be free to show that there is such a need. They must therefore have the moral right to scrutinise and criticise existing institutions and practices. This is a Hohfeldian power right. Its correlate is the liability to critical scrutiny of those who are in authority in existing institutions and practices. They have no moral immunity right exempting them from such scrutiny, and, when it is justified, they have an obligation to respond constructively to criticism. The right to criticise, however, is only one aspect of the wider right to freedom of expression and inquiry. From the standpoint of agnostic humanism, this wider right is justified because it increases the opportunities of human beings to make the most of human life.[4] How to make the most of human life is an open question to which there is no final or definitive answer. Hence the need for freedom of expression and inquiry, so that every possibility can be discussed and critically assessed. This has implications for the interpretation of the human right to freedom. An interpretation which includes freedom of expression and inquiry is more enlightened than one which does not.

8.4.4   A qualification must be made to what has been said about a community's particular morality incorporating the standpoint of agnostic humanism. In an actual community, this may well be a matter of degree: the question being not whether, but to what extent, that standpoint is incorporated. This is because, as we saw in Chapter 3 (see 3.4.2), a community's particular morality is the outcome of its history and is likely to contain discrepancies. Consider contemporary Western national communities. Historically they were professing Christian communities, although in most cases there was by no means unanimity either within or betweeen them about the correct interpretation of Christian teaching. Recently they have been becoming increasingly secularised, and with that increasing secularisation the standpoint of agnostic humanism has come to be increasingly incorporated into their respective particular moralities. This means that demands for social change which presuppose a more enlightened interpretation of human rights than that currently prevailing will receive a mixed reception. They will be morally acceptable to those who are already *de facto* agnostic humanists, morally unacceptable to those who are still seriously trying to live according to Christian teaching and for whom the currently prevailing interpretation embodies that teaching as they understand it. An example is the demand, in what historically has been a Roman Catholic country, for legislation authorising civil marriage and divorce.

The demand is for an expansion of the right to freedom. People are to be legally entitled to marry without a religious ceremony, to terminate their marriage under certain specified conditions and thereafter to remarry. The specified conditions must include adequate provision for any children of the marriage, so that the human right of children to care is not violated. There are two main reasons why the right to freedom thus expanded is more enlightened. The first has to do with the right to civil marriage, the second with the right to divorce and to remarry. The first recognises the extra-rational character of religious belief, and that there is no rational justification for requiring non-believers to go through a religious ceremony. The right to divorce and to remarry recognises that marriages can break down and that there is no rational justification for denying people the opportunity to try again with different partners. The enactment of these rights into law in no way detracts from the intrinsic value of marriage, but its vicissitudes and the pain of an unhappy union are recognised and legal remedies made available. Nor is the position of practising Roman Catholics adversely affected. They continue to be legally entitled to marry and to maintain family life according to Catholic teaching. The fact that civil marriage and divorce have now become legally available does not mean that they are required to avail themselves of them. On the contrary, they have a moral obligation, arising from their religious commitment, to refrain from doing so. But the position of non-Catholics has improved. They are no longer required to accept the Roman Catholic version of marriage: a version which they do not share and which Roman Catholics have no rational justification for imposing upon them.

If practising Catholics are unconvinced by these arguments, that does not invalidate them. But it may adversely affect the prospects of changing the law to permit civil marriage and divorce. Whether it does depends upon the political power of Catholics and more especially of the Church. One indication of the extent to which a community's particular morality incorporates the standpoint of agnostic humanism is the political position within it of organisations committed to maintaining religious or ideological orthodoxy. The more the standpoint has come to be incorporated, the less the political power of such organisations, and the better the prospects for reforms reflecting a more enlightened interpretation of human rights. The prospects for such reforms are better where, as in contemporary Western nations, the form of government is democratic. Democratic political procedures provide for the criticism and reform of existing institutions and practices. A democratic form of government is, however, no guarantee that the standpoint of agnostic humanism is widespread in the community. The Irish Republic has had a democratic form of government for two generations. During this period no less than previously, its particular morality has remained centred upon Roman Catholicism. At the time of writing, there is no civil marriage or divorce in the Irish Republic.

8.4.5   My account of human rights as a minimum standard enables two questions to be asked about every community. Does its way of life, with its particular morality, institutions and values, deny any of the seven main human rights to any human being? How enlightened is the interpretation of each human right currently prevailing within it? The traditional doctrine of natural rights enables a question resembling the first to be asked: does the community's way of life deny any of those rights held to be natural to any human being? But it does not allow the second question to arise at all. This is because it fails to see that universal moral rights must be contextually interpreted. It fails to see this because, as we saw earlier, it fails to appreciate the significance of moral diversity and of the distinction between principles and rules. Neither the UN Declaration nor the European Convention enables the second question to be asked. That is, however, not surprising, since neither is concerned with human rights properly so-called – that is, universal moral rights (see Introduction). Neither of the two questions is excluded by the qualified, limited relativism which moral diversity entails. Answering them contributes to the understanding of that diversity. They do this by enabling the current state of human rights in actual communities to be critically assessed. To know that a community's present way of life denies certain human rights to certain human beings is to know that there is an important respect in which its way of life is morally defective. To know that the currently prevailing interpretation of human rights in a community is in various respects unenlightened is to know that there are ways in which its way of life can be improved even if there is little likelihood of such improvements coming about in the foreseeable future.

Supporters of the traditional doctrine of natural rights believed that it provided a moral foundation for politics, and were primarily concerned with its application to politics. Both the UN Declaration and the European Convention are political documents in the sense that they are primarily concerned with the scope and limits of government action. The implications for politics of my account of human rights have still to be considered. Before turning to that and as a preface to it, two matters are worth touching upon. The first is that it does not follow that, because the currently prevailing interpretation of human rights in a community is in various respects unenlightened, there must be some members who are dissatisfied with it. They may all accept it unreservedly, knowing it to be integral to a way of life which they value and are determined to preserve. Visitors to such a community who have acquired or been brought up with a more enlightened interpretation are not justified in trying to spread this among their hosts: for instance, by trying to get devout Catholics to agitate for civil marriage and divorce, or orthodox Muslim women to protest against purdah. My account of human rights does not justify what to the members of the community must appear as presumptious meddling. If a community's way of life commands widespread support among its members, then, subject to one proviso, the principle of civility requires respect for it from everyone else. If the prevailing interpretation of human rights is in various respects unenlightened, that is a matter for the members, not for outsiders. The proviso is that the community's way of life does not deny any of the seven main human rights to any human being. To the extent that it does, it morally forfeits respect. What outsiders can and should do about it is another question, but more about that in the next chapter.

The second arises out of something touched on near the end of the last chapter (see 7.3.5). Reference was there made to the case of a polarised community: that is, one which is deeply and painfully divided along racial, religious, linguistic or economic lines. It was there pointed out that, if people cannot agree about the terms upon which they are to live together, they will be unable to agree about the legal rights which they ought to have. A corollary to this is that they will be unable to agree about the interpretation of human rights. The interpretation which in fact prevails will be that which is acceptable to the dominant group: to Europeans in South Africa, to white Americans in the 'old South', to Protestants in Northern Ireland. This will be imposed upon the subordinate group: Africans in South Africa, blacks in the American South, Catholics in Ulster. In particular, because the subordinate group rejects the status in the community imposed upon it by the dominant group, there will be disagreement between them about the requirements of proportionate equality. They will have different ideas about the respects in which they are equal and unequal to one another, and there will therefore be no basis common to both groups for interpreting the right to fair treatment. It follows that human rights cannot provide the basis for healing the division in a polarised community. But it is still helpful in trying to understand the character of that polarisation to ask the two questions about the state of human rights in the community. What can be learned from answering them, however, can better be appreciated after the implications for politics of human rights properly so-called have been considered.

9 Human Rights and Politics

9.1 ON THE NATURE AND SIGNIFICANCE OF GOVERNMENT

9.1.1 Human rights are moral not political rights. People not only can live, but historically have lived, together without formal political organisation: for example, in communities of food-gatherers, hunters and nomads. There are therefore no political rights which people have solely in virtue of being human, no political rights which belong to them at all times and in all places. Only when contextual interpretation requires it can any human right be a political right. Today, however, nearly all human communities are governed communities. They take the form of nation states, of which there are now more than 150. This political organisation of social life has implications for the contextual interpretation of human rights. To understand them, something must be said about the institution of government, and in particular about its moral basis. We have already seen (in 8.2.2) that the principle of 'social responsibility' gives to a community a corporate power right which entitles it, through agents acting on its behalf, to organise and regulate the activities of its members to the extent that this is necessary to maintain and promote its interest. These agents are its government. A community has a government, that is to say, if there is within it an agency to which the exercise of its corporate power right is formally entrusted.

The correlate of a community's corporate power right is the liability of its members to have their activities organised and regulated. 'Social responsibility' requires them to accept this liability because it requires them to play their part in maintaining and promoting their community's interest, and to give it precedence over their personal and sectional interests whenever there is a conflict (see 2.3.2 above). Hence they have an obligation to obey the government, which, being entrusted with the exercise of the community's corporate power right, has authority to organise and regulate their activities. But, as an agency within the community, the government no less than the members is committed to the union of common with particular morality which constitutes the community's actual morality. It is entrusted with the exercise of the community's corporate power right and 'honourable conduct' requires it to be faithful to that trust. The scope of its authority is limited to what is necessary for the community's interest, which is also the interest of its members *qua* members although not always *qua* private persons. It must not shrink from unpopular measures if they are required by that interest. But 'justice' requires it to allocate fairly the sacrifices and burdens which such measures involve. To enable human rights to be interpreted in political contexts, however, the moral basis of government must be extended beyond the actual morality of a particular governed community to include universal morality. We already know that the requirements of the former are subordinate to those of the latter (see 8.1.1 above). Every government, whether or not it acknowledges them, is subject to the requirements of universal morality. Not only do they oblige it to do as much as it can to protect the human rights of everyone subject to its jurisdiction: they also oblige it always to respect and therefore never to do anything to violate the human rights of all with whom it has any dealings, those of foreigners no less than those of its own subjects. Before more can be said about the interpretation of human rights in political contexts, some other matters must be considered.

9.1.2   The interest of a community has both an internal and an external side. On its internal side it is an interest in all those conditions within the community which are most likely in the circumstances of the present and foreseeable future to enable all its members, not just particular groups and classes, to live as well as possible. In the modern world such conditions include, as a minimum, domestic peace and order and enough of the material necessities of life to maintain all of the population in physical and mental health, together with methods of production and distribution adequate to supply them (see 2.3.1 above). On its external side it is an interest in all those conditions abroad most favourable to its corporate security and prosperity. In the modern world, again as a minimum, these include safety from external attack, and access to foreign markets and to sources of raw materials not available at home. As the custodian of the community's interest at home and abroad, the government must have supreme authority within it to organise and regulate the activities of its members. But authority alone is not enough. If internal peace and order and external security are to be maintained, the government must have a monopoly of coercive power within the community. The community's corporate power right must entitle it to recruit, organise and maintain both police and military forces. But at all times both the police and the military must be subject to the government's authority. The coercive power they constitute is legitimate only so long as it is exercised under that authority.

We saw in Chapter 1 (see 1.1.2 and 1.3.1) that a legal system must contain secondary as well as primary rules. This, together with what was said in Chapter 7 about 'the rule of law' (see 7.1.3), shows what is necessary to make government possible. Government must be established by and derive its authority from the secondary rules of constitutional law. Its authority is supreme in virtue of 'the supremacy of law', the first of the three specific principles of 'the rule of law'. Hence, for government to be possible, a community must have a system of positive law and be morally committed to 'the rule of law'. This is, however, an oversimplified account. I have referred to government as an agency without distinguishing between its three branches: the legislative, the executive and the judicial. I have said nothing about the distinctive authority possessed by each. A full treatment of the institution of government would have to discuss these matters. Here, however, two comments must suffice. The first is to point out that legislative, executive and judicial authority presuppose constitutional law as their source.[1] Henceforth I shall use the term 'political authority' to refer to them collectively. The second is to emphasise the importance of the independence of the judiciary. Without it there is no protection from the abuse of legislative and executive authority and of the coercive power which reinforces executive authority.

Because political authority must be conferred by constitutional law, it follows that government properly so-called must be constitutional. A revolutionary government is therefore not strictly speaking a government at all. Through revolutionary action it has abolished or suspended the constitution and can have no *de jure* authority. At most it can have *de facto* authority in virtue of widespread popular support. To become legitimate and acquire *de jure* authority, it must establish a constitution and conform to its procedures. Many of today's legitimate governments began as revolutionary regimes, the government of the United States being perhaps the most famous example.[2] Like the community it governs, a government is morally committed to 'the rule of law'. What about an absolute monarchy? It is constitutional in the sense of being subject to constitutional laws prescribing hereditary succession to the throne. It is absolute in the sense that the monarch is above the law. He has an absolute immunity right conferred upon him by the constitutional axiom 'The king can do no wrong', exempting him from all legal proceedings irrespective of what he does and what is done in his name. The presumption is that the monarch will uphold 'the rule of law' in the exercise of his authority, and his coronation oath may well commit him to doing so. But, if he or his servants are corrupt, his subjects have no legal remedies. Absolute monarchy may be constitutional, but as a form of government it is defective. If 'the rule of law' is to be upheld, the constitution must ensure that no one is above the law. Those with political authority no less than those over whom they exercise it must be subject to legal proceedings. The importance of this for the legal protection of rights, including human rights, is obvious.

9.1.3   We can learn more about poltiical authority by considering briefly a distinction between what I shall call 'custodial' and 'operational' authority. They are two ways of being 'in authority'. To have the custody of something is to be responsible for preserving and maintaining it. 'Custodial' authority is the authority which is necessary in a social context to carry out this responsibility. It is exercised over those people whose activities in that context must be organised and regulated to enable the responsibility to be carried out. Examples are a warden's authority in a hostel, a referee's in a game, and parents' in a family. The hostel is in the warden's custody, the rules of the game in the referee's, and the welfare of their children in the parents'. The warden's authority is exercised over the residents, the referee's over the players, and the parents' over their children. To be subject to custodial authority is to be subject to 'side constraints'.[3] The scope of custodial authority is limited to what is necessary for the responsibility of the particular custody to be carried out. Provided that the residents comply with the warden's requirements, they are free to lead their own lives and pursue their own activities. Provided that the players keep to the rules and obey the referee, they are free to adopt whatever tactis and make whatever moves they think best. Children are required to submit to parental control of their conduct, but it is they, not their parents, who are growing up, and as they grow up much of what they do and experience necessarily lies outside parental control.

To have operational authority is to be 'in authority' in a team of action.[4] An example is managerial authority in a commerical enterprise. The enterprise is the team of action and the management is in operational authority within it. That authority is excercised over the employees, whose role is to serve the enterprise by performing the tasks assigned to them by the management. Other examples are the command structure in a military unit, or on board ship, or in a fire brigade. A foreman in a work group has operational authority over the workers, a bureaucracy over the clerical staff. In each case there is a team of action with specific things to do. What makes each team capable of doing them is the operational authority within it. Those with that authority plan, organise and direct what is done by the members of the team acting together in combination. Without operational authority, they could not act together and so could not constitute a team. Operational authority does not consist of side constraints upon the activities of those subject to it. The members of the team are not free to pursue their own activities provided that they comply with it. *Qua* members, they have no activities of their own to pursue. They have only their respective parts to play in the combined activity of the team: parts which are assigned to them by, and performed under the direction of, those in operational authority in the team.

That political authority is custodial not operational is implicit in 'freedom under the law', the third of the three specific principles of 'the rule of law' (see 9.1.2 above). The law imposes side constraints upon the activities of those subject to it. Where it is silent, they are free to act according to their own choice and decisions. I anticipated this conclusion earlier in this chapter when I referred to government as the custodian of its community's interest. Because government is subject to 'the rule of law', the measures it takes to maintain and promote that interest must be legally authorised. They include measures to organise and maintain teams of action: for example, the police, the armed forces, social-welfare services and an education system. No community is as such a team of action. It is a group of people living together, not a group of people acting in combination to do specific things. But people who live together must satisfy their biological needs if they are to survive. For this purpose they must form teams of action, or, in the case of a simple community, a single team of action – for example, of food-gatherers, of hunters, of herdsmen. It follows that in every community there must be operational authority to run the teams of action necessary for its survival. For obvious reasons there must also be custodial authority in the form of parental authority.

But, as we have seen, there does not have to be political authority. Social life is possible without it (see 9.1.1 above). It is needed whenever social life becomes too complex for the members of a community to decide for themselves as individuals how best to maintain and promote its interest. Without political authority, social life is likely to remain on a small scale and close to the margin of subsistence, or so the examples of communities of food-gatherers, hunters and nomads suggest. Political organisation can, however, be a matter of degree. A community may have the rudiments of government in the form of a customary legal system and a judiciary, without the legislative and executive authority which constitutes 'full-blown' government. To what extent the social life of medieval Europe was politically organised is a question which cannot be pursued here. The answer turns upon how far the feudal system was one of custodial authority as well as being one of operational authority. The custodial character of political authority has implications for the contextual interpretation of human rights. But a characteristic feature of that distinctively twentieth-century phenomenon the totalitarian state is that within it the community is thought of as primarily a team of action and political authority as primarily operational. But more about that and its implications for human rights in a moment.

9.2   POLITICAL RIGHTS AND HUMAN RIGHTS

9.2.1   There can be political rights only in a politically organised community or state. They are the rights possessed by the government and the governed in their respective capacities. What they are in detail depends upon a state's particular form of government. We already know (see 9.1.2) that government is established by and derives its authority from positive law, and that both government and governed are morally committed to 'the rule of law'. We saw in Chapter 7 (see 7.1.3) that, if a community is to maintain a system of positive law, every member must have a right to the equal protection of the law and a general right to legal liberty; that is, to freedom under the law. These are contained in two of the three specific principles of 'the rule of law': equality before the law, and freedom under the law. There are therefore two political rights which in virtue of being subject to political authority every member of a state must have, irrespective of its particular form of government. They are the two constitutional rights to the equal protection of the law and to freedom under the law, 'constitutional' for reasons which will be given in a moment. Those who govern are entitled to do so through having been appointed by procedures laid down in constitutional law: for example, hereditary succession to the throne in a monarchy, election by universal suffrage in a democracy. Their particular rights as governors, what in particular they are entitled to do in virtue of their various offices, are prescribed by the law. But, being morally committed to 'the rule of law', they have an obligation always to act lawfully and, in particular, always to respect the constitutional rights of all their subjects.

The right to freedom under the law is a general liberty right, limited only by the general obligation to obey the law. It is also an immunity right. You are entitled to immunity from any interference with your freedom of action which is not legally authorised. The right is inherent in the custodial character of political authority. We saw in the last section (9.1.3) that law imposes side constraints upon the activities of those subject to it. Provided they comply with these, they are free to pursue their own purposes. This is why the right to freedom under the law is a constitutional right. It is part of what defines the status of a legal person: that is, a person subject to and the beneficiary of legal authority. You cannot have the status without having the right. The right to the equal protection of the law is primarily a claim right upon the executive and judicial branches of government. But it is also a power right entitling the right-holder to sue for civil wrongs. It is a constitutional right because it too is part of what defines the status of a legal person. To be a legal person is to be entitled to the impartial application of legal rules and therefore to the same protection which they afford to all who are subject to the law. It is, however, logically prior to the right to freedom under the law. If you are not entitled to the equal protection of the law, you cannot be entitled to immunity from any interference with your freedom of action which has not been legally authorised. You have no legal remedy against anyone who illegally interferes with your freedom of action, because, being denied the equal protection of the law, you have no legal remedies at all.

9.2.2 We saw in Chapter 7 (see 7.1.3) that the sources of the two constitutional rights are two principles of common morality interpreted in the context of positive law. These are 'justice as fair treatment' and 'freedom from arbitrary interference'. We saw in Chapter 8 (see 8.1.1) that these are also principles of universal morality. The rights to fair treatment and to freedom from arbitrary interference which they contain are universal moral rights — that is, human rights (see 8.1.5 and 8.2.3 above). Hence the two constitutional rights are what these two human rights become when interpreted in political contexts. This can be shown in another way. As human beings, all the people subject to a government's jurisdiction have the right to fair treatment. Suppose that a government witholds from some of them the protection of the law which it accords to the rest. This is unfair, because those to whom the protection is denied are as much in need of it as those who receive it. Although equal in the relevant respect, they are being treated unequally. In order to respect the human right to fair treatment of all subject to its jurisdiction, a government must extend the protection of the law to them all without exception. That means according to all of them the status of legal person, in virtue of which each of them is entitled to the equal protection of the law. This is what the human right to fair treatment becomes when interpreted in political contexts. But their status as legal persons also entitles them to freedom under the law. They have the right to immunity from any interference not authorised by the law. Suppose that a government interferes with the freedom of action of some of them without having the legal authority to do so. Such interference is arbitrary because not legally authorised. It is a violation not only of the right to freedom under the law of those who suffer it, but also of their human right to freedom from arbitrary interference. The right to freedom under the law is what the human right to freedom from arbitrary interference becomes when interpreted in political contexts.

Being a member of a state and having the status of a legal person within it are not the same. All members are legal persons, but not all legal persons are necessarily members. Some may be travellers in transit, some visitors, others resident aliens. If a government is to respect the rights to fair treatment and to freedom from arbitrary interference of all who are subject to its jurisdiction, it must not confine the status of legal person to members but accord it to all who enter its territory for as long as they remain. This does not mean that all who want to enter must be admitted. As the custodian of its community's interest a government is justified, if in its judgement that interest requires it, in controlling the entry of foreigners and prescribing the terms on which they can stay. The right to freedom from arbitrary interference does not entitle foreigners to unrestricted admission to any state they choose. Restrictions upon their entry are not arbitrary if they are in the community's interest. But 'fair treatment' requires that such restrictions should be impartially applied and must them-selves be fair. It also requires that the terms upon which those admitted are allowed to stay must be fair.

9.2.3   It is of course not only the terms upon which foreigners are allowed to stay which must be fair. So must be all the laws which the government is responsible for enforcing. They must take account in their prescriptions of all relevant equalities and inequalities. A qualification must also be added about freedom from arbitrary interference. It is not enough for interference with any legal person's freedom of action to be legally authorised. The legal side constraints which a community's corporate power right entitles its government to impose must be in the community's interest. If they are not, they are arbitrary. These considerations show that an important proviso about the content of the law must be added to what has been said about the status of legal person and the two constitutional rights which are part of that status. No law must be unfair to any legal person and none must arbitrarily interfere with the freedom of action of any legal person. If all who are subject to a government's jurisdiction have the status of legal person, if the proviso about the content of the law is satisfied, and if the government enforces the law honestly and impartially, then, so far as the government is concerned, the human rights to fair treatment and to freedom from arbitrary interference of all subject to its jurisdiction are being respected. It is doing all that can be required of it.

It is, however, not only these two but all seven human rights that universal morality requires a government to respect. The proviso must be expanded to meet this requirement. That means adding two further requirements – one negative, the other positive. The negative requirement is that no law shall prescribe conduct which is incompatible with respecting any of the seven human rights; the positive, that so far as possible the law shall protect human rights by making violations of them criminal offences and the civil law give practical effect to the entitlements they confer. We saw in Chapter 7 (see 7.3.4) that the rights which a community's positive law ought to secure to its members are those which serve the purposes of positive law, security and social co-operation. Security is the concern of the criminal law. It directly protects the right to life by prohibiting the taking of human life except in self-defence and as a legally authorised punishment. It contributes to the protection of the rights to honourable treatment and to civility by prohibiting theft, fraud, robbery and violence. Where resources permit, civil law can contribute to social co-operation by making legal provision for social-welfare services, thereby giving practical effect to the right to aid and the right of children to care. It can also contribute to protecting the right to civility by providing legal remedies for negligence, breach of contract, libel and the like. However, lack of resources and the fact that they have not contributed to their cost justify a government in excluding travellers, visitors and resident aliens from all or some social-welfare services.

9.2.4   Violations of human rights can be more or less serious.[5] Lying, rudeness and favouritism are violations of the rights to honourable treatment, to civility and to fair treatment. But, while frequently occurring in personal relations, they are not often serious. For the most part, they fall outside the scope of publicly enforceable rules. Hence they fall outside the legal protection which government can give to human rights. That is limited to what can be brought under such rules and, within this category, to what is serious: that is, violations of a kind which do serious harm to their victims. We saw in Chapter 7 (see 7.3.4) that in addition to the right to freedom from arbitrary interference, the right to life is necessary if there are to be any rights at all. But, although the right to life is one which the positive law of every state ought to protect, that does not make it a political right. The same is true of the human rights to aid, to honourable treatment, to civility and of children to care. While positive law can help protect them and give effect to what they entitle people to, that does not make them political rights. This is because they are not rights which are constitutive of the relationship between government and governed. They do not define the status of legal person, although they are rights which *qua* human beings all legal persons have.

The 'Bills of Rights' which are part of the constitutions of many states today are properly described as bills of the fundamental rights of the citizens of those states. If, as likely, they contain the two constitutional rights, they can truly be said to include two human political rights. But, unless they are confined to the two constitutional rights, they are not bills of human political rights, because they are not limited to the political rights which belong to human beings whenever and wherever they are subject to political authority. Human beings within a state who are denied the status of legal person and the two constitutional rights which define it are subject not to political authority but merely to political power. The rights to vote, to contest elections and to political free speech are rights of citizenship under a representative form of government, and in a democracy of all adult members of the state. But they are not human political rights, because they are not part of what defines the status of legal person. People can have that status and be members of a state without having those rights: for example, in a hereditary monarchy or aristocracy, or under a form of limited representative government in which citizenship is confined to a particular class. This is not to deny that representative democracy is desirable wherever social, economic and cultural conditions make it possible. It provides better remedies for human fallibility than any other form of government, and by extending citizenship to all members of the state makes possible a more enlightened interpretation of human rights. But that does not make the rights of democratic citizenship human political rights. They are not constitutive of the relationship between government and governed at all times and in all places, because not a necessary part of the status of a legal person.

9.2.5 In the last chapter I pointed out that the idea of human rights as a minimum standard enables two questions to be asked about every community. Does its way of life, with its particular morality, institutions and values, deny any of the seven main human rights to any human being? How enlightened is the interpretation of each human right currently prevailing within it? (See 8.4.5.) When the community is a state, these questions must be asked about its law and government. They are among its principal institutions and have a direct bearing upon respect for human rights within it. The discussion of this section has implications for the first question. It breaks into two. Are any human beings subject to the government's jurisdiction denied the status of legal person and the two constitutional rights? Are the requirements, negative and positive, of the proviso about the content of the law satisfied? This last also breaks into two. Does any law prescribe conduct which is incompatible with respecting any of the seven main human rights? Does the criminal law do all that it can to protect human rights? Questions must also be asked about how law and government work in practice. The status of legal person and the two constitutional rights may be formally guaranteed to everyone by the constitution. But, if the judiciary is corrupt, the right to the equal protection of the law may be violated so regularly in the case of a certain class of litigants that it is effectively denied. In the old South in the USA, all-white juries rarely if ever convicted a white man of an offence against a black, however strong the evidence pointing to a conviction.

When discussing the second question in the last chapter (see 8.4.5), I used two examples: equal educational and career opportunities for men and women, and civil marriage and divorce. Where the first exists, the interpretation of the right to fair treatment is more enlightened; where the second, the interpretation of the right to freedom from arbitrary interference. Whether in a state there is provision for civil marriage and divorce is a legal question. The law is likely also to be concerned with the actual educational and career opportunities open to men and women, and, if they are to be made equal, legal measures will be required. Asking how enlightened the currently prevailing interpretation of human rights in a state is necessarily involves inquiring into the content of its positive law and into how its law and government work in practice. This, together with what was said in the last paragraph, show that answering the two questions in the case of an actual state requires much detailed information. It cannot be undertaken here. But there are a number of political issues, both domestic and international, to the understanding of which the idea of human rights as a minimum standard has something to contribute. The rest of this chapter will be devoted to indicating what that is in the case of some of the more important of them. As we shall see, the idea has some value as an aid to the diagnosis of social and political ills, but it has rather less as a remedy.

9.3   DOMESTIC POLITICS AND HUMAN RIGHTS

9.3.1   We have seen that if 'the rule of law' is to be upheld, all those in a state with political authority must be subject to the law. To the extent that this is not the case – for example, in an absolute monarchy – the status of legal person is not secure. Not only the two constitutional rights but all human rights are at risk. Those who are above the law can violate them without their victims having an effective legal remedy (see 9.1.2 above). Under a revolutionary regime all human rights are necessarily at risk. This is because, as we have seen (in 9.1.2), a revolutionary government can have only *de facto* not *de jure* authority. 'The rule of law' is inoperative and there can be no status of legal person. The same is true in a dictatorship which is a stabilised revolutionary regime. This does not mean that revolution can never be morally justified. It may be the only way of ending a regime which, while nominally constitutional, has degenerated into a brutal and corrupt tyranny under which human rights are not only at risk but frequently violated. But it is important not to have any illusions about revolution. Because it entails putting all human rights at risk, it can be morally justified only as the lesser evil: that is, when human rights are not only at risk but are subject to frequent serious violations, or, in the case of some of the population, denied altogether.

All totalitarian regimes are dictatorships, but by no means all dictatorships are totalitarian. Earlier (in 9.1.3) I referred to a characteristic feature of totalitarian states: that in them the community is regarded primarily as a team of action and political authority as primarily operational. The purpose of the team is to construct a new social order according to ideological prescriptions: for example, to build socialism.[6] This is done under the direction of the totalitarian government, which has supreme operational authority over the team. Hence, under totalitarianism, the relation between the regime and its subjects is more like that between 'management' and 'managed' than between government and governed. Under a constitutional regime human rights are not at risk in the relation between management and managed because the latter have the status of legal persons and the protection which it affords. What the management can require of them is morally and legally limited to what is compatible with respecting that status. Under totalitarianism, 'the rule of law' is inoperative and there is no status of legal person. Consequently there are no legal and moral limits to what the regime as 'management' can require of its subjects as 'managed'. Their sole *raison d'être* is to serve the regime, the justification for this lying in the ideology which is the regime's moral foundation. The violations of human rights under totalitarianism – especially of the rights to life, to fair treatment, to freedom from arbitrary interference, and to civility – are notorious and need no comment here. Suffice it to point out that, because political authority is thought of as primarily operational, the occasion for and likelihood of such violations is all the greater.

9.3.2 Revolutionary government presupposes constitutional government in the sense that, unless a constitutional regime already exists, it can neither be abolished nor suspended by revolution (see 9.1.2 above). The origins of government logically cannot lie in revolution. Nor can they lie in conquest, although a particular regime may be inaugurated after the conquest of a hitherto ungoverned people by an already existing state (colonial regimes are an obvious example). A revolutionary government can become legitimate by establishing a constitution and conforming to its procedures (see 9.1.2 above). This may be some version of the constitution it has suspended or a brand new one. But in either case there must already be within the community a tradition of living according to law, and *a fortiori*, a practical understanding of 'the rule of law'. Such a tradition can be transmitted to a conquered people by conquerors within whose own community it already exists (as happened in the provinces of the Roman Empire). But, just because it is a tradition, it cannot be created *de novo*. It is not necessary for social life as such. There are many nation states today, notably in Latin America, in which it is far from being well established. How it can become established, what social, cultural and moral prerequisites must be met, are complex questions which cannot be pursued here. Suffice it to say that, in any community in which living according to law is not a well-established tradition, the status of legal person can at best be insecure, so that little or no effective legal protection can be given to human rights.

In the last chapter (see 8.4.5) I pointed out that in a polarised community human rights cannot provide a basis for healing the divide. The polarised groups cannot agree about their interpretation and that which prevails is that which is acceptable to the dominant group. Consequently human rights cannot receive effective legal protection, because there is disagreement about what counts as protecting them. Within the dominant group the tradition of living according to law may be well established, but the content of the law will reflect the social polarisation: apartheid in South Africa, racial segregation in the old

American South, the Special Powers Act in the former devolved regime in Northern Ireland. Members of the subordinate group may obey the law out of prudence, but they will not be morally committed to the regime it maintains. The origins of polarisation must be sought in the history of each polarised community, but knowledge of those origins, while affording a better understanding, cannot yield a remedy.

What is rather misleadingly called 'power-sharing' is sometimes recommended as a remedy. What is meant is that political authority should be shared between representatives of the polarised groups. The recommendation ignores what I shall call the paradox of power-sharing, which briefly is this: when power-sharing is needed, it won't work; when it will work, it isn't needed. The mutual hostility which occasions the need for it prevents it from working, while in the absence of such hostility ordinary political procedures will suffice. Power-sharing can indeed work if enough people on each side of the social divide are tired of polarisation and are willing to compromise in order to find common ground for co-operation. But power-sharing cannot create that willingness, nor can human rights. Invoking them cannot settle serious social and political disputes, because their contextual interpretation presupposes the absence of such disputes. What has been said in this and the last two paragraphs shows the limitations of the idea of human rights. If it is to make a significant contribution to the life of a state, two conditions must be satisfied. The first is that, within the community, the tradition of living according to law must be well established. The second is the absence of serious social and political conflicts. The idea of human rights can indeed aid in the diagnosis of social and political ills, but it is not a remedy for them.

9.3.3   Racial discrimination is a characteristic feature of a racially polarised community. I have already referred to apartheid and to racial segregation in the old American South (see 9.3.2). Racial discrimination is discrimination by the dominant racial group in a community against a subordinate racial group solely on the basis of the racial differences between them. Members of the former deny to members of the latter opportunities which they themselves enjoy in such fields as education, employment, housing and leisure. This is a violation of the human right to fair treatment, because equals are being treated unequally. As fellow human beings the members of both groups are equal in moral status, but the treatment which the members of the dominant group accord to the members of the subordinate group is different from and inferior to that which they accord to themselves. Purely physical differences such as colour, as distinct from differences of character and capacity, logically can have no moral relevance and so cannot justify unequal treatment. A theological justification of racial discrimination such as that propounded by the Dutch Reformed Church is morally defective. It fails to meet the requirements of the universal minimum moral standard.

A caste system is a hereditary hierarchical social order and hereditary differences are physical differences. But, provided that two conditions are satisfied, such a system does not of itself violate the human right to fair treatment, or any of the other human rights. The first is that the community is not polarised but united in maintaining a way of life in which the caste system is an integral part. The second is that the status assigned to each caste by the hierarchical social order gives to each caste a realistic opportunity of living well according to the values of the community's particular morality. There must be no 'untouchables'. A caste system which satisfies these two conditions satisfies the requirements of universal morality, but the social order which it constitutes, with its stratified rigidity, is far from being enlightened. That is not, however, a matter which can be pursued further here. Another physical difference between human beings is difference of sex. What has just been said about a caste system is equally applicable to any social order in which male and female roles are differentiated, social and political authority being the prerogative of one sex and submission to that authority the duty of the other. Again, provided that the two conditions are satisfied, so are the requirements of universal morality. Where the authority rests with men, feminists, with good reason, would condemn such a social order as unenlightened. They would, however, be mistaken if they contended that, of itself, it violated human rights.

Subject to an important proviso, compulsory religious uniformity does not violate any human rights. This is that the religion is genuinely universal, all human beings coming within its scope solely in virtue of being human. The killing of heretics and of those who refuse to see the light after it has been shown to them is not wanton. According to 'true believers', error has no rights. The duty of its victims once they have been informed of the truth is to accept it and mend their ways. The attitude of 'true believers' is that of those who accept the first answer to the question about religious diversity (see 4.1.2 above). While this is far from being an enlightened attitude, it meets the requirements of universal morality. As 'true believers', all human beings are fellow human beings. What is true of compulsory religious uniformity is also true of compulsory ideological uniformity, so long as the proviso about universality is satisfied. Universal ideological orthodoxy does not violate any human rights. As fellow adherents, all human beings are fellow human beings, but, if in either case the compulsion is imposed by a dictatorial regime, human rights will not only be at risk but are likely to be violated. Their violation, however, arises not from the requirements of compulsory religious or ideological uniformity but from the fact that those who impose the compulsion are above the law. Whether such compulsory uniformity can actually be secured except under a dictatorship is doubtful, but its possibility is at least conceivable. Hence the need to distinguish between the requirements of uniformity and the means of securing it, so far as the violation of human rights is concerned.

9.3.4   Earlier in this section (see 9.3.1) I pointed out that under a constitutional regime in the relation between 'management' and 'managed' the latter no less than the former have the status of legal persons and the protection which it affords. What the management can require of the managed is morally and legally limited to what is compatible with respect for that status. This suggests that, under a constitutional regime in which the proviso about the content of law is satisfied, the human rights of all who engage in commercial transactions are not at risk. Some qualifications, however, are necessary. In commercial transactions people deal with one another neither as fellow members of a community nor as fellow human beings, but simply as buyers and sellers. The principle of 'fellowship' has no application. I will sell to you only if you can pay. If you cannot, the fact that you are in distress and need what I am selling is commercially irrelevant. Nor are commercial transactions sufficient to ensure the implementation of the principle of 'child care'. Universal morality requires it to be implemented irrespective of commercial considerations. What is good commercially is not always, as such, good socially. A community's interest is not confined to conditions favourable to commercial prosperity. Government action is needed to regulate commercial transactions for the sake of non-commercial values such as health, social welfare and education, and conservation. This is a matter about which more clearly needs to be said. Here, however, it is enough to point out that, while commercial transactions can and should be limited to what is compatible with respect for human rights, they do not themselves provide for that respect in all cases. Both the right to aid and the right of children to care are excluded from a purely commercial perspective.

9.4   INTERNATIONAL RELATIONS AND HUMAN RIGHTS

9.4.1   In the last chapter I said that the global impact of modern technology means that, if humanity is to survive, let alone prosper, some form of international community is essential. I also said (see 8.2.2) that, while the United Nations is a far from perfect embodiment of a universal human community, it at least provides a context for the international application of social responsibility as a principle of universal morality. That principle, together with beneficence, requires national governments to interpret their responsibilities as members of the United Nations in ways which will make it a better embodiment of a universal human community – its present deficiencies in that respect being attributable not to any inherent defects in its structure and organisation, but to moral defects in some member nations and a less than complete commitment by many of them to the United Nations as an international community. We have now to consider the implications of the idea of human rights as a minimum standard for the conduct of international relations by governments genuinely committed to the United Nations and to realising its community potential. As a first step something must be said about the rights and obligations of nation states as members of an international community.

In virtue of that membership, national governments as agents of nation-states are committed to acting on the principles of common morality in all their dealings with one another. They have the rights and obligations contained in those principles, which, in the context of an international community, are the rights and obligations of corporate persons. The right to life is the right to national existence. This includes an immunity right and a power right. The former is the right to immunity from the jurisdiction of foreign governments and from coercion by them, the latter the right to resist such jurisdiction and coercion. The right to fair treatment includes a claim right to a fair hearing in international disputes and an immunity right from discrimination in international trade. The right to aid includes claim rights to help in natural disasters and to assistance in establishing and maintaining a viable national economy. The right to freedom from arbitrary interference includes a right to immunity from foreign interference in internal affairs, together with a power right to resist such interference. It also includes a liberty right to pursue domestic policies of the government's own choice, this being a corollary of the immunity right to non-interference. The right to honourable treatment includes a claim right to the observance of treaties and international agreements, and a right to immunity from foreign subversion. The right to civility includes a claim right to be treated according to established diplomatic procedures. The obligations correlative to these rights consist of the acts and forbearances necessary to respect them. As members of the international community, all governments are under these obligations in all their dealings with one another while having the rights to which they are correlative.

9.4.2 In the last chapter I pointed out that individual human beings are members of an international community only in virtue of their membership of individual nation states. Any human beings who, because of race, colour or creed, or for any other reason, are denied membership of the nation states in which they live, or who do not live in nation states at all, are thereby denied membership of that international community (see 8.2.2 above). This means that membership of an international community does not of itself commit a national government to respecting the rights of foreigners as individual human beings. It is committed only to respecting their rights as members of foreign nation states which are themselves members of the same international community. *Qua* member of an international community, a national government is not committed to respecting human rights as such. But universal morality requires it to respect them always and everywhere. It has an obligation not only so far as it can to protect the human rights of its own subjects, but in its foreign policy always to treat all foreigners as fellow human beings and therefore always to respect their human rights. Because of its universality, the requirements of universal morality take precedence over those of the international morality of an international community. National governments have an obligation to exercise their rights as members of that community only in ways which are compatible with respecting human rights always and everywhere.

Does this mean that a national government which violates the human rights of some of its own subjects – for example, through racial discrimination or by imprisoning alleged dissidents without trial and torturing them – thereby morally forfeits its immunity right to non-interference? According to international morality, that right disables foreign governments from interfering in its internal affairs. Does the human right of the victims to aid put foreign governments under an obligation to help them, if necessary at the expense of the right to non-interference? They clearly have an obligation to do what they can to help by peaceful means. Such means, however, are limited to granting asylum to refugees, to initiating or supporting commercial and cultural boycotts, and to trying to persuade the offending government and its supporters of the wrong they are doing.[7] These are attempts to influence domestic policy rather than a direct interference with it. Why must help be confined to peaceful means? Why should not foreign governments not themselves guilty of serious human-rights violations declare war on the offending government and either force it to mend its ways or replace it by one which will respect the human rights of all its subjects? If a government is committing genocide against an ethnic minority of its subjects, in what other way can foreign governments help?

According to the principles of fellowship, freedom from arbitrary interference and civility, physical force against human beings is justified only to resist unprovoked physical force. In the context of an international community, this means that a state is justified in going to war only in self-defence against aggression from another state and to assist a state which is already the victim of aggression. Foreign governments are therefore justified in declaring war on the offending state only if it is committing aggression against other states. According to international morality, the fact that it is violating the human rights of its own subjects is not in itself a justification. It morally forfeits its immunity right to non-interference only if it is committing aggression, and if interference in its internal affairs is necessary to stop it. Can what is wrong according to international morality ever be right according to universal morality? Only if war against the offending state is a lesser evil than the violation of human rights of which that state is guilty. But in warfare the combatants cannot respect one another's human rights. They are enemies, the aim of each being the physical subjugation of the other. Hence war as a means of securing respect for human rights has the drawback that it necessarily involves not respecting them.[8] We already know that in the modern world some form of international community is essential for human survival (see 8.2.2 above and 9.4.4 below). War by its nature endangers an international community. When undertaken to resist aggression it may be the lesser evil. But, as a means of securing respect for human rights, it is likely to be a greater evil than the violation of them in a particular state.

9.4.3 International law and the conventions of diplomacy provide a framework for the contextual interpretation of the rights of nation states. But, while this framework can help to contain international conflicts, it lacks the authority and power to settle them. Hence the ubiquity of war as the ultimate arbiter of international conflicts. The existence of an international community does not prevent international conflicts. In the economic sphere, national self-interest and an international community's interest are not identical.[9] A nation's interest abroad is in conditions which will enable it to prosper, not in conditions which will enable all nations to prosper. There is no international pre-established harmony which guarantees that what promotes one nation's prosperity necessarily promotes the prosperity of all. But, while there is often an economic dimension, not all international conflicts are economic in origin. Many arise from deeply felt grievances about past wrongs, real or imagined; many from long-standing religious and, especially today, ideological hostility. Others again arise in the aftermath of revolution and civil war. International law and diplomatic conventions may be insufficient to enable the parties to an international conflict to agree about the interpretation of their respective rights and obligations. What to one nation is aggression is to another the legitimate defence of its vital national interests, or the justified rectification of a past wrong. When what counts as fair is in dispute, appeals to the right to fair treatment will be unavailing.

The international community today is comparable to a polarised community writ large. Not only are there many conflicts of national interest: different traditions of culture and civilisation have generated different and in some respect conflicting particular moralities. Most nation states today acknowledge the rights and obligations of membership of an international community. Too much, however, should not be expected from this acknowledgement. Nor, after what has been said in this section, should too much be expected from the idea of human rights. Yet it should not be wholly discounted, for it receives at least some recognition in international relations today. In conventional warfare, the distinction between combatants and non-combatants is widely acknowledged. So are the rights of neutrals and of prisoners of war. The moral basis of the first is the human right to life; of the second, the human right to fair treatment; of the third, the human rights to life, to honourable treatment and to civility. There is also widespread recognition internationally of the human right to aid of the victims of natural disasters and accidents and of the casualties of war and revolution.

9.4.4   We have seen (in 9.4.2) that, although in warfare the combatants cannot respect one another's human rights, war undertaken to resist aggression can be the lesser evil. Universal morality, however, imposes an additional requirement. The human rights of enemy non-combatants and of neutral foreigners must always be respected. The destructive power of modern nuclear weapons means that in nuclear warfare this requirement cannot be met. The distinction between enemy combatants and non-combatants is obliterated. Neutral foreigners have to suffer nuclear fall-out and the ensuing environmental damage. Hence, according to universal morality, nuclear war can never be the lesser evil, because to resort to it is to disrgard the right to life of enemy non-combatants and of neutral foreigners.[10] International morality points to the same conclusion. An international community can tolerate conventional war because it allows neutral foreigners to remain substantially unharmed. But this is not true of nuclear war. No nation can be morally justified in protecting its own existence by means which do serious harm to neutral nations. Nor does universal morality justify a nuclear second strike in response to a nuclear first strike. It is sheer vengeance and we already know that there is no human right to revenge.

We have seen (in 9.4.3) that most national governments today acknowledge the rights and obligations of membership in an international community, and that the idea of human rights as a minimum standard receives some recognition by many of them. That nuclear war is morally unacceptable is not, however, admitted by national governments with a nuclear capacity. For them to admit it would be to admit that their nuclear defence policies of deterrence are based on bluff. They are unlikely to admit this to themselves, let alone to potential enemies. Today the roughly equal nuclear capacities of the North Atlantic Treaty Organisation and the Warsaw Pact governments, and the 'mutually assured destruction' which it entails mean that it is not in either side's interest to initiate nuclear warfare. While these conditions hold, prudence, let alone morality, requires the maintenance of nuclear peace. But prudence also encourages each side to try to achieve nuclear superiority over the other. Hence the 'arms race' in which both are currently embroiled. Prudential considerations foster short-run stability but long-run instability. But such instability cannot be in the interest of an international community. International morality requires the governments on each side to transcend their mutual hostility to the extent necessary to enable them to agree on practical measures to halt the arms race. How to meet this requirement is a challenge to creative international statesmanship.

The requirement is also one of universal morality, since, if humanity is to survive, some form of international community is essential (see 8.2.2 and 9.4.1 above). But meeting it entails acquiescing in, although not condoning, the violation of human rights and perhaps even their denial, notwithstanding the respect for human rights always and everywhere required by universal morality. Such acquiescence is necessary to reach agreement with dictatorships and totalitarian regimes about practical measures to halt the arms race. Universal morality sanctions it as the lesser evil. The idea of human rights as a minimum standard is less than a complete guide to the conduct of international relations. But it is vital for the understanding of international moral issues – showing, for instance, why nuclear war is morally unacceptable. This is not dissimilar to its significance in domestic politics. It is an aid in the diagnosis of social and political ills but not a remedy. To understand both the significance and the limitations of the idea of human rights has been the aim of this book. To try to make it carry more weight than it can bear is a mistake. But to deny that it can carry any at all, to dismiss it as wholly vacuous, is also a mistake.

Notes

INTRODUCTION

1. I pass over the question of whether there is a communist tradition of culture and civilisation, for two reasons. One is that, since communism has been imposed upon the peoples who live under it, whether it can be considered a tradition is questionable. Admittedly both Christianity and Islam were imposed upon many peoples in the first place but over centuries came to be accepted. There has not been enough time since the imposition of communism for this to happen. The other is that, since communist ideas and values originated in the West, there is a case for regarding communism as a Western heresy. But I shall not pursue that here.
2. This and the subsequent quotations from MacIntyre are all from *After Virtue: A Study in Moral Theory* (London: Duckworth, 1981) pp. 67ff.

CHAPTER 1: RULES, PRINCIPLES AND CONDUCT

1. A similar distinction is drawn by H. L. A. Hart in *The Concept of Law* (Oxford: Clarendon Press, 1961).
2. See J. R. Searle, *Speech Acts* (Cambridge University Press, 1969).
3. Jeremy Bentham, *An Introduction to the Principles of Morals and Legislation* (1789).
4. A. V. Dicey, *Introduction to the Study of the Law of the Constitution*, 8th edn (London: Macmillan, 1920).
5. John Rawls, 'Two Concepts of Rules', *Philosophical Review*, 1955.
6. This appears to be Peter Winch's view in his book *The Idea of a Social Science* (London: Routledge & Kegan Paul, 1958) and in his essay 'Authority' in *Political Philosophy*, ed. A. Quinton (Oxford University Press, 1967). He does not distinguish between rules and principles. Rather he seems to assimilate them, and that, for the reasons given above, cannot be right.
7. I take self-discipline to be more than self-control because it involves attention to and concentration upon particular tasks, rather than merely controlling one's feelings.
8. Plato makes this point both in the *Gorgias*, during the discussion between Socrates and Gorgias, and in *The Republic*, book I, during the discussion with Polemarchus.

CHAPTER 2: MORALITY AND SOCIETY

1. See J. O. Urmson 'Saints and Heroes', in *Essays in Moral Philosophy*, ed. A. I. Melden (Oxford: Basil Blackwell, 1958).
2. What is said here is confined to the logical relation between 'obligation' and 'saintliness' and 'heroism'.

3. See Immanuel Kant, *Fundamental Principles of the Metaphysic of Morals*, tr. T. K. Abbott, 10th edn (London: Longman) section 2.
4. In some cases, others can release him: for instance, a promisee can release a promisor from his obligation but the promisor cannot release himself.
5. See A. J. M. Milne, *Freedom and Rights* (London: Allen & Unwin, 1968) ch. 3, for a fuller discussion of these matters.
6. Thomas Hobbes, *Leviathan*, ed. Oakeshott (Oxford: Basil Blackwell, 1946) p. 82.
7. Ibid., p. 82.
8. Plato, *The Republic*, tr. H. D. P. Lee (Harmondsworth: Penguin, 1955) book 1.
9. See ibid., book 2.
10. What has been said here about the interest of a community and the interest of its members is a statement of analytic truth. It states some of the implications of the concepts of 'community', of 'membership' and of 'interest' as they are ordinarily used. 'Interest' is taken to mean an interest in conditions which are favourable for, or advantageous to, the subject whose interest it is.
11. Technological innovation leading to increased productivity may make it possible in the course of time for all to have more, but it will take time and, in the short run, what is said in the text stands.
12. Cf. H. Sidgwick's account of egoism in *The Methods of Ethics*, book 1, 7th edn (London: Macmillan, 1967).
13. See Searle, *Speech Acts*, and also his essay 'How to Derive an "Ought" from an "Is"', repr. in *Ethics*, ed. P. Foot (London: Oxford University Press, 1967).

CHAPTER 3: MORAL UNIVERSALITY AND MORAL DIVERSITY (i)

1. This may not always be formulated explicitly in terms of the concept of 'obligation', but the central idea in that concept, that of 'the right thing to do', is universal.
2. This term was coined by Maurice Ginsberg. See his 'The Diversity of Morals', in *Essays in Sociology and Social Philosophy* (London: Heinemann, 1957) vol. I.
3. Geographical, climatic and economic factors have also played a part. How they have done so is, however, a matter for detailed empirical inquiry and falls outside the scope of this book.
4. John Rawls, *A Theory of Justice* (Oxford University Press, 1971).
5. Aristotle, *Nicomachean Ethics*, book 5. I am here thinking along the same lines as Aristotle and am obviously indebted to him. 'To each his due' is my version of his 'particular justice'. The common ground between us is 'proportionate equality', but in my exposition of that principle in the next section of this chapter, I do not follow him in detail.
6. It is part of the concept of 'compensation' that the kind and degree must be in proportion to the culpable harm suffered. Too much, too little or the wrong kind is not compensation properly so-called. The idea of fairness is thus an integral part of the concept of 'compensation', and this reinforces the points in the text: that decisions about the kind and amount of compensation must be made according to the proportionate-equality principle.

7.   I leave aside the special case of an association the purpose of which is the promotion of the welfare of children.

8.   As a constitutive rule, the prohibition of rape is comparable to the prohibition of theft. Without the latter, there could be no such institution as property at all. Without the former, there could be no sexual 'conduct' properly so-called: that is, no orderly practice of sexual relations.

CHAPTER 4: MORAL DIVERSITY (ii): RELIGION AND IDEOLOGY

1.   What is said here is only what is necessary to understand religious morality. It is not a complete account of the nature of religion. However, I think what is said is correct so far as it goes and should find a place in an adequate account.

2.   I borrow Sir James Jeans's title but without committing myself to any of the substantive doctrines of his book.

3.   It may be objected that a community which compels a section of its members to live according to a religious creed which they do not share is for that reason a most unenlightened community. Agreed, but it is still a community, albeit an unenlightened one. More about this later: see 8.4.3.

4.   H. A. L. Fisher, *A History of Europe*, vol. I: *Ancient and Medieval* (London: Edward Arnold, 1943) ch. XIV, p. 170.

5.   A high proportion of the population of Britain today profess to be Anglicans. But of these only a low proportion, about 10 per cent, are regular church-goers.

6.   Karl Marx and Friedrich Engels, *The German Ideology*, trs. from the German, ed. by S. Ryazanskaya (Moscow: Progress Publishers, 1964), Karl Mannheim, *Ideology and Utopia* (London: Routledge & Kegan Paul, 1966).

7.   P. Corbett, *Ideologies* (London: Hutchinson, 1965) p. 11.

8.   Alasdair MacIntyre, *Against the Self-Images of the Age* (London: Duckworth, 1971) p. 5.

9.   Kenneth R. Minogue, *The Concept of a University* (London: Weidenfeld & Nicolson, 1973) p. 151.

10. See John Hospers, *Libertarianism: A Political Philosophy for Tomorrow* (Los Angeles: Nash, 1971) for a lucid and forceful statement.

11. See Karl Marx and Friedrich Engels, *The Communist Manifesto* (1848).

12. See Robert P. Wolff, *In Defence of Anarchism* (New York: Harper 1970).

13. See H. J. Laski, *A Grammar of Politics* (London, 1925); and G. D. H. Cole, *Social Theory* (London: Library of Social Studies, 1920).

14. Quoted by W. B. Gallie in *A New University: A. D. Lindsay and the Keele Experiment* (London: Chatto & Windus, 1960).

15. Sir Isaiah Berlin, *Two Concepts of Liberty* (Oxford University Press, 1958) p. 52.

16. See Eric Hoffer, *The True Believer* (New York: Mentor Books, Harper & Row, 1951).

CHAPTER 5: MORALITY AND THE 'CATEGORICAL IMPERATIVE'

1.   Immanuel Kant, *Philosophy of Law: An Exposition of the Fundamental Principles of Jurisprudence as the Science of Right*, tr. W. D. Hastie (1887) p. 33.

2.   These are my words not Kant's, but they successfully capture his meaning.
3.   According to Kant, this is not so. Because lying cannot be universalised, its prohibition is absolute. There is an obligation to tell the truth, even to a would-be murderer in search of his intended victim. See Immanuel Kant, *Fundamental Principles of the Metaphysic of Ethics*, tr. T. K. Abbott, 10th edn (London: Longman).
4.   Ibid., p. 56, Section II.
5.   G. E. Moore to the contrary notwithstanding: if I understand him, Moore contends in his *Ethics* (Oxford University Press, 1958) that something can have intrinsic value even if there is no one who values it, which is at variance with our ordinary ideas about intrinsic value. What I have said here is based upon C. I. Lewis's account in his *Analysis of Knowledge and Valuation* (La Salle, Ill.: Open Court Publishing, 1950).
6.   Cf. Shylock in *The Merchant of Venice*, III.i: 'Hath not a Jew eyes, hath not a Jew hands, organs, dimensions, senses, affections, passions, fed by the same food, hurt by the same weapons, subject to the same diseases, healed by the same means, warmed and cooled by the same winter and summer, as a Christian is? If you prick us, do we not bleed? If you tickle us, do we not laugh? If you poison us, do we not die? And if you wrong us, shall we not revenge? If we are like you in the rest, we shall resemble you in that.'
7.   Aristotle, *Politics*, book 1.

CHAPTER 6: THE IDEA OF RIGHTS (i)

1.   D. D. Raphael, *Problems of Political Philosophy* (London: Macmillan, 1970) pp. 68–70.
2.   This is a corollary of the principle of beneficence.
3.   Karl Welman, 'A New View of Human Rights', in *Human Rights*, ed. S. Kamenka (London: Edward Arnold, 1978).
4.   The examples are mine, not Hohfeld's. They include moral as well as legal rights in order to show that his analysis holds of rights as such, irrespective of their source.
5.   Raphael, *Problems of Political Philosophy*, pp. 68–70.
6.   This regulation was in effect during the Second World War, as I know from personal experience. So far as I know, it is still in force today.
7.   This does not mean that no immunity right can be universal. As we shall see in Chapter 8, there are some which are.
8.   Or, in the case of a legal right, having a contractual undertaking performed.

CHAPTER 7: THE IDEA OF RIGHTS (ii): ON THE SOURCES AND SIGNIFICANCE OF SOCIAL RIGHTS

1.   We have already seen in 1.3.1 that law and morality contain rules and principles. That the same is true of custom will be seen in section 7.2.
2.   For all references in this sub-section to the logical characteristics of constitutive and regulative rules, see 1.1.2 above.

3. If ecclesiastical authority has jurisdiction within a community with a system of positive law, it must be recognised and itself be authorised by the system. The same is true of the jurisdiction of international agencies.

4. Such power rights entitle people to protection from illegal government action: for instance, to sue officials for acting *ultra vires*. This illustrates Hohfeld's point that what appears to be a single right turns out to be a cluster of rights. However, the general right to the equal protection of the law is first and foremost a claim right.

5. This information is elliptical. A fuller statement is, 'What is said to the priest in the confessional, is said in absolute confidence and he must therefore never betray it.' For the sake of brevity, I use the elliptical formulation.

6. Statements of brute facts contain necessary descriptive truths as well as contingent truths. If John Doe is 6 feet tall, it is necessarily true that he is more than 5 feet tall. This is entailed by the constitutive rules of arithmetic. The point is not that the contingent truths in statements of brute fact do not entail necessary truths, but that these truths are not prescriptive.

7. Fyodor Dostoyevsky, *The House of the Dead*, tr. Constance Garnett (London: William Heinemann, originally published 1915).

8. Compare this with what is said in 4.1.4 above, about the origins of religion.

9. Among other things, a full account would have to say something about custom in relation to tradition. This cannot be pursued here. Suffice it to say that a tradition is more than merely a custom. It contains principles and values which are transmitted from generation to generation: for instance, a tradition of voluntary service, the traditions of a school, a regiment, a profession.

10. This is only a brief indication of the rights contained in the principles of common morality. They will be discussed at length in the next chapter.

11. This applies only to elective rights. Demand for respect for non-elective rights, made necessarily by an adult member on the right-holder's behalf, entails no commitment by the right-holder, who is not capable of commitments. The passive character of non-elective rights is a relevant difference.

12. On this, see the passage from Sir Isaiah Berlin quoted in 4.2.4 above.

13. More clearly needs to be said about animal rights, but not in a book limited to human rights.

14. Among these rules are those setting minimum standards for the implementation of principles. For instance, the right to compensation for negligence requires a rule setting a minimum standard of care (see 1.3.1 above).

15. The idea of an international community is touched on briefly in the next chapter (see 8.2.2).

16. More needs to be said about this, especially in connection with trade unions and the 'closed shop', but it cannot be pursued here.

CHAPTER 8: THE IDEA OF RIGHTS (iii): HUMAN RIGHTS

1. Whether capital punishment is an appropriate penalty for murder is a controversial question. But, while it may be inhumane, it is not wanton killing, and that is the point here.

2. Or at least as they were in the British Army.

3. By a 'moral code' I mean the actual morality of an individual community. As we have seen (in 3.4.3), this is always a union of common morality with a particular morality.

4. Cf. J. S. Mill, *On Liberty* (1859) ch. 2, for his case for freedom of speech, and also F. Schauer, *Free Speech: A Philosophical Enquiry* (Cambridge University Press, 1982).

CHAPTER 9: HUMAN RIGHTS AND POLITICS

1. I use 'constitutional law' in an extended sense to cover the conventional secondary rules of an unwritten constitution such as that of the United Kingdom.

2. The government of the Soviet Union also originated in revolution, but, owing to its treatment of its subjects, it cannot be called constitutional today, despite the existence of a written constitution.

3. I borrow the term 'side constraints' from Robert Nozick's *Anarchy, State and Utopia* (Oxford: Basil Blackwell, 1974) without committing myself to any of the substantive doctrines in his book.

4. See Bertrand de Juvenal's *Sovereignty* (Cambridge University Press, 1957) in which the notion of a team of action is briefly touched upon.

5. I have already referred to this in the case of the right to fair treatment (see 8.1.6).

6. This is not to say that socialism necessarily entails totalitarianism. I do not deny the possibility of democratic and therefore constitutional socialism.

7. Commercial boycotts may well harm the state imposing them, which is why governments are reluctant to resort to them. This reluctance can be morally justified on the grounds that a government's first duty in foreign policy is to promote its state's own interest, provided that in doing so it does not directly violate the human rights of any foreigners. It is also often contended that commercial boycotts harm the victims they are intended to help. These matters cannot, however, be pursued here.

8. This is not to deny that combatants can and should respect the human rights of non-combatants and of prisoners of war, and also of all foreign neutrals.

9. See 8.2.2 above for what the interest of an international community is an interest in.

10. It may be objected that mass bombing in the Second World War obliterated the distinction between enemy combatants and non-combatants. This, however, only shows that conventional warfare becomes morally unacceptable when such methods are used.

Index